Russell Austin

20-07 21st St.

L.I. City 5, N.Y.

Astoria 4-1273

A PLANNED ECONOMY
OR
FREE ENTERPRISE

BY E. LIPSON

THE ECONOMIC HISTORY OF ENGLAND

Vol. I. The Middle Ages. *Eighth edition*
Vols. II & III. The Age of Mercantilism. *Fourth edition*

THE HISTORY OF THE
WOOLLEN AND WORSTED INDUSTRIES

EUROPE IN THE XIXTH CENTURY *
1815–1914
Seventh edition

EUROPE 1914–1939 *
Third edition

* These two also in one volume, *Europe in the Nineteenth and Twentieth Centuries*

ADAM AND CHARLES BLACK : LONDON

A PLANNED ECONOMY
OR
FREE ENTERPRISE

The Lessons of History

BY

E. LIPSON

SECOND EDITION

"*There is no new thing under the sun.*"
ECCLESIASTES

ADAM & CHARLES BLACK
4, 5 & 6 SOHO SQUARE LONDON W.1
1946

FIRST EDITION 1944
SECOND EDITION 1946

MADE IN GREAT BRITAIN
PRINTED BY R. & R. CLARK, LIMITED, EDINBURGH

PREFACE TO THE FIRST EDITION

I HAVE long been convinced that the historical method of approach can make its own contribution to the discussion of current issues—partly because it enables us to take long-term views, and to discern the design of the pattern in the apparently chaotic movements of the human shuttle; and partly because we may not only derive inspiration from the experiences of the past but also profit by their salutary warnings. This book therefore endeavours to ascertain what light our history can throw upon the situation in which we find ourselves to-day.

I have given an account of England's first planned economy with some degree of fullness in order to draw attention to the many illuminating parallels between our own and former times, for the continuity of economic development makes the past in a sense the mirror in which the present in its essentials is reflected. Many of our problems—unemployment, the balance of trade, the maintenance of agriculture, the relations between the state and private enterprise—are not new problems; and to see them in their historical setting may assist us in our search for a solution. At the same time I have taken the opportunity to lay before the reader a picture of the older English society differing in many material respects from that which has become traditional.

In the concluding chapter I have attempted to apply the lessons of history in outlining a programme of post-war reconstruction. This programme is not offered as a complete expression of our aspirations for the future social order. It is a complex of practical objectives in harmony with the underlying trends of our national growth, representing an instalment which lies within our immediate compass, and on which a substantial measure of agreement may be possible.

As this book is designed for the general reader, references have been omitted; for the statements made in chapters II-IV full documentation will be found in my *Economic History of England*, Vols. II & III ("The Age of Mercantilism"). It is proper to say that these chapters are adapted from the Introduction newly added to Vol. II of that History. I have drawn, in chapter V, upon some paragraphs in my book, *Europe 1914–1939*.

For permission to reproduce (in Appendix II) an Article which I contributed to the columns of *The Times*, my acknowledgments are due to the Editor.

E. LIPSON

May 1944

PREFACE TO THE SECOND EDITION

THE general election of 1945 gave the British people an opportunity to decide on the political complexion of the government by which their affairs were to be administered during the period of reconstruction after the second world war. However varied may have been the motives which actuated the electorate, its verdict has been generally recognized as a mandate for the adoption of the policy of a planned economy—that is, the central direction of the national resources. In these circumstances the theme which is the subject of this book has now become a concrete political reality. I have pointed out that everything depends on the nature of the planning; and I have endeavoured to indicate the guiding principles which should determine the scope and methods of a planned economy. Our task is to harmonize the traditional forces which have moulded economic life with the changing needs of a virile community and the demands of an awakened social conscience. If we are to avoid the economic chaos into which the nations drifted between the two world wars, it behoves us more than ever to study and to profit by 'the lessons of history'.

E. L.

August 1945

CONTENTS

[*contd.*]

A PLANNED ECONOMY OR FREE ENTERPRISE

THE LESSONS OF HISTORY

CHAPTER ONE

INTRODUCTION

I PROPOSE in the opening chapters of this book to give an account of England's first planned economy [1], with the hope that the lessons which can be drawn from its history may throw light upon our present situation and afford a measure of guidance in the solution of the economic problems now confronting us. I shall endeavour to describe its character and achievements, the reasons for its adoption, and the historic framework within which it operated. I shall also trace the rise of individualism which inaugurated an era of free enterprise in the place of a planned economy. All the portents point to the possibility of another planned economy in a not very remote future. It is therefore of more than academic interest to inquire whether a planned economy is alien to the English tradition, and whether individualism is something other than the fruit of an acquisitive spirit. The historical survey is designed to answer these and other questions.

The scope of England's first planned economy was two-fold. It sought firstly to determine in what ways the national resources should be employed; and secondly to preserve the traditional fabric of economic life which in former centuries was organized on a corporate basis. In both respects it came into conflict with an insurgent indi-

[1] I have explained the meanings which I attach to the terms planned economy, free enterprise and private enterprise, in an Appendix at the end of the book.

vidualism which ultimately succeeded in bursting the bonds that cramped its growth. To explain the far-reaching significance of the conflict, I may begin by indicating the main factors which have contributed to the making of English society. One is the factor of co-operation : the other is the factor of individualism. The Englishman is generally looked upon as an individualist *par excellence*, accustomed to plough a lonely furrow in the conduct of his economic affairs ; and it may therefore seem strange to picture him as a member of a disciplined community acting in the closest relations with his fellows, though the team spirit displayed in games is a relic of an ancient tradition. In the England of the nineteenth century the tide of individualism attained its high-water mark : in the England of the present day the tide is fast receding. Many branches of the national economy are beginning to assume a corporate aspect : individualism is not extinguished but it is being brought increasingly under control. A new England is in the process of formation, yet it can be considered new only if we compare it with the England of the ' Industrial Revolution ' and the nineteenth century. In reality, it is an England which is returning to the spirit of an older regime based on co-operation, where economic behaviour conformed to a set pattern and all the pursuits of the individual were regulated in collaboration with his peers—until eventually the competitive instinct proved too strong for the restraining hand of the legislature and he was liberated from the shackles of authority.

The theme of the present book is this dual trait in the English character—the communal and the individualist. Each has played a decisive part in our national growth. When one trait develops at the expense of the other, either economic progress which (hitherto at any rate) has depended primarily on individual enterprise, or social welfare which is due to communal enterprise, is likely to suffer. We must learn to reconcile these conflicting claims, and to steer the ship of state between the Scylla of economic stagnation and the Charybdis of abrupt social disturbances. After all, what really matters in the economic as in every other sphere of life is not the speed at which we move but the direction in which we are moving. In the final analysis the problem of reconstruction is how we can establish the basis of an ordered commonwealth, in which stability and security have their rightful place as well as progress.

It may surprise some of my readers to learn that England once had a planned economy, which was gradually undermined by the growth of individualism. Other countries, however, have not been slow to perceive that the foundations of England's greatness as a commercial and industrial state were laid before the nineteenth century. When I was engaged in writing an economic history of England I tried to build up a specialist library in the subject. I found difficulty in obtaining the economic literature of the seventeenth and eighteenth centuries since it was both rare and costly. Items in my own possession trebled in value within a few years. I discovered that the principal buyers of this literature were the libraries of Moscow and Tokyo, which believed that there was still something to be learnt from England's first planned economy and from the statecraft of the mercantilist epoch.

Our comparative neglect of the earlier phases of our economic development can be easily explained. Partly it is due to the prevailing misconception which regards the 'Industrial Revolution' as the beginning of modern economic life, just as the French Revolution is viewed as the beginning of modern political life. Partly it is due to the biassed interpretation of the classical economists, which led to the dismissal of our first planned economy as unworthy of serious consideration, although it endured for several centuries and was deeply rooted in the traditions which had moulded our national evolution. The picture which I endeavour to present differs fundamentally from that which has held the field for more than a hundred and fifty years. Adam Smith wrote his famous book at a time when the foundations of the mercantile system were crumbling and the doctrines of *laissez-faire* were in the ascendant. His treatment of the older economic policy was not objective because he wished to discredit it. He condemned it root and branch as based upon a complete fallacy, though in acknowledging that national security was more important than opulence he largely conceded the main principle at issue. The time seems ripe to repair our neglect of the history of England's first planned economy; and we shall do well to embody in our reconstruction programme what was best in it while discarding the features which proved injurious.

I have devoted one chapter to a review of the policy and errors of the two decades which bridge the two world wars, for the causes of the economic malaise that followed the first world war have a direct bearing on the problems arising out of the second world war. In spite of the baffling complexity of the period the lessons of history are here writ plain. Looking back upon those pregnant years which shattered all our high hopes of a world of peace and plenty, we can now see how the fateful sequence of events made inevitable a renewal of the titanic conflict. In the political sphere the isolationism of the United States, the impotence of a League of Nations supported only by moral sanctions, the drawing apart of France and England and the encouragement thereby afforded to the aggressive states, resulted in a temporizing and fumbling policy which helped to produce the very disasters it sought to avert. In the economic sphere opportunism was even more marked. The criticism that can be justly directed against our policy is that it was a makeshift policy dictated by expediency or panic, and failed to take account of all the relevant national and international factors. Each 'solution' of a problem brought graver problems in its train. Whether our abandonment of free trade and the gold standard was wise or not is fairly debatable, but the sudden recourse to 'ad hoc' expedients upset the world economy, intensified economic nationalism, and raised in a more acute form the issues of colonies and of access to raw materials.

Admittedly we face the days that lie ahead of us with one advantage which we did not possess in 1919, though it has been very dearly purchased : we have taken many leaps in the dark and have accumulated a vast fund of experience through an astonishing range of experiments. In these twenty years (1919–39) which witnessed the collapse of national currencies and saw in operation the most ambitious schemes of national self-sufficiency, we boxed the economic compass. Under the influence of a catastrophic depression (1929–33) we tried every conceivable device of monetary and commercial policies, cut ourselves loose from the safe anchorage of gold, joined the circle of protectionist countries, discarded the 'orthodoxies' in which our economic philosophy was steeped, and gave the fullest scope to innovations which shrank from no heresies. If we profit by our experiences we shall bring to the immense tasks of reconstruction a confidence born of a stern discipline and bitter training in the school of adversity. We have shown during the second world war that we have learnt how to avoid the extravagant rates of interest which prevailed in the first world war, as well as to curb inflation of prices. It may be taken for granted that vigorous efforts will be made to prevent prices from multiplying nearly threefold as in 1920, and unemployment fourfold as in 1921 and fivefold as in 1932. But it remains to be seen whether we shall succeed in fitting a nationalist policy into the framework of international co-operation.

The concluding chapter of the book presents in broad outline a reconstruction programme which seeks to apply the lessons of history to our post-war problems. There is a danger that the guiding concepts of our future policy may become obscured in a bewildering mass of legislation. For this reason it is essential to see our problems as a whole and to shape the lines of economic statecraft, both internal and external, in accordance with clearly-defined principles. We must keep our goal steadily before our eyes, avoid the clash of conflicting objectives, and establish the standards by which to measure the claims of private interests masquerading under the cloak of public virtue.

In these pages I make frequent allusions to 'the lessons of history'. Yet there is a school of thought which has no use for history except perhaps as an intellectual recreation to satisfy a sense of curiosity about the past. Its standpoint is expressed in the aphorism that the only lesson to be learnt from history is that there is nothing to be learnt. This was not the opinion of the Greek historian Thucydides, who is usually considered the greatest of the political historians. He wrote his work, as he expressly tells us, in the conviction that the future, in view of the uniformity of human nature, will tend to bear a strong likeness to the past. He sought in his own words to be "judged useful by those inquirers who desire an exact knowledge of the past as an aid to the interpretation of the future, which in the course of human things must resemble if it does not reflect it". He even went so far as to put into one of his speeches the remark that "there is no advantage in reflection on the past further than may be of service to the present". The student of medicine, of law, of business practices, is accustomed to study 'cases', so that he may deduce general principles which can be applied to the fresh 'cases' which perpetually arise in a severer or milder form and with varying symptoms. History too is a case-book, which provides many lessons from which we can derive profit. Nevertheless in handling the problems of the present—which is history in the making—we tend to disregard what can be learnt from the past. We prefer to rely upon our own dearly-bought experiences. Experience is doubtless a great teacher, but (it has been truly said) her fees are high.

No one can study economic development without being impressed by the many parallels which can be drawn between the past and the present. History may not repeat itself in the sense that exactly identical situations are reproduced, for there are necessarily variations in the scale, tempo of change, and complexity of human affairs. None the less the past does throw a strong reflected light upon the present. Familiar problems are always recurring : the same phenomena appear again and again : the old errors of policy crop up with distressing frequency. The conflicting claims of individualism and a corporate society, the notion of a planned economy, the interweaving of politics and economics, the efforts to achieve national security by economic self-sufficiency, tariffs, trade associations, the relations of capital and labour, limitation of output, rates of interest, monetary exchanges, currency, prices, wages, and unemployment—all these things were the subject of lively discussion in the seventeenth and eighteenth centuries. We cannot afford to ignore what was then said and done ; if we have done so hitherto, this is owing largely to the erroneous belief that before the 'Industrial Revolution' England was a backward agricultural country with little industry or trade. The following chapters will furnish abundant indications that the reverse is the truth. Not only did capitalism, factories, large-scale production, world-wide markets, credit instruments, cartels, the alternation of booms and slumps, the industrial proletariat and trade unions exist prior to the invention of power-driven machinery, but war produced precisely the same maladjustments which we have experienced in our own day—inflation of war industries, disturbance of the monetary exchanges, expansion of the currency, rise in prices and widespread unemployment. We are accustomed to think, for example, that unemployment is a modern phenomenon. Actually it is at least four centuries old, and writers who explain the reasons and remedies for trade depressions will find most of their original ideas anticipated in the report of a royal commission on unemployment framed as early as 1622.

There are remarkable resemblances between the past and the present not only in economic organization but also in economic statecraft. As I have written in a recent book [1] : "There is a striking similarity between the economic statecraft of the present day, which we may term neo-

[1] *Europe 1914–1939*.

mercantilism, and the mercantile system as it existed in the seventeenth century. Both are inspired by the same fundamental purpose—the attainment of economic self-sufficiency as the corollary of political independence. Both have recourse to the same methods of achieving their purpose—the discouragement of imports, the policy of a balanced trade with each particular country, the prohibition of the export of gold, the manipulation of the currencies, the promotion of key industries, and the regimentation of economic life in order to divert the productive energies of the community into the appropriate channels. If the economists of the seventeenth century were to return to the Europe of our own times, they would find themselves in a familiar atmosphere ; if Adam Smith came back he would feel that *The Wealth of Nations* had been written in vain. Thus under changed conditions the world has reverted to an economic system which it was thought to have discarded for ever. The historian may exclaim with Ecclesiastes : 'There is no new thing under the sun' ".

It is, in fact, one of the outstanding lessons of history that it teaches the permanence of national economic policies so long as there is preserved the setting of nation-states. Experience has shown that the concept of a world economic system, as contemplated by nineteenth-century idealists, cannot be pursued in isolation from the political conditions which prevail. Hence an enlightened trade policy, if it is to have its roots in something more stable than Utopian idealism, must be co-ordinated with a regrouping of political forces, in which the sovereignty of nation-states survives as a specific guarantee of a particular way of life but is untainted by any suspicion of predatory instincts. In short, in the nineteenth century free trade was viewed as the antechamber to the millennium, as the prerequisite of universal peace ; whereas to-day it appears as a consequence rather than as a cause of international solidarity and good will. It is evident, then, that much can be learnt from the economic ideas and practices prevalent in former ages. They are the essential substance of our own modes of thought, for they affect us alike in the measure of our agreement and in the measure of our dissent.

Although the present is the heir of the past, there is a natural tendency to look askance at any attempt to link up past and present. The historian, like the shoemaker, must therefore expect to be admonished to stick to his last. There are several reasons for this attitude. One is that endeavours to pry into the future, or even to indicate the signposts on the road traversed by the present, have not hitherto been attended with conspicuous success. The historian needs to see the chequered pattern as a whole before he can unravel the multi-coloured threads of which it is woven. Confronted with a changing panorama of world-shaking events, he lacks the first requirement of a seeker after truth—a sense of detachment and a quiet atmosphere in which surface movements are ignored and attention is concentrated on the underlying trend. The interpretation of 'contemporary history' presents difficulties which sometimes seem almost insuperable. Theoretically we should be better informed about the world in which we live than about the past, for the knowledge of which we are dependent on written and often meagre records. Actually this is not the case. To see events in their true perspective we need the distance of time, just as we need the distance of space to see the mountain as a whole. The eddies and cross-currents that swirl around us in a distracted Europe confuse our judgment. The kaleidoscopic character of the international situation makes it difficult to interpret its real significance and to relate it to the eternal verities. The colourful and picturesque incidents which crowd upon us in a breathless succession oppress the mind. Life seems a bewilderment, and humanity appears to be building its edifice on shifting sands. It is only when the chaotic movements have worked themselves out to their appointed end that we can appraise their meaning, and determine their true place in the general scheme of evolution.

Apart from the difficulties inherent in any attempt to

apply the lessons of history to the rapid transformations of the present, there is another reason for the reluctance to pay heed to its teachings: instead of a balanced survey of all the facts and factors, economists and publicists are inclined to select the material which appears to support their pre-conceived notions. And a third reason is that the data, even when used objectively, are often insufficient for making sound inferences. For instance, those who discuss current problems certainly draw upon the experience of the inter-war period (1919–39), but the period is too short and its character too singular to provide the basis for safe generalizations. It can be plausibly argued that the collapse of the 'automatic' mechanism of free enterprise precludes any possibility of its restoration. Or the thesis can be maintained with equal force that the 'chaos' of these two decades was abnormal, the aftermath of an unparalleled war, and therefore affords no trustworthy guidance for the future—it merely proves that a 'peace economy' cannot stand the strains and stresses for which it was never meant, and therefore the supersession of free enterprise can only be justified on the assumption that war, with brief intervals of 'armed peace', must be accepted as an inexorable and inescapable fact of our destiny. Moreover the accepted interpretations of the conclusions to be drawn from the inter-war period tend to suffer from the temptation to find a single, or primary, explanation of complex economic movements; for example, the gold standard, the rate of interest, the cessation of international lending, technology, etc. One is reminded of the efforts made by ancient philosophers to discover a sole explanation of the manifold phenomena of the Universe.

The historical approach to the study of our present-day problems enables us to take a wider sweep and a larger canvas, to see the confused welter of modern happenings in their proper perspective, that is, in their relation to long-term trends. Just as a man who looks back on his early life through the vista of the years can discern in it a recognizable pattern in which different threads are interlaced to form a coherent design, even though from day to day his vision may be clouded by the confusion of passing events and by the uncertainties of the immediate future, so also there is an unmistakable pattern in the affairs of a nation. If we can determine the aspect of the pattern we are more likely to form a correct idea of the direction in which we are moving, and even perhaps forecast the shape of what still lies hidden in the womb of time. True, the unpredictable constantly recurs to upset the calculations based on short-term views. War or the emergence of a dynamic personality appears to give a new twist to national development; but while the tempo of change may be accelerated natural forces reassert themselves, for the pattern fashioned by the loom of time inevitably moulds the future. In short, the past is the antechamber through which we must pass to enter the hall of true knowledge—where we may perceive in the development of mankind not a casual series of unrelated episodes but something of a design. In this design conscious human agency undoubtedly plays a part, though imponderable elements (whose nature we are only beginning dimly to comprehend) shape our ends rough-hew them how we may. Furthermore the past, in broadening the basis of our experiences, helps us to gauge the accuracy of our diagnosis of the world in which we live. The complexity of human affairs seems to baffle all the efforts at analysis. Nevertheless if we learn to take long views, we are better equipped to measure the real importance of contemporary events, and to devise solutions of our problems which are in harmony with the basic factors of our national growth.

Indeed without an adequate appreciation of the historical background—the indispensable condition for understanding our own age—we shall be gravely handicapped in handling the issues of post-war reconstruction. It is easy enough, as we have learnt from the experiments of recent years, to devise a series of makeshift expedients producing contradictory effects and reducing the economic system to chaos. It is easy enough to devise logical schemes (like the paper constitutions of Abbe Sieyès during the French Revolution) which have little chance of survival because they are not rooted in the national tradition. But it is more difficult to bring knowledge and experience to bear upon the heritage which we have received from the past, and to introduce modifications which are the fruits of deliberate purpose and yet are in harmony with the general pattern as it unfolds itself through the generations. For this reason the pursuit of historical truth may become one of the factors of human progress, since the illumination of the past may help in some measure to diminish the obscurity of the present and to lighten the darkness that veils the future.

For England, perhaps more than for any other country, the study of the past has a special significance. We are a precedent-loving nation, and if it is sometimes a source of weakness it is probably in a greater degree a source of strength. As a consequence our way of life is built upon firm foundations. It rests upon the body of traditional influences handed down from generation to generation, enriched and modified by the accumulation of fresh experiences and an ever-increasing clearness of vision and insight into our national purpose. We treasure what is most valuable in our heritage, yet we seek to harmonize it with the requirements of a progressive community. On the surface we often appear unduly conservative in our social and political structure because we cling to forms and institutions that seem to have outlived their day, but we invest them with a new meaning, whilst behind the façade we make the adjustments which enable us to march with the times. No country in the world exhibits more vestiges of its mediaeval past. Nevertheless England abolished serfdom several centuries before most European countries ; she was the home of the ' Industrial Revolution ' ; she was the first to develop the capitalist system on a large scale ; and her socialist thinkers preceded Karl Marx. Hence the contrast drawn between France and England is not without justification—that in the former the more things change the more they remain the same ; in the latter the more things remain the same, the more they change. In the evolution of England's national life the old and the new are inextricably blended. Thus the sense of history has become as the very breath of her nostrils.

History has long been recognized as a school for statesmen ; but the public, too, have the right to expect guidance in interpreting the 'signs of the times' from those whose historical insight may enable them to apply the lessons of the past to the problems of the present. A democracy cannot abdicate its responsibilities, and it must remain the final arbiter even on economic questions. To discharge its functions effectively it needs to be well-informed ; and history, though one of the principal sources of instruction, is not the only avenue to a full understanding. Unfortunately the complexity of modern civilization and the constant extension of the bounds of knowledge are producing a growing cleavage between specialists of every kind and the public. The former, it has been aptly remarked, know more and more about less and less ; while the latter know less and less about more and more. Economics, in particular, is fast becoming a sealed book to all but the initiated owing to its terminology and its employment of a mathematical apparatus. A distinguished philosopher, the late F. C. S. Schiller, once remarked to me that in his early days every educated man was accustomed to read either Adam Smith or John Stuart Mill. Nowadays, he deplored, the general reader could not understand the modern works on economics, and as a result he lacked the ability to detect even glaring economic fallacies. This is extremely regrettable since practical issues cannot be relegated to the exclusive province of the economic expert—and for two important reasons.

In the first place, no practical issue is ever purely economic. There are all kinds of extraneous forces at work which affect economic behaviour and bring it within the orbit of political, social and spiritual influences. We are returning to an older standpoint in recognizing that there are other values in life besides economic values, which are mainly concerned with the efficient use of the factors of production. The problems of reconstruction cannot therefore be viewed solely from an economic angle. On the contrary, we have always to bear in mind the over-riding considerations of national security, social stability and international co-operation, all of which may involve sacrifices of material wealth. Thus a strategic economy may divert the national resources into less profitable channels; for instance, raising commodities at home which can be produced more cheaply abroad. The workers may prefer an economic system which ensures steady employment to one which yields a higher but more intermittent income. The community may pursue a 'good-neighbour policy' instead of following the dictates of self-interest. In short, man does not live by economics alone; and there are qualitative standards other than the measuring-rod of wealth. In the second place, as a guide to practical affairs economic science is subject to the limitations imposed by an analysis which has to assume hypothetical conditions. The deductive economist may feel not indisposed to concur with the deductive philosopher, Herbert Spencer, who once defined a tragedy as a hypothesis killed by a fact.

We may conclude that a democracy ought not to hand over its responsibilities to economists, whose function it is to explain how the economic system works but not to prescribe remedies. Still less should a democracy place itself unreservedly in the hands of business leaders, although it might be supposed that the latter can be relied upon to know what is best for industry. Actually the views of business men do not necessarily coincide with what is best for the nation, for example, when they favour high tariffs; or they may run counter to other pressing economic needs. Moreover industry often has a vested interest in the *status quo*, just as the professions have in traditional knowledge and methods. In addition industrial experts are sometimes unduly rigid in their ideas. "Don't talk to me about ships of iron", said the chief constructor of one of the royal dockyards a century ago, "it's contrary to nature". In

1920 a prominent cotton manufacturer, warned by a professor of economics of the impending crash, retorted : " This boom will last ten years ".

The objection may be raised that the public are less qualified to pronounce judgment on economic than on political affairs, but until the extension of the franchise it was denied that the public were competent to decide on political affairs. There appears to be no adequate reason why an informed public opinion should not concern itself with broad questions of policy relating, among other things, to tariffs and subsidies, trade associations, the requirements of a strategic economy, the progressive amelioration of labour conditions in respect of hours, wages, regular employment and factory hygiene, and above all, the respective merits of a planned economy and of free enterprise. In the realm of more technical matters the public can apply standards of efficiency based on the achievements of progressive undertakings at home and abroad. One thing, however, needs to be stressed. Unless public opinion is well-instructed and well-balanced it will not be sound. This pre-supposes clear thinking on national issues, and lays a special obligation upon the leaders of thought in the press and elsewhere. If one half of our troubles in the years 1919–39 were due to causes beyond our control, the other half arose from a failure to think out our problems and to view them in a true light, that is, in the framework set by history, tradition and psychology. Even to-day a medley of proposals is being canvassed which takes no account of the long-term trends in national development. A bewildered public asking of the Wise :

> " What Lamp had Destiny to guide
> Her little Children stumbling in the Dark ? "

may exclaim with Omar Khayyám :

> " Myself when young did eagerly frequent
> Doctor and Saint, and heard great Argument
> About it and about : but evermore
> Came out by the same Door as in I went."

Among the lessons of history which this book is designed to illustrate, perhaps the most pregnant—and certainly one with far-reaching implications—is that economic development is a continuous process. The keynote of our national life in the economic as in the constitutional sphere is its continuity: there is always a constant tide of evolution in which the old is blended almost imperceptibly with the new. Accordingly we must conceive of economic society as a living organism which grows and functions by unceasing adaptation to an ever-changing environment. Every generation is the heir of the past, and in turn bequeathes the setting wherein its successors may work out their own specific contribution to human advancement. A survey of the older English community discloses an aspect widely remote from the idealized picture which is usually drawn; and it shows that the so-called 'Industrial Revolution' constituted no sudden breach with the existing order. Between the middle ages and the nineteenth century lies a period of two hundred and fifty years, which may conveniently be designated as the age of mercantilism. It was the epoch of a planned economy, but it also gave birth to a regime of free enterprise. The latter not only shattered the corporate structure of society, replacing it by an individualist structure which bore many of the capitalist traits associated with modern England, but at the same time it destroyed the traditional conception of the place of the state in relation to the national economy. A study of mercantilist England affords convincing evidence that our problems are not new problems, as is apt to be imagined, and our handling of them must be in harmony with the historic pattern imprinted on our island story.

Another lesson to be learnt from the past is that there appears to be a cycle in human affairs. A community does not achieve progress by a continuous movement in the same direction: it moves forward, then it recedes though never to the original position. As with the individual, in whom satiety provokes a desire for something different, so with the nation. National growth is governed by the law of action and reaction : it is owing to the oscillations of the pendulum that equilibrium is maintained. Each generation tends to react against the ways of thought and the practices of the preceding generation. It is critical of the accepted dogmas and often it goes to the extreme in its repudiation. And the greater the rebound of the pendulum in one direction, the more certain will be its recoil in the opposite direction. The rise of individualism was a protest against a society organized on communal lines and controlled by a planned economy. Now we are beginning to turn again towards a corporate economic life. To avoid undue reaction in the future our aim should be to preserve what is best in our present economic system, the spirit of enterprise, and to fuse it with the team spirit, so that self-interest may be held in check by the ideal of public service and devotion to the commonweal.

One invaluable lesson of history is that economics cannot be isolated from politics. In the years 1919–39 the interplay of political and economic factors was so intricate and involved that it becomes difficult to unravel the tangled web of cause and effect, each impinging upon the other in an unbroken sequence. It was impossible to determine whether political insecurity, which prevented closer co-operation between the nations, was the source of the general economic malaise or whether the latter was the disturbing element which drew them apart. Many illustrations can be given of the interaction of politics and economics in generating the instability which ultimately culminated in a second world war. The outstanding example is the pursuit of national self-sufficiency in the thirties. This was due partly to economic forces (set in motion or accelerated by the great depression of 1929–33), which prevented the free movement of men, commodities and capital ; and partly to the political aspirations of totalitarian states to establish their economy on a war footing. To find a way out of the impasse European statesmen had debated, even in the twenties, the fundamental problem whether politics should take precedence of economics or the reverse. Some held that constructive effort should first of all be made on the political plane. Others averred that political rapprochement would be the natural consequence of more cordial relations in the domain of commercial policy. The truth appears to be that economics and politics are like two blades of a pair of scissors : neither can function properly if separated from the other. Without a freer international trade we can hardly hope to achieve genuine political solidarity, yet the sense of political security is the vital condition of economic co-operation. The two policies need to be co-ordinated : if they are pursued on conflicting lines they will neutralize one another. The disturbed atmosphere will be reproduced which prevailed after the first world war, when contradictory influences struggled for mastery—efforts to unite the peoples of the earth recently locked in deadly strife being matched by efforts to set new barriers between them. Peace treaties should therefore lay the foundations of an improved economic, as well as political, system of international relationships. Members of the society of nations, if they seek to live in harmony with each other, must be prepared to make substantial concessions and to subordinate self-interest to the general ' weal '. If two world wars have failed to drive home the folly of cupidity, then a further succession of wars will bring its inevitable nemesis in universal impoverishment.

All planning for reconstruction pre-supposes the maintenance of peace. True, the possibility of another war cannot be excluded from our calculations ; and in sketching an economic programme I have stressed the view that national security must be one of the major factors shaping our future economic policy. Yet a world satiated with blood is painfully anxious to make an end of war, and it behoves us therefore to appraise correctly the political and economic situation as it existed between the two world wars for the light which it may throw on the genesis of war. I shall examine the economic aspect in a subsequent chapter : here a word may be said about the political aspect. It is the paradox of the inter-war period (1919–39) that it opened with the most sanguine expectations of close international collaboration and ended in a renewal of nationalist strife. I do not subscribe to the opinion that all the troubles of the period are to be traced to an unjust peace settlement. The peace treaties were not arbitrary instruments reflecting the views of a handful of rancorous plenipotentiaries : in the main the clauses were taken unaltered from the reports of nearly three-score commissions of experts. That some injustices may have been done is perhaps true : it is beyond human wisdom to frame a peace instrument which does absolute justice to all concerned [1]. Frequently the choice lay between a greater or a lesser evil. The majority of the territorial changes were in accordance with the nationalist sentiment of the regions affected, although there were notable exceptions (in the circumstances not easily avoidable) to the right of self-determination. It is difficult to resist the conclusion that the decisive cause of the second world war lay less in the nature of the peace settlement than in the failure to enforce it, especially in regard to disarmament. " The right course is not to chastise them rigorously when they do rise, but rigorously to watch them before they rise, and to prevent their ever entertaining the idea ". This was the counsel of Thucydides who believed that there were lessons to be derived from past experiences.

One difficulty in preserving peace is that as the coming generation grows to manhood it tends to forget the horrors of war ; so we can have little assurance that two or three decades hence the victorious powers will be prepared to take effective action to uphold any peace treaty whatever its character. Perhaps the most appropriate ' war memorial ' would be the preservation of a bombed building in every locality to serve as a visual reminder of the meaning of modern warfare. Nevertheless, to hold nations down by force of arms is at best only an interim policy. The foundations of the new international order must rest on something

[1] An examination of the peace treaties, together with the ' Observations ' made by the German peace delegation and the ' Reply ' of the Allies, will be found in my book on *Europe 1914–1939*.

less transient than the fleeting passions of vengeance and fear. No political arrangements in themselves can provide adequate guarantees that peace will be maintained. To avoid the recurrence of wars, it is also necessary to remove the economic friction which helps to breed wars. This implies international co-operation, which (as I shall show later) was conspicuously absent in the decade that preceded the second world war.

The study of the past may be presumed to throw light upon a question of cardinal interest—whether economic statecraft can control or deflect the processes of evolution, or whether there are natural laws in operation which are impervious to human agency. The influence exerted by personality upon history has been much debated. On the one hand this influence is magnified by those who believe that history is the biography of great men. On the other hand the influence of personality is apt to appear negligible, or at least comparatively unimportant, in the eyes of the economic historian aware of great tidal movements, of vast currents, which seem to pursue their way to a predestined end regardless of puny efforts to stay their course. Admittedly we must not always expect to find evidence of a conscious human purpose in the weaving of the social pattern: the movements of the shuttle may be determined by impersonal imponderable forces. But to recognize that society is a living organism, whose growth is governed by the laws of its being, does not mean that we are the blind puppets of destiny or that we must resign ourselves to economic fatalism. One can scarcely question the overwhelming importance of economic factors in the life of a nation. None the less constructive statesmanship, if wisely directed, is not perhaps so impotent as a purely economic interpretation of history may tend to suggest. As Morley has pointed out: "Great economic and social forces flow with a tidal sweep over communities that are only half-conscious of that which is befalling them. Wise statesmen are those who foresee what time is thus bringing, and endeavour to shape institutions and to mould men's thought and purpose in accordance with the change that is silently surrounding them ".

Within the appointed limits set by natural forces it would appear to be within our power to mould circumstances, but two provisos must be fulfilled. The first is that we do not run counter to national psychology and traditions. To give an example. It is probable that there would have been no Bolshevik Revolution without Lenin, whose influence prevailed upon his party to accept a programme which involved an abrupt transition from a feudal to a socialist society and from autocracy to a ' dictatorship of the proletariat ', and which eliminated at a stroke two historic stages—capitalism and democracy. Yet the very violence of Lenin's reaction against Western institutions was producing within two decades a swing of the pendulum. Russia had begun to return to economic and political concepts which had been too hastily discarded by the architects of the Soviet state. These modifications may eventually result in a form of society not perhaps materially different from what would have been evolved by the operation of natural forces. Indeed if we take long views we may question whether the fruits of any revolution could not have been achieved at an infinitely less cost in human suffering and disorganization. The French Revolution involved an orgy of terror and twenty years of war : its essentials could have been secured in the early stages without proceeding to such lengths. It is worth while to observe that economic conditions have undergone a greater transformation in England, who was spared a political revolution, than in France who had a succession of them. Apart from the fatal inability to control the course of a revolution or foresee its consequences, the basic factors in evolution are bound to reassert themselves with the inevitable oscillations of the pendulum. The second proviso is that prudent statesmanship does not lose sight of a very important lesson of history—namely, that in the long run a nation is not made prosperous by policies but by the capacity, energy and versatility of a people, and that a misdirected policy may stultify instead of stimulate these fundamental qualities. In our discussions of a planned economy this supreme consideration should be the touchstone of all the projects which come under review.

CHAPTER TWO

ENGLAND'S FIRST PLANNED ECONOMY

THE subject of the present chapter is England's first planned economy. It is worth our attention because it furnishes the background to our own problems—the future relations between the state and free enterprise in the shaping and execution of a reconstruction programme. Its importance for this purpose is heightened by the fact that it was not improvised in response to some transient ideology but was moulded through the centuries by the forces of tradition and progress. In it, therefore, are mirrored the fundamental traits of the national character—the respect for basic concepts combined with a flexibility which permits of adaptation to the needs of an ever-changing society. It also possesses interest of another kind. It covers a memorable epoch in our island story—the spacious days when adventurous pioneers encompassed the globe and men of vision laid the foundations of the Empire, when the struggle for freedom established on a secure foundation the inalienable rights of the individual, when great poets, philosophers and scientists gave to mankind the imperishable fruits of their genius. An epoch so fertile in every branch of human endeavour must assuredly have had an economic setting which was in keeping with the restless active spirit of the age, together with an economic life pulsating with strength and vitality.

The first planned economy did not spring Athena-like from the brain of a legislator : it was not forged at a single stroke. It resembles the English constitution in that it is not to be found in any single document. Its interpretation must be built up from innumerable fragments of legislation which burden the statute-book with a mass of intricate economic detail, as well as from the 'Discourses' of mercantilist writers. Its growth was gradual, for it was the product of historical forces as old as English society itself. Indeed to the modern generation, reared in an atmosphere of free enterprise, perhaps its most arresting feature was that its roots lay deep embedded in the national way of life, because for many centuries England was organized on a communal basis and the individual carried on his economic activities within the framework of a corporate society with village courts, urban gilds and oversea trading companies. If at the present day the concept of a planned economy has gained in principle so large a measure of acceptance, this may well be due not only to a recognition of the altered conditions of world economy but also to an instinct—particularly potent in a precedent-loving people—that it is in harmony with our national heritage. And the decline of England's first planned economy was as gradual as its growth. It did not fall like the walls of Jericho by the sound of a trumpet, nor like the temple of Gaza by the strength of a Samson—it was certainly not destroyed by Adam Smith. Long before the 'Industrial Revolution' it was honeycombed by the insidious penetration of individualism, and it wilted away in a regime of free enterprise which was alien to its fundamental concepts. In general it functioned from the middle of the sixteenth to the close of the eighteenth century. One part, the protection of agriculture, actually survived to the middle of the nineteenth century. Another part, the protection of industry, was revived as recently as 1932 when England definitely reverted to mercantilism which other countries had never really abandoned. A variety of legislative measures relating to labour conditions supplies connecting links with yet a third part. Thus there is a continuity both in our economic development and in the fundamental principles of our economic statecraft, which blends past and present into a coherent unity.

There were three sides to the first planned economy. The commercial aspect was embodied in what is termed the mercantile system or economic nationalism ; while the industrial and agrarian aspects, though not known by any distinctive name, were based on similar principles. They were closely inter-related in the respect that a traditional outlook moulded public policy towards each of the three branches of the national economy, and the subsequent trend in the direction of *laissez-faire* was dictated in all three cases alike by the growing influence of individualism.

§ 1. *Industry*

At the opening of the nineteenth century when *laissez-faire* was enthroned as the fashionable philosophy, a president of the United States delivered an inaugural address in which he said: " With all these blessings what more is necessary to make us a happy and a prosperous people? Still one thing more, fellow citizens, a wise and frugal government, which shall restrain men from injuring one another, shall leave them otherwise free to regulate their own pursuits of industry and improvement, and shall not take from the mouth of labour the bread it has earned ". The province of the state as visualized by Thomas Jefferson represented an ideal which in his day had won almost universal recognition. It became the practice to fling scorn upon the old-fashioned principles which held sway in the olden days. " The reign of Queen Elizabeth ", it was confidently proclaimed, " though glorious was not one in which sound principles of commerce were known ".

To avoid doctrinaire criticisms of the first planned economy, we must view the past in relation to the actual framework of society in former centuries and not measure it by the standards of the present from which we are already beginning to depart. The conception of freedom which predominated in the early years of the nineteenth century, when the state relied upon the play of unfettered competition and enlightened self-interest to achieve social harmony, was not necessarily suited to a different environment. In earlier ages the English people did not believe in an unregulated industrialism, or that it was the duty of the government to hold aloof as much as possible from economic affairs. On the contrary, they were convinced that the divergence of public and private interests called for state intervention in order to protect the community from the harmful side of individualism. To understand the viewpoint which was then current, we must take into account the prevailing attitude of mind. In the first place, industry was still conceived as in the middle ages in the light of a public service. It was an ' art '—we should now term it a ' profession '—and, as in a modern profession, a code of conduct was laid down and suitable conditions were imposed designed to protect alike the interests of the public as consumers and of the skilled workers as producers. In the second place, the tradition of communal control in the economic sphere was deeply rooted in the historic consciousness of the English nation. There was never a time in the memory of men when the principles of *laissez-faire* had reigned, or when men had been left at liberty in their pursuit of a livelihood. In the middle ages agriculture had been regulated by the village courts, industry by the craft gilds, commerce by the merchant gilds at home and by trading companies abroad. The Englishman was reared in a society in which his business was not his business alone, and in which his economic life was no less subject to supervision than his political or religious life.

The early mercantilist state [1], as it grew to maturity, inherited the communal traditions bequeathed by the middle ages. It came into existence at a time when profound changes were taking place in the industrial landscape. The growth of capitalism, the dispersion of the textile manufacture over the countryside and the emergence of new enterprises outside the jurisdiction of the urban authorities imperilled the whole structure of industry as it

[1] It is convenient to use the term mercantilist state to designate the state which is associated with the first planned economy. Two phases of the mercantilist state must be distinguished since public policy underwent a considerable modification after the Civil War. The first phase embraces the reigns of Queen Elizabeth and the Early Stuarts. The second phase comprises the epoch of the Later Stuarts and the Early Hanoverians.

had been built up in the middle ages on a gild basis. Accordingly the intervention of the state was imperatively demanded if the time-honoured sanctions of a rigid industrial discipline were to be preserved from extinction. It is seldom that governments are entirely free agents. As a rule they are confronted with practical problems which they can only handle within the limitations set by the circumstances of their age [1], and public opinion was not yet prepared for the abandonment of the old order. To avert its imminent break-up, the central authority was impelled to assume wider responsibilities and to share with the local communities their main economic functions. Early mercantilist legislation was in its essentials nothing more than the application, on a national scale, of the orthodox practices which had been followed for several centuries by municipal bodies. And much that may now seem to us inexplicable and arbitrary becomes intelligible, when it is viewed in relation to the historic conditions of which it was at once the fruit and the logical sequel. It will be seen in a subsequent chapter how in the course of the seventeenth century men began to challenge the principle of state regulation of industry ; and how a century before Adam Smith men were already proclaiming the doctrine of economic freedom. This development, however, did not take place until the Civil War had shaken the very foundations of society and created a new balance of political forces. Not until after a convulsion of the first magnitude did the business community of England venture to claim openly the right to manage its affairs without official guidance. At the moment I am concerned with the normal functioning of public policy prior to the Great Rebellion.

In the sphere of industry the avowed aim of the first planned economy was to bring capitalism under control. The industrial entrepreneur was subject to restrictions in

[1] The rulers of a country seldom enjoy the opportunity of creating a new social fabric, and normally they are constrained to act on 'short-term' considerations. The Russian Revolution is conspicuous as the unique exception.

six different ways. First : he was not at liberty to decide the terms on which he hired his labour, since he was bound by legal rates of wages. Secondly : he was not at liberty to expand or contract his demand for labour in response to a fluctuating market for his wares, since pressure was exerted on employers to keep their men at work. Thirdly : he was not at liberty to draw freely upon the available labour, since he might only employ trained workmen who had served an apprenticeship. Fourthly : he was not at liberty to manufacture his goods as he pleased, since he must conform to standard measurements and standard qualities. Fifthly : he was not at liberty to determine the prices of all his products in accordance with the laws of supply and demand or the 'rigging' of the market, since prices were sometimes fixed by public authority. Sixthly : he was not at liberty even to carry on his trade in certain circumstances, since it might be put into the hands of monopolists, who could either refuse him the right to continue in business or exact from him oppressive fees for doing so. Let us look more closely at these various manifestations of state control of industry : we may perhaps find in them something to imitate as well as something to avoid in the handling of our own industrial problems. And first as to wages.

The grievance of low wages was as old as the capitalist system itself. It was voiced in a fifteenth-century pamphlet *On England's Commercial Policy*—one of the earliest expressions of industrial discontent known to us—which indicated that at this very early date capitalism lent itself easily to exploitation.

"The poor have the labour, the rich the winning".

The evil was accentuated by the failure of wages to keep pace with the advance in prices produced by the influx of American silver into Europe. A famous ballad, which is said to have been chaunted about the streets in the time of Charles II., recited in rude rhymes the grievances of the workers in cloth against their employers.

"In former ages we us'd to give,
So that our work-folks like farmers did live;
But the times are altered, we will make them know
All we can for to bring them all under our bow;
We will make to work hard for sixpence a day,
Though a shilling they deserve if they had their just pay.
And this is a way for to fill up our purse,
Although we do get it with many a curse".

While the monarchy, acting through the agency of the Privy Council, sustained its grip upon the economic life of the country, the regulation of working-class conditions was considered the province of the state. It refused to recognize the claim of the wage-earners to combine together in order to promote their interests, yet as a compensation it did not leave them unprotected. It shouldered, in principle at least, the responsibility for safeguarding the welfare of the workers because it interfered in matters affecting wages, employment and technical training. The right of the state to lay down appropriate standards of remuneration for the working community became a fundamental concept of the industrial order. The famous enactment known as the Statute of Apprentices (1563) [1] empowered the justices of the peace in every county and city to fix maximum wages, calculated to "yield unto the hired person both in the time of scarcity and in the time of plenty a convenient proportion of wages": later in the reign of James I. was instituted the first minimum wage law on the English statute-book [2].

The question how far the authoritarian regulation of wages existed in practice has been much discussed. Wage assessments in one branch or another of industry have a continuous history for over two and a half centuries (1563 to 1824), and they have been revived in the twentieth

[1] The system of state regulation of wages goes back to the middle of the fourteenth century, though in earlier times it was apparently limited to unskilled labour outside the craft gilds.

[2] The act of 1604 applied to the woollen industry, then the premier industry of the country.

century ; but the machinery was most commonly put into operation in the first hundred years. Its efficient working depended primarily upon the hold which the central authority maintained over the local magistrates. Under Elizabeth and the Early Stuarts the government displayed a genuine solicitude for distressed artisans, and showed itself ready to support the interests of workmen against their employers, so that the procedure cannot be regarded as purely one-sided. Cases of intervention were especially frequent in the reign of Charles I. when an active social policy was pursued. In some instances state interference was attended by economic reactions which neutralized its benevolent intentions, for an increase in wages might lead to unemployment and the government was then forced to give way. The lesson was thus demonstrated that economic problems cannot be solved piecemeal, that rates of wages react on prices, prices react on demand, and demand reacts on employment. Yet it is not surprising that the statesmanship of the seventeenth century was baffled by interactions which are still a source of perplexity.

The system of wage assessment has been criticized on various grounds. Historians were wont to denounce it as an instrument for degrading and impoverishing the labourer : economists condemned it as a violation of the principles of *laissez-faire* : employers stressed the technical difficulties of a uniform scale : workers sometimes claimed that wages should be governed by merit. I think that there are valid reasons for drawing certain broad conclusions. First : state control provided a safeguard against undue oppression. The occasions on which the wage-earners themselves pressed for official rates may be interpreted as an indication that it was not considered to work unfairly in their interests. When the 'Industrial Revolution' menaced the handicraftsmen with a rapid deterioration in their standard of life, their first instinct was to turn to the traditional machinery by which that standard, as they believed, had been supported in the past. It is reasonable to infer that the system of wage regulation was not viewed by the working men in a hostile light nor associated in their minds with any embittered memories. Secondly: the system did not prevent a rise in wages since assessments which ran counter to the popular sentiment remained inoperative. "The poor", it was said towards the end of the seventeenth century, "laugh at them and cry: 'statute work against statute wages'. For laws will not make nor influence prices in open market". Thirdly: the attempt to vary the remuneration of labour according to the cost of living proved unsuccessful, and a fall in prices enabled the working class to maintain its traditional standard of life with less effort. A later generation indeed flung scorn upon the orthodox theory of wages that the price of labour should be determined by the price of food. "The squires of Norfolk", said Edmund Burke, "had dined when they gave it as their opinion that [wages] might or ought to rise and fall with the market of provisions". In the eighteenth century the theory came to be held that wages depended, like other commodities, upon supply and demand. It is noteworthy that in this, as in many other respects, we are returning to an older standpoint. In recent years wage agreements have shown a marked tendency to relate the rates of wages to the cost of living: in some cases they have even embodied the principle of a sliding scale in which wages are automatically regulated by the cost-of-living index [1]. Thus they imply a categorical rejection of the view that labour should be treated as 'a commodity'.

I turn next to the policy adopted in regard to unemployment. The growth of capitalism created the problem of unemployment as far back as the sixteenth century, for the more extended the market the greater is the liability to commercial fluctuations. The capitalist takes on fresh hands when trade is brisk and dismisses them when trade is dull: the ebb and flow of commerce react with a regular

[1] It is of interest to observe that the principle of a sliding scale in which wages were regulated, first by the price of the product and subsequently by the cost of food, was adopted by the London [Quaker] Lead Company near the end of the eighteenth century.

rhythm upon industry and produce at one moment an expansion, at another moment a shrinkage, in the volume of employment. In addition, the abnormal interruptions which we call commercial crises were already a prominent feature in the age of mercantilism; and the 'Industrial Revolution' only intensified, it did not originate, the phenomenon of trade depressions. This explains why the early economists viewed with apprehension the rapid progress of industry. They saw clearly that England's commerce in becoming world-wide was affected by the vicissitudes of a world economy, and that the course of her economic life was profoundly disturbed by occurrences remote from her shores. Hence they preferred to see the prosperity of the country broad-based on land rather than on the shifting foundations of trade. Even in the seventeenth century tariffs and wars were revealed as factors of cardinal importance. The efforts of 'the neighbouring nations in Europe' to establish their own manufactures made the continental market precarious; and their adherence to a protectionist policy furnished one of the main arguments for developing a colonial empire in order to provide an alternative market for English products. Moreover England seldom enjoyed a protracted spell of peace; and the industrial situation was adversely influenced by the succession of wars. They inflated certain branches of the national economy such as iron and ship-building, interrupted the normal channels of trade, disturbed the monetary exchanges, and brought in their wake unemployment and destitution. It is not surprising then that war was denounced as 'one of the greatest calamities'. It was observed in *The Spectator* (1711) that "if the profit and loss by wars could be justly balanced, it would be rarely found that the conquest is sufficient to repay the cost". Another writer (1734) pointed out that war usually ruined the vanquished, "and what we who conquered got by it the taxes will amply testify". Modern discussions on the economic folly of war have not materially added to these eighteenth-century reflections.

The attitude of the state towards the problem of unemployment has varied in different ages. Under the Tudors and Early Stuarts the prevailing tendency favoured intervention. The period extending from the Civil War to the close of the nineteenth century was marked by *laissez-faire*. The twentieth century witnessed the revival of the principle of intervention though in an altered form. The reason for state action in the first epoch was partly that it carried on the traditions of the craft gilds, partly it was due to the fear of social unrest, and partly there was a genuine desire to protect ' the poor man's labour, his inheritance '—to quote a seventeenth-century phrase. The methods of official intervention were both legislative and administrative. The legislative method was to secure continuity of employment by insistence on long engagements. In the middle ages it was usual to bind workmen for lengthy periods, sometimes for three or four years. The practice was given legal force in the Statute of Apprentices (1563) which enacted that no person should be taken into service for less than a year. The hiring of farm workers at the annual fair, or ' statute ', lasted into the nineteenth century and in some places it survives at the present day. A Yorkshire farmer in the reign of Charles I. related that at one ' statute hiring ' he " heard a servant asked what he could do, who made this answer—

' I can sowe,
I can mowe,
And I can stacke,
And I can doe,
My master too,
When my master turnes his backe ' ".

The administrative method was to find work for the unemployed or exert pressure upon employers not to turn their men adrift but to keep them at work. There are repeated examples of authoritarian intervention to warn employers against throwing their men out of work under penalty of a summons before the Privy Council. " Those who had gained in profitable times", the government admonished capitalist producers, "must now be content to lose for the public good until the decay of trade was remedied". One of the most memorable depressions in English history lasted several years (1620–24), when the export trade in cloth declined by one-third and unemployment was on a national scale. "The whole commonwealth suffereth", it was announced in a proclamation. In some cases the magistrates bore testimony that the employers were alive to their responsibilities. "The clothiers here do yet continue to keep their poor in work as in former times they have done, although it hath been to their great losses; and so they are contented to do as long as they may occupy their trade without undoing of themselves". Money was borrowed to pay wages; and it was recorded that "one Will Bennett, a very ancient and good clothier, doth offer to live by brown bread [1] and water rather than his great number of poor people should want work, if he had means to keep them in work". Other measures were taken to deal with the situation. Merchants were ordered to lay in stock; manufacturers were protected by a moratorium from their creditors; and the magistrates were instructed to start relief works. Finally a royal commission composed of twelve persons was set up in 1622—the first of its kind to make a detailed investigation of the causes of unemployment. Its comprehensive report presents a contemporary analysis of a phenomenon destined to become a recurring feature of England's economic development.

The third restriction laid on industrial entrepreneurs was the obligation to employ trained labour. By making technical training on the basis of apprenticeship compulsory for all engaged in industry, the state supported the claim of qualified workmen to be protected against cheap labour, and the claim of consumers to be protected against unskilled workmanship—but a check was imposed on capitalism since it curtailed the supply of labour. The Statute of Apprentices, which invested apprenticeship with general legal

[1] White bread instead of rye was already 'the bread of our forefathers'.

sanction, remained on the statute-book for two and a half centuries (1563–1814). Its observance was primarily a matter of local custom, and there was an infinite variety of practices in different parts of the country. One example may serve to illustrate the dissensions provoked by breaches of 'the law Queen Betty made'. The bakers of Rye complained that in spite of 'good and wholesome laws' requiring 'each sort of people' to "use the trade and living wherein they have been lawfully trained up", brewers turned bakers without having served an apprenticeship "contrary to all law, equity and good conscience". The authorities, finding that "by no reasonable persuasion those brewers would leave baking", and that the principal offender who baked and brewed "is (God be thanked) grown to good wealth, and the whole company of the bakers thereby utterly impoverished", issued a decree that "the state of a commonwealth is preferred before the private gain of a few".

The economic functions of the state were not confined to regulating the conditions of labour in respect of wages, employment and training: they also embraced the sphere of production by prescribing the technical processes of manufacture. The minutest rules were framed regarding the nature of the materials, the use of mechanical appliances and the form of the finished products. Every branch of industry was in some degree brought under control, though the one chiefly affected by national regulation was the woollen manufacture—the favourite child of the legislature which lavished upon it unremitting care and attention. In order to ensure 'true making', cloth had to conform to a certain length, breadth and weight: it was also forbidden to mingle different kinds of wool, or use various ingredients in dyeing, or employ mechanical devices such as gig mills and tenter-frames for finishing and stretching the fabric. In short, an intricate network of rules was devised which was intended to standardize industry, that is, to establish a uniform standard of quality and dimensions. A later age condemned attempts to standardize industry on the plea that it hampered individual enterprise. Much of the criticism was just, because the community had by then grown ripe for a larger measure of economic freedom and for greater elasticity in the working of the industrial system. We must not, however, infer that in former centuries the individual could have been safely left in the conduct of his business affairs to the promptings of enlightened self-interest. Nowadays the maxim of trade runs—" The interest of the seller is sufficient security to the buyer for fair dealing " ; and it is believed that competition will promote its fulfilment. Whether or not this is true the state of industry in earlier times, at all events, justified a policy of regulation if not necessarily the particular forms which it favoured. In the seventeenth century it was a byword 'to shrink as northern cloth' ; and the reputation which Bradford, now the metropolis of the worsted industry, had gained for fraudulent work may be gauged from a verse in a Methodist hymn :

" On Bradford likewise look Thou down
Where Satan keeps his seat ".

There are sufficient indications that official supervision was needed with a view to foster elementary ideas of honesty and give credit to manufactures by the prevention of abuses ; while it also harmonized with the gild tradition that industry should be 'orderly governed'. And the discipline imposed by the gilds and by the state may well have played its part in schooling the producers of wealth in habits of self-restraint, and in instilling into them a sense of those economic virtues on which alone can be built up an enduring reputation for sound workmanship and just dealing. In the modern trend towards the standardization of products (the necessary concomitant of mass production), in the rapidly expanding volume of legislation for purity (especially in food) and workmanship (especially in house-building), and in recent proposals that the state should encourage improvements in quality and design, we have in essence a reversion to an earlier viewpoint.

Among the legacies bequeathed by the mediaeval gilds to the mercantilist state was the principle of price regulation [1]; and we are likely in the near future to witness a marked revival of the control of prices in the case of the necessities of life. The conviction of consumers that price movements were due to the machinations of middlemen gave birth to a series of experiments intended to secure stability of prices. Commodities of which the price was fixed by the state at one period or another include cloth, silks, ale, wines and tea, but the conspicuous examples of continuity of policy were the two primary necessaries of bread and coal, for here a serious rise in prices easily assumed the proportions of a national catastrophe. Attempts to govern the price of bread extend from the thirteenth to the nineteenth century. They were intended, explained Davenant at the end of the seventeenth century, to " give the common people the benefit of plenty ", the weight of bread increasing as the price of corn fell. He was not in favour of price regulation for all commodities but drew a distinction between those of a uniform character, such as bread, and those capable of improvement by " skill, art and care ". In the former case he considered that limitation of the price " may be for public advantage ", yet in the latter it was " impracticable and a bar to industry ". Coal, like bread, came within the first of these two categories. It is safe to say that no economic question in the seventeenth and eighteenth centuries agitated the public mind more persistently than the price of coal, and the repeated though fruitless efforts made by the authorities for over two hundred years to check its continuous advance represent an illuminating episode in the age-long conflict between producers and consumers for control of the market. The extortions of coal merchants were lampooned in one of Crowley's ' Epigrams ' on a sixteenth-century ' Colier of Croydon ':

> " Men thyncke he is cosen to the Colyar of Hell ".

Nor were bakers, wine-sellers and ale-wives more popular

[1] There is also an example of state control of dividends. The maximum amount of dividends of the East India Company was fixed in the eighteenth century. This constitutes a precedent for state control of the dividends of ' utility ' companies at the present day.

in earlier days. In the middle ages bakers who broke the 'assize' of bread were drawn upon hurdles through the streets of the town with the defective loaf hanging round their necks: the seller of unsound wine was compelled to drink a draught of the wine which he sold and the remainder was then poured over his head—a poetic form of justice: the fraudulent ale-wife was liable to be placed in the 'cucking-stool'. The municipal authorities showed themselves lax in their enforcement of these penalties; and on one occasion at Coventry the commons rose and threw loaves at the mayor's head because he neglected to punish the bakers.

The sixth restriction on manufacturers was the most deeply resented of all the restraints placed on industrial capitalism. No feature of the economic policy of the early mercantilist state has attracted more attention than the ill-starred industrial experiments known as the patents of monopoly, and nothing has done more to bring it into discredit. Under the patent system the state bestowed the control of an industry on an individual or a group of individuals acting in a corporate capacity. The delegation of governmental functions to private persons seeking their own profit tended to create a kind of feudalism in industry. At the present day public opinion is beginning to look with favour upon the idea of establishing corporate bodies to administer important national services: these bodies are specially constituted to ensure that they serve not the interests of their members but those of the community. The patent system was something radically different, since the 'projectors' into whose hands was confided a branch of industry or trade were concerned only to exploit their opportunities for personal gain. Apart from the oppressive and self-seeking conduct of the agents whom the Crown employed in its projects for stimulating industrial development, grave mistrust was also aroused on account of the suspicion which attached to the sincerity of its motives. A protectionist policy, intended to make England economically independent of foreign countries, was associated with a fiscal policy of finding new sources of income which would make the executive politically independent of the legislature. The attempt to combine in a single scheme aims widely dissimilar was invariably disastrous. A genuine, if mistaken, national object lent colour to specious proposals for raising money, while the lure of revenue warped the government's judgment and blinded it to the rocks which lay ahead. It must be noticed, however, that the pecuniary motive was not entirely without justification, for the Crown could reasonably claim that the loss of customs duties on prohibited articles should be compensated by an excise on the commodities produced at home. Unfortunately the patents were so ill-managed that the sum extracted from the consumers was out of all proportion to the amount which reached the exchequer, the greater part being intercepted by the monopolists. The fundamental defect of the patent system lay, in fact, in the malpractices of its administrators and even a good patent could be rendered noxious by the servants of the patentee.

None the less we shall miss much of the significance of the patents of monopoly, if we concentrate our attention solely upon the tortuous fiscal proceedings of the Crown or upon the extortions of its agents. There was another side to the patents, and it constitutes their true importance as an episode in English economic development. This side reflected a real desire to introduce new industrial arts—just as to-day we are confronted with the necessity of supplementing the staple export industries with the highly specialized products of modern technology in order to keep abreast of the changing needs of a world market. In the sixteenth century England was behind the Continent in several branches of industry, for example, cloth-finishing, glass-making, paper-making and mining. Her dependence upon other countries ran counter to the maxims of economic nationalism ; and some of the patents at any rate were deliberately intended to free England from her handicaps, and make her self-sufficing so far as her natural resources permitted. The soap patent, for instance, provided that no foreign soap should be imported and that native soap should be made with home-grown materials. Similarly, the salt and glass patents professed to encourage English manufactures. The fostering of infant industries is of course a normal objective in protectionist states, but nowadays it is accomplished by means of tariffs and subsidies. The peculiarity of the mercantilist methods was that they strove to achieve self-sufficiency by the prohibition of imports, coupled with the concession of exclusive privileges to an individual or company. Thus they vested complete control of the market in the hands of a single producer, because protection from external competition was combined with the suppression of independent enterprise at home: the sequel, as may be readily imagined, was a considerable advance in prices. A parallel situation arises in our own economy when a combine which has established a virtual monopoly in the domestic market fortifies its position by entering into agreements with international cartels.

I have sought to show that the claim of the state to regulate the industrial life of the community was in harmony with a deep-seated tradition. Another sign of the essential continuity of economic outlook is afforded by the survival of the craft gilds. These institutions, which have played a great part in English economic life, are often mentioned at the present day when it is a growing practice for trade associations to arrogate to themselves the name of historic bodies widely different in composition and functions. The mediaeval craft gild may be defined as a group of producers associated together in the pursuit of a common calling. It comprised not only employers but also employees (journeymen and apprentices), who looked forward to the day when they would take their place among the masters of the gild as fully qualified craftsmen. It was first and foremost an industrial organization but religious duties, the performance of pageants, the care for the poor and the education of the young were no less part of its functions than its economic activities. The latter included the regulation of wages and hours of labour, the systematic inspection of workshops, and efforts to reconcile the interests of producers and consumers by insistence upon sound workmanship, good quality and a just price reasonable alike to buyer and seller. Thus the craft gilds embodied a whole way of life, economic, social, religious and artistic, into which the individual was completely absorbed, and which gave him in the eyes of the world both status and prestige.

It is sometimes the usage to speak of the 'decline' of the craft gilds after the sixteenth century. The term must be understood to mean that the growth of new centres of industry, where the writ of the gilds did not run, deprived the crafts of their former predominance in the industrial order. It must not be taken to imply that the craft gilds ceased to be of any account in the national economy, for they continued to perform some of their functions. The persistence of the gild regime is shown by the numerous grants of incorporation which both the Crown and Parliament made during the seventeenth century to newly-formed or old-established crafts. The erection of these companies indicates how strongly entrenched was the traditional idea of the corporate rule of industry. The dominating sentiment still supported in principle the exercise of authority in economic affairs. It held, to quote a contemporary view, that the craft gilds had "worked great good in respect that the government of every artificer and tradesman being committed to men of gravity, best experienced in the same faculty and mistery, the particular grievances and deceits in every trade might be examined, reformed and ordered". In accordance with this sentiment various proposals were advanced in the seventeenth century for the general reconstitution of industry on the basis of trade associations armed with powers of control and search. These proposals, which in a modified form are again becoming articulate in many quarters, would have reversed the course of development since the close of the middle ages. They failed to materialize and in consequence the advancing tide of individualism swept on with unrestrained force.

§ 2. *Commerce*

In the years that lie between the world wars (1919–39) two problems were outstanding—the balance of international payments and the trend towards economic self-sufficiency. These problems were not new problems though circumstances now gave them a prominence which they had not enjoyed for a century. They were the staple topics of discussion in the age of mercantilism, to which in this respect our own age exhibits a striking resemblance. In a subsequent chapter I shall have occasion to consider them in their current bearings, for upon the nature of their solution depends the whole structure of international economic relationships after the second world war. It is however an indispensable preliminary to the proper understanding of these problems that we should view them in their relation to England's first planned economy, of which they constituted an integral feature. The present section, therefore, is designed to indicate what part was played in the domain of public policy, firstly by monetary factors and the balance of trade, and secondly by the pursuit of economic self-sufficiency.

For many centuries England adhered to a commercial system known as the mercantile system, and we have long been accustomed to take our interpretation of it from *The Wealth of Nations* : indeed, there are not wanting credulous disciples at the present day who attribute the overthrow of mercantilism to the teachings of this work. Adam Smith was unquestionably a great intellectual force, but as in the case of other outstanding figures the real nature and extent of his influence have been obscured by legendary accretions and by the repetition of well-worn clichés. On many fundamental points it is necessary to reconsider afresh the traditional views—more especially, mercantilist opinion on money ; the reasons for the adoption of free trade ; and the movement towards *laissez-faire* in industry. Here I shall speak of the first, while later I shall endeavour to show

how the current notions on the other two points also need to be modified.

The mercantile system is defined by *The Oxford English Dictionary* as " a term used by Adam Smith and later political economists for the system of economic doctrine and legislative policy based on the principle that money alone constituted wealth ". John Stuart Mill wrote: under the mercantile system " it was assumed . . . that wealth consisted solely of money ". Nothing has done more to discredit mercantilism than the unquestioning acceptance of the interpretation placed upon it by these two economists whose writings formed the economic bible of successive generations of Englishmen. For many decades it has been regarded as axiomatic that the whole structure of mercantilist doctrines and policy was grounded upon a confusion of money with wealth. Yet it is, on the surface, a singular notion that a system of economic policy which endured for several centuries should have had its basis in pure fantasy ; or that the business men of the seventeenth century—whose education was often much wider than that enjoyed by their modern successors, for they sometimes knew Hebrew, Greek and Latin, and (like Mun, Child and Dudley North) could compose instructive economic ' Discourses '—should have entertained delusions about money and wealth which are patently absurd. It can be demonstrated that the bulk of mercantilist writers did not believe in the crude fallacies generally attributed to them. They did not misconceive the true nature of wealth which they elucidated in comprehensive terms as ' every kind of useful possession ', nor were they ignorant of the true functions of money. I have quoted elsewhere [1] many representative authors from the early sixteenth century onwards, whose writings reveal clearly that money was not identified with wealth, and that its principal purpose—to serve as an instrument of exchange—was recognized in an unmistakable way. Abundant statements on the nature of wealth and money can be cited in support of the view that the general body of mercantilist

[1] In *The Economic History of England*, vol. iii.

thought (1550–1750) was not built on a Midas-like conception of wealth—' the narrowing lust for gold '. Although occasional lapses and unguarded phrases may be found in ' Discourses ' which were not intended as economic treatises, the instructed opinion of the seventeenth century was interpreted by the historian of the Royal Society (in 1667) when he criticized the ' Spaniards in America ' because their ' chief design ' was the transportation of bullion, which was so profitable that they neglected ' many other of its native riches '. Nor was this enlightened attitude confined to a few thinkers in advance of their times. In a parliamentary debate in the reign of James I. it was pronounced " a general opinion that any kingdom that is rich in staple commodities must needs be rich ". (We are apt even to-day to lose sight of this fundamental truth.)

It is of course undeniable that one object of England's first planned economy was the acquisition of the precious metals—not owing to any confusion with wealth but because they were indispensable as instruments of exchange at home and for the liquidation of the adverse balances which might arise in the course of foreign trade. Although credit instruments (bills, cheques and bank notes) were in use, paper money could not wholly take the place of metallic coins—after all gold was retained in circulation in England down to the first world war. The precious metals had become more plentiful through the discovery of America, but mercantilist governments were moved by a genuine fear of the country lapsing into scarcity again ; and their persistent anxiety was based on actual conditions. Currency difficulties were incessantly cropping up because the supply of circulating medium was not always adequate for the needs of industry and trade. Davenant—who enjoyed perhaps greater authority than any other seventeenth-century economist—voiced the real mercantilist viewpoint when he declared, on the one hand, that the ' true riches ' of a realm consisted of industrious inhabitants and natural products ; and on the other, that there must be enough money " to keep the wheels of the machine in motion ", that is, for the payment of rent, wages, commodities and taxes. An insufficiency of specie to drive the nation's trade starved commerce of its 'radical moisture' and lessened its volume. Modern economists have expressed a similar view that a large command of resources in the form of currency renders business easy and smooth.

The mercantilists were not only concerned to prevent a scarcity of money; they also wanted to keep its quantity ever increasing since a rise in prices was favourable to industry. Our respect for the acumen of mercantilist writers is heightened when we find that already in the early seventeenth century they drew attention to the economic stimulus of an expanding currency. Indeed the mercantilist emphasis on treasure largely had its roots in the historical fact that the more abundant supply of the mechanism of exchange in the sixteenth century unquestionably served to lubricate the mechanism of production. In addition the government had an interest in augmenting the amount of precious metals in circulation, for in time of war it was enabled to make essential purchases with a commodity universally acceptable. Hence the argument for a plentiful stock of money as the 'life of commerce' was reinforced by the needs of national defence, which demanded the sinews of war. In this connexion it may be recalled that the German government down to 1914 kept a war chest at Spandau[1]. One final consideration must not be overlooked. The currency system was ultimately part of a general protectionist system framed to obstruct the 'excessive import' of foreign commodities and ensure that the latter were paid for with native goods instead of money. I shall describe in another chapter how the idea of balancing commodity exports and imports with each country was resurrected between the two world wars—with precisely the same end in view.

A famous controversy sprang up between two schools of thought as to the best method of conserving and aug-

[1] In both world wars the British government financed its purchases abroad partly by the sale of foreign securities.

menting the national stock of the precious metals. The bullionist school favoured restrictions on their export—this was the method actually adopted (as regards gold) by all countries, including our own, in the thirties of the present century. The mercantilist school believed that the precious metals could be sent out of the country like any other commodity provided a favourable balance of trade, a surplus of exports over imports, brought money back into the country. The conclusion followed that the government should regulate not the flow of precious metals but the stream of commerce, directing it into channels which would secure a favourable balance of trade. With the virtual extinction of the bullionist school in consequence of a historic change in English monetary policy—when the export of foreign coin and bullion was legalized (1663)—the mercantilist doctrine triumphed and the balance of trade became the touchstone of national prosperity, as it is likely to be once again in the coming decades. Its practical influence was profound. It furnished the arguments for the severe curtailment of intercourse between England and France on the ground that the balance of trade with France was unfavourable to us; and it was the partial revolt of economists against its teachings which inaugurated the first phase of the free trade movement. The mercantilist theory of foreign commerce, while it marked an advance upon the crude doctrines of the bullionists, tended to foster a one-sided view of oversea trade since it measured its value by its balance rather than by its volume and character. To-day foreign commerce is vital to our existence because it supplies us with foodstuffs and raw materials. But until the 'Industrial Revolution' England raised her own food supply and the raw material for her greatest industry (the woollen manufacture), and banking and credit facilities were still incomplete; it was therefore natural that foreign commerce should often be esteemed for the addition which it made to the stock of precious metals. It was the obvious means of accumulating gold and silver when a country had no mines of its own.

In these days when the balance of international payments has become one of our outstanding problems, we are enabled to understand the concern of the mercantilists to ensure a favourable balance with a more sympathetic insight than was displayed by their critics, the classical economists. An unfavourable balance means a drain of gold abroad to pay for the excess of imports over exports ; and a decrease in the quantity of money in a country causes changes in the general level of prices which may produce serious social reactions and bring on an industrial crisis. It is no doubt true (as the orthodox economists averred) that in ' the long run ' the gold will come back provided the fall in prices stimulates exports and diminishes imports, thus turning the balance in the country's favour and restoring equilibrium. The mercantilists, however, were exercised with what happened in ' the short run ', that is, with the consequences entailed during a period of transition by a contraction in the volume of the currency ; and governments to-day adopt a precisely similar attitude, which partially explains why they seem nearer in spirit to the mercantilist viewpoint. The shrewd business instinct of seventeenth-century England —" There are able heads in England to consult on matters in trade ", it was remarked in the reign of Charles II.—was seeking to avert what actually occurred after the war of 1914–18, namely, the maldistribution of gold among the nations. The restrictions which in recent years were placed by all states alike on the export of gold show that the movement of gold continues even in the twentieth century to exert a potent influence upon the economic situation.

In the light of our own experiences, we may perhaps feel less disposed to concur in the judgment which it has hitherto been the practice to pass upon mercantilism—that it was based upon a fallacy. The *fons et origo* of this condemnation was Adam Smith's assumption that no official ' attention ' was needed to " supply us with all the gold and silver " required. Actually the modern device of raising the bank rate in order to protect the gold reserves is only the counterpart of the methods adopted by the mercantilists to secure an adequate amount of the precious metals for the proper functioning of the economic mechanism. And the position was the more difficult in earlier centuries inasmuch as England could not freely import bullion from abroad owing to the embargo laid by certain European countries (for instance Spain, and at one time even Holland) on the export of the precious metals. Moreover three great branches of foreign trade—East India, Baltic and Levant—depended on the export of bullion, of which the supply had necessarily to be replenished from other sources. Herein lay one reason for the importance attached to the balance of trade as 'a national object'. A favourable balance with one country enabled England to support an adverse balance with another country whose products were vital to her, such as iron and naval stores.

Pre-occupation with the subject of money has had the unfortunate effect of fostering a distorted conception of the mercantile system, and obscuring its more essential aspect as a planned national economy based on self-sufficiency. To appreciate the true significance of mercantilism it must be viewed not *in vacuo* but in relation to its antecedents. A correct historical perspective will take account of the evolutionary process which brought the mercantilist state into being, and it will seek to interpret its many-sided phenomena in the light of its genesis and development. Mercantilism is town economy writ large. By this I mean that the industrial and commercial activities of the community ceased to be organized on an urban basis, and local interests were merged in those of the country as a whole. The ascendancy which the towns enjoyed in remoter times lapsed when a national regime replaced a municipal regime as the mainspring of economic growth: disintegration, which had been the feature of the older society, began to yield to consolidation. The transition from the town economy which prevailed in Early England to the national economy dominant in the age of mercantilism had already made marked progress in the later middle ages. The process of unification, as it crystallized in the gradual concentration of economic forces in the state, is seen in a variety of directions—in the assimilation of municipal practices to a uniform standard ; in the legislation which regulated on a nation-wide basis the woollen industry, the conditions of labour, the assize of bread, the assize of weights and measures, the currency and the customs system ; in the break-down of the barriers to internal trade ; and in the formulation of a common policy in external trade. Nevertheless, while the state represented a more comprehensive view of society, now bound together in a community of economic life, it inherited the municipal armoury of ideas and weapons. It moulded itself upon the example set by the towns and applied the existing machinery on a larger scale. The unit was no longer the borough with its genuine sense of solidarity though narrow range of vision, but the nation ; yet the enlargement of the unit left unchanged the concepts in which the older structure was rooted, until they were modified under the insistent pressure of individualism.

A comparison of town economy and national economy enables us to discern the essential continuity of economic policy. In the stage of a town economy every borough strove to become a complete entity, a self-dependent body. It displayed jealousy of other burghal communities towards which it conducted itself after the fashion of an independent city state armed with active powers of aggression and defence ; it sought to institute a monopoly of industry over an extensive area ; and it imposed trading disabilities on the strangers within its gates. In the stage of a national economy the body of tradition created by municipal practices was incorporated within the framework of state action. Its pivotal features, and especially the basic principle of exclusiveness, remained unaltered in so far as they implied the aim of self-sufficiency. The underlying idea was to establish the strength of a state by making it independent of other states in the economic sphere : to use modern terminology it pursued a strategic economy based on power rather than a welfare economy based on abundance. The development of the national resources was designed to promote national security, and 'consideration of power' took precedence over 'consideration of plenty' (the antithesis is Bacon's). It should be observed that the notion of self-sufficiency—or autarky as it is now often termed—does not imply economic isolation, that is, the complete severance of all economic ties with other countries. It does not, therefore, debar international trade—the interchange of commodities between countries. The mercantilist ideal was that a community should rely upon its own resources, agricultural and industrial, essential for its existence. This meant that normally it must produce its absolute necessities in respect of foodstuffs and manufactured articles to the fullest extent possible, and it must also possess its own mercantile marine. In addition it should utilize commercial relationships with other countries to supply deficiencies which could not be made good at home, in return for the export of its own surplus products.

Accordingly the real kernel of the mercantile system lay in the protection of agriculture, industry and navigation; and the criterion applied to foreign trade was its reaction upon the other branches of the economic system. The accumulation of treasure was not one of the fundamentals of mercantilism. Its subordinate place in the mercantilist scheme may be gauged from the fact that the statute-book is burdened with innumerable acts relating to tillage and manufactures and shipping, but only one law of importance concerns treasure and this (as early as 1663) affirmed the right to export foreign coin or bullion: previous to its enactment free trade in gold and silver had been in practice conceded through the issue of licences. No stronger proof is needed that the mercantile system was grounded, not on a confusion of money with wealth, but on the attainment of a balanced economy which in the interests of national security sought to achieve economic independence as the corollary of political independence.

To interpret mercantilism in the sense of economic nationalism does not involve the conclusion that it is necessarily a better system than its antithesis—international economic co-operation. The former aspires after self-sufficiency. The latter rests upon a more advanced principle, the international division of labour where each country concentrates its energies upon the pursuits for which it is best adapted and exchanges its surplus products for those of other countries—thereby affording the possibilities of a higher standard of life through a greater command over the bounty of nature and the resources of human skill. Now that the mirage of self-sufficiency has again cast its spell over a distracted world, and even found influential advocates in our own midst, the following quotation from a seventeenth-century writer is worth pondering. "To say, as many are apt to do, that England can live of itself without the assistance of any foreign nation is to give it not the least commendation beyond any other country. But to say, and that truly, that England by the industry of its inhabitants employed in shipping, plantations, mines, manufactures, pastures and tillage, doth not only abound in all sorts of commodities as native meat, drink, clothes, houses and coaches fit for the necessities, ease and ornaments of life, but can outvie most nations of the world for the vast plenty in varieties of wines, spices, drugs, fruits, silks, pictures, music, silver, gold, precious stones and all other supports of grandeur and delight, that is to speak it a truly civilized and glorious nation indeed". Economic nationalism is in fact the counterpart of extreme political nationalism; yet it must be recognized (as its recrudescence in recent years suggests) that it has a measure of justification where security is lacking, which its doctrinaire critics have failed to appreciate.

The resources of England, however, were inadequate to provide her with the raw materials required in certain industries, and her dependence upon alien sources infringed the cardinal maxim of the mercantile system. Hence the importance which was attached to the foundation of colonies, for they afforded the means by which foreign commodities could become 'native' to the realm: they opened up the vision of an empire knit together by economic ties in which each part sustained and nourished the whole, and the mother country and the colonies were made complementary to one another. Thus, in harmony with the fundamental principles of mercantilism, the conception of a self-supporting country eventually broadened into that of a self-supporting empire—a conception which in some quarters is being resurrected to-day. The idea of imperial economic relationships was firmly entertained ; and there was a consensus of opinion that the colonies existed to bring benefit to the parent state in consuming its manufactures, in employing its ships and in supplementing its resources in raw materials.

The legal structure of the mercantile system rested upon three pillars—the corn laws, the protection of industry, and the navigation acts. Of the corn laws I shall speak in the next section : they prove that the mercantilist state, while it was at pains to stimulate manufactures, endeavoured to avoid a one-sided development of the national economy. Adam Smith's famous dictum—that the discovery of America and a passage to the East Indies by the Cape of Good Hope raised the mercantile system " to a degree of splendour and glory which it could never otherwise have attained ", by making the towns of Europe become the manufacturers and carriers for Asia, Africa and America—led him to the conclusion that the object of mercantilism was to enrich a nation " rather by trade and manufactures than by the improvement and cultivation of land ". Yet in the case of England, at any rate, it was perhaps the most instructive feature of mercantilism that it did not sacrifice agriculture to industry but sought to preserve something of a balance between them : the soil still fulfilled its natural function of providing food. Of the navigation acts—which imposed the obligation to employ native ships in order to foster the growth of a mercantile marine—it need only be said here that they were a legacy of the middle ages since the policy of safeguarding the carrying trade dates from the fourteenth century. The methods of protecting industry were similar to those adopted in the case of agriculture, namely, the discouragement of certain kinds of imports by prohibitions or heavy duties and the encouragement of certain kinds of exports by the payment of bounties.

The system of promoting the producer's interests has been regarded as the " decisive novelty in mercantilism " and its " most important original contribution to the history of economic policy " ; but the protection of native manufactures was not peculiar to mercantilism. It was an integral part of mediaeval statecraft and it gradually crystallized in a succession of measures against imports. This feature of mercantilism was actually a deeply-rooted phenomenon, and in essence it was an extension of the spirit which had led the burghers of each mediaeval town to erect barriers against every other town—the instinct to protection from being civic had become national. The transition was in progress in the course of the fourteenth and fifteenth centuries, and it was finally consummated in the mercantile system which thus reflects the continuity of economic ideas adapted to the conditions of a changing environment. The mercantilist argument in favour of protection as stated in the preface to James I.'s Book of Rates has a familiar ring—" If it be agreeable to the rule of nature to prefer our own people before strangers, then is it much more reasonable that the manufactures of other nations should be charged with impositions than that the people of our own kingdom should not be set on work ". Apart from the pressure of vested interests, manufacturers and artisans alike, the basic motives for protection in the middle ages and the succeeding centuries down to the present day have always been the fear of unemployment coupled with the desire to foster infant industries. " All the nations of Europe ", declared *The British Merchant* (1713) in words that are scarcely less true to-day than when they were written, " concur in this maxim that the less they consume of foreign commodities the better it is for them ". What is distinctive of mercantilism, as compared with earlier times, is the more systematic application of a protectionist system in all spheres of the national economy in order to develop native productive sources of every kind, and it was due to the conscious pursuit of the ideal of self-sufficiency.

It is necessary to observe that the mercantilists did not disapprove of all imports or approve of all exports. Their discrimination between different branches of trade suggests that they were guided by ' general maxims ' which furnished the criterion whether any branch was beneficial or prejudicial. They encouraged the export of manufactured articles but frowned upon the export of raw materials. It is true that the shipment of coal abroad was permitted (subject to a heavy duty) but the staple commodity of the realm, wool, was rigorously kept for the home market. The manufacturers claimed the right to monopolize the raw material produced at home, of which Dryden boasted in *King Arthur* :

> " Though Jason's Fleece was fam'd of old,
> The British wool is growing gold ;
> No mines can more of wealth supply ".

And they prevailed in their demand that it should not be sent abroad to feed the looms of their foreign rivals, " so that we may not be killed with arrows from our own quiver ". The protection of the woollen industry was the most tenacious doctrine in the economic creed of the mercantilist state ; and for two centuries it was a leading principle of English commercial policy to stop the export of the chief raw material. The embargo remained in force down to the third decade of the nineteenth century despite the persistent efforts of the wool-growers to secure its repeal. In the case of imports the mercantilists regarded as ' eminently bad ' the wares which competed with home products ; they deprecated, as the author of the *Libelle of Englyshe Polycye* did in the fifteenth century, ' things of mere luxury and pleasure ' ; yet they recognized the utility of commodities with which the nation could not dispense (raw materials) or which could be re-exported. On this basis was constructed an elaborate protective network of prohibitions and high tariffs on foreign manufactured goods, combined with the removal of duties on foreign raw materials : at the same time the export of most native products was stimulated by fiscal immunities—the remission or reduction of duties—as well as by the institution of bounties. The embargoes laid on the transportation of machinery and on the emigration of skilled artisans were other links in the chain of protection similarly devised to safeguard the English producer against his alien competitors.

The system of protection had its counterpart in the efforts to promote by direct means the domestic consumption of native manufactures. A strong agitation in favour of the compulsory wearing of English cloth sprang up in the seventeenth century. In the course of a parliamentary debate opposition was voiced on the plea that it was " hard to make a law whereby we shall not know our wives from our chambermaids ". After the Restoration it was enacted that the dead must be buried in woollen cloth.

> " Since the Living would not bear it,
> They should, when dead, be forc'd to wear it ".

Again when the cap-makers complained that men had left off wearing caps, Parliament ordered everyone above six years old ' except ladies and gentlemen ' to wear ' a cap of wool ' on Sundays and holidays, because the wearing of caps was ' very decent and comely '. An eighteenth-century pamphleteer commented sarcastically on the efforts at enforced consumption : " No other law is wanted to complete the business but only one, that our perukes should be made of wool ". The state endeavoured to regulate not only the apparel but also the diet of its subjects. After the Reformation the policy of ' Fish Days ' was adopted, requiring abstention from meat on certain days in the week—" so the sea-coasts shall be strong with men and habitations, and the fleet flourish more than ever ". One fish, the herring, which played an important part in the fate of empires—the decline of the Hanseatic League and the rise of Holland—was held in particular repute as the 'king of fish'. "No clothing comparable to the English bay nor pheasant excelling a seasonable English red herring", was the verdict of Spaniards in the seventeenth century. And the housewife had at her command recipes for its preparation which ran into many scores.

Every social and political system contains within it the seeds of its own decay, and once it is in process of disintegration the antiquated vestiges of a worn-out regime readily evoke adverse comments. Part of the criticism directed against the mercantile system is based upon an erroneous interpretation of its aims. Part reflects the inability to grasp the fact that a nation is a living organism whose growth is determined by historical conditions which the rulers of a community must take into account in their conduct of public affairs. In every phase of economic development the new is interwoven with the old; and the trend of statecraft necessarily depends upon the degree to which traditional influences still retain their potency. Only as the new asserts itself at the expense of the old does a marked modification in statecraft become feasible.

To form a just and balanced estimate of the mercantile system two things need to be borne in mind. In the first place, as I have sought to explain, mercantilism when viewed as an historical category appears in a different light from that in which it is commonly depicted. It represented a situation in which the city state of mediaeval times had developed into a national state without shedding its exclusive and self-centred character. In the second place, the aims and achievements of mercantilism must be appraised, not by a minute scrutiny of economic literature of varying degrees of merit and authority, but by a comprehensive grasp of public policy as it was framed in acts of Parliament and administrative regulations. We may, for instance, discount the erroneous opinions on the subject of money—which were not unknown then as now—when we find that they were not reflected in actual mercantilist practice; and other examples exhibit the divergence between economic ideas and economic realities. More fairly we can criticize the mercantile system for pursuing aims which were mutually contradictory. The navigation acts were intended to foster a mercantile marine but they hampered industry and commerce upon which the carrying trade depended : the protection given to one branch of industry was often detrimental to other branches : the old colonial system served to limit rather than extend the capacity of the colonies to absorb the products of the mother country. A study of these inherent contradictions in mercantilism conveys the impression that it was largely nebulous and opportunist. The flux of human affairs and the needs of an ever-changing environment cut athwart the systematic working out of a planned economy based on specified and unvarying principles. We must therefore avoid the supposition that there was consistency or uniformity either in the conception or execution of the national programme, though there was unmistakably an underlying purpose. Another valid criticism of the mercantile system is that it looked with envy upon the prosperity of other countries—at one time Spain, then Holland, subsequently France ; and it did not recognize (as is often the case to-day) that a trading nation benefits by having wealthy customers even if they are also competitors. Its standpoint was that of a merchant who sees his opportunity in the misfortunes of a rival. The conception of a fixed volume of trade implied that the economic progress of one state was achieved at the expense of others, and that its elimination would automatically enable its rivals to grasp a larger share for themselves. The elastic nature of trade warns us against such facile assumptions. The commercial jealousies between nations proved a fertile source of wars, for which a heavy price was exacted in the dislocation of industry, the increase of unemployment and the erection of workhouses. Yet even at this early date a more enlightened view of commerce was gradually taking shape in a trend of thought wherein the world was conceived as an entity, of which the different markets were mutually dependent.

When we turn from the aims to the achievements of the mercantile system we find a sharp division of opinion. The critics belittle its practical importance. They view its legislative programme as an empty futility which pursued a mirage, the accumulation of precious metals : they maintain that it diverted the national energies into channels where they were less profitably employed : they attribute to its operation the disruption of the first colonial empire. Another school of thought discerns in mercantilism a vital element in the explanation of England's industrial, commercial and maritime pre-eminence. It holds that the expansion of her industry and oversea trade, the supremacy of her naval power, and the building up of an empire bound together by political and economic bonds, all testify to the success and wisdom of mercantilist policy.

My own estimate of the mercantile system starts with the recognition that England in the seventeenth and eighteenth centuries did make immense strides. The crux of the problem is to determine how far this notable advance was due to a planned economy. In general, economic effects are produced by the interplay of a variety of factors and it is difficult to measure the precise significance of any particular element. It is apparent that mercantilism does not furnish the sole or even the main explanation of England's industrial and commercial growth, because foreign countries lagged behind although they had recourse to similar expedients. Other influences besides legislative interference were at work, and they serve to show how intricate are the threads that weave the economic pattern. The first was the energetic and resourceful character of the business leaders, who were drawn from all sections of the community since trade was not considered a bar to ' gentility ' : I have already spoken of their creative powers as evinced in their organizing abilities, speculative instincts and technical insight. The second was the scope afforded to freedom of enterprise by the gradual relaxation of the traditional restraints. The third was the reign of law, " the best inheritance that the subject hath ", which protected the liberty and property of the individual. The fourth was the stability of the political institutions and security from invasion—" Nature has given us the best frontier in the world ", observed an eighteenth-century writer. The fifth was the abundance of natural products—especially corn and wool—and the early exploitation of the mineral wealth in coal. The sixth was the geographical situation in relation to Europe and America combined with a multitude of convenient harbours. The seventh was the adventurous spirit which encompassed the globe and opened up new markets for manufactures. The eighth was scientific discoveries in agriculture and mechanical inventions in industry. The ninth was the settlement of aliens. The tenth was the flexibility of the fiscal system which kept the burden of taxes proportioned to the expanding wealth of the nation, coupled with the general disappearance of tolls in internal trade. The eleventh was the rise of a banking system which afforded opportunities for the deposit and employment of capital. The twelfth was the cumulative effects of centuries of uninterrupted economic growth. This impressive array of the factors which enabled England to outstrip her rivals in the race for industrial and commercial supremacy makes it impossible to assert that her economic ascendancy rested on the mercantile system. When a seventeenth-century writer affirmed that " no nation in the world is naturally so adapted for a mighty trade of all sorts as England ", it was her natural advantages which he had in mind.

Nevertheless we must not under-estimate the genuine importance of the policy pursued by mercantilist statesmen. It can scarcely be questioned, for instance, that tariffs may materially assist an infant industry, though bestowing bounties fulfils the same purpose without raising prices to the consumer. In the sphere of agriculture the institution of bounties on corn exported abroad achieved positive results in encouraging the farmers to retain land under the plough. England became ' a famous kingdom for corn ' ; and whether or not this was owing mainly to a succession of favourable seasons and to technical improvements stimulated by the increase of the urban population, yet mercantilism may claim some of the credit. In other directions the results attained by legislative measures were more problematical. There are grounds for dissenting from the opinion—shared even by Adam Smith who considered them 'the wisest of all the commercial regulations of England'—that the acts of navigation, which provided the framework of naval policy for nearly two centuries, promoted the growth of shipping. Again in the treatment of Ireland, where the clamour of sectional interests produced an abundant crop of repressive legislation, mercantilism conceived in the narrowest spirit yielded the fruits which have long embittered the relations between the two countries.

One memorable feature of mercantilist policy finds a place in all the histories written on both sides of the Atlantic; and its proper elucidation is imperative not only in the interest of historical truth but for the removal of misconceptions which have been a barrier against close and sympathetic collaboration. What is termed the old colonial system was often selfish, even ungenerous, and it was nearly always unwise or inexpedient. Nothing that happened in the seventeenth century was more momentous in its consequences for the future destiny of mankind than the settlement of the New World by emigrants from the Old; but no one could foresee the incalculable significance of this impact of America upon Europe, and it was natural that the colonies should be viewed not as the nucleus of a new civilization but as the by-product of the old civilization. England's colonies were never intended to be like those of Ancient Greece, which cherished the sacred fire taken from the hearth of the parent state to remind them of their common origin, while they retained complete independence in the management of their domestic concerns. The English settlers in the New World also carried with them the sacred fire in the form of a knowledge of law and the ordered liberty that springs from law, but in addition they preserved an organic connexion with the mother country from which they were sprung. The 'Acts of Trade', which governed the economic relations between England and her colonies, had injurious effects that were not always negligible. They had the unfortunate result of inducing the colonists, as Franklin bitterly protested, to "reflect how lightly the interest of all America had been estimated here when the interests of a few of the inhabitants of Great Britain happened to have the smallest competition with it". They were condemned by the Elder Pitt who expressed his conviction that "the whole commercial system of America may be altered to advantage. You have prohibited where you ought to have encouraged; and you have encouraged where you ought to have prohibited". And Burke went to the root of the matter when he claimed that a great empire cannot be supported "upon a narrow and restrictive scheme of commerce".

None the less economic grievances were not the principal cause of the American Revolution. It is incorrect to say that England lost her first empire "in consequence of an attempt to maintain the monopoly of colonial trade". This notion now grown into a hoary legend is not supported by modern scholarship. In order to judge the system on which the British Empire was based for two centuries in a true historical perspective, it must be interpreted in the light of the services rendered to the oversea dominions. England furnished the plantations with their first settlers: she found the capital for their development: she ensured them a preferential market for their produce: she safeguarded their trade-routes: she defended them from hostile attacks. Thus the old colonial system, though it assumed that the mother country was entitled to reap substantial benefits from her possessions, was far from being one-sided. Under it the colonies enjoyed reciprocal advantages in the shape of the protection, the credit and the market of the parent state. In one important commodity, tobacco, the colonists were given a monopoly of the English market at the expense of the English farmer whose interests were sacrificed. The ruthless destruction of tobacco-planting in England is a forgotten page of history. It took nearly a century to stamp it out; and the services of the militia and even of the regular troops had to be requisitioned year by year to trample down the growing crops. The maintenance of an unpopular policy in the face of widespread opposition at home was clearly due to the conviction that the welfare of the plantations was bound up with the retention of their market in this country. All things considered it may be fairly debated whether—in spite of the subordination of their economic interests to the welfare of the motherland—they did not derive from the connexion ample compensation for the sacrifices which it entailed. In any case their disabilities, however irksome they may seem on paper, could not have seriously retarded their growth: otherwise it is improbable that they would have been enabled to achieve their political emancipation. The Declaration of Independence (which indeed makes no reference to the 'Acts of Trade' beyond an allusion of doubtful significance) was born more of a sense of economic strength than of economic weakness. But I think that the lesson may be fairly drawn from the history of the first British Empire that ties of sentiment and common traditions are more likely to prove an enduring basis for a commonwealth of nations than an artificial interlocking of economic interests, which tend in the long run to breed friction rather than create good will.

Finally, in any appraisement of the mercantile system we must never lose sight of the interaction of politics and economics. No economic question was approached from a purely economic standpoint. The corn laws were a means to maintain the nation's supply of food in the event of war: the fostering of the iron industry was advocated for the sake of arms and munitions: the navigation acts were intended to build up the maritime power of the kingdom: the prohibition of the export of wool was expected to inflict 'a deadly wound' upon the national enemy, France: the old colonial system was partly planned to secure the political subjection of the oversea settlements. To this concept that economic issues must be subordinated to a larger view of the national interests our own generation is, in principle, once again returning.

§ 3. *Agriculture*

England has always been vexed with an agrarian problem. It is particularly acute in our own day when husbandry has become the Cinderella of English industries. Her ugly sisters, with their monstrous apparatus of factories and mines and crowded urban areas, strut the stage and hold the attention of the audience. The pleasant smiling fields of the countryside are only brought to the consciousness of the town dweller in the course of an occasional excursion : to him, at their best, they are playgrounds for his lighter moments. Yet it is beginning to dawn upon public opinion that the place of agriculture in the national economy constitutes a matter of grave urgency. One school of thought maintains the standpoint that farming must take its chance like any branch of industry. Its decline is an indication that capital and labour are finding a more fruitful outlet for employment in other directions. To divert capital and labour, by artificial expedients, to spheres in which they are less profitable is to misapply the national resources, reverse the natural trend of economic enterprise and sacrifice sober realities to idealism. The other school of thought regards our economic fabric as dangerously one-sided : the former balance between agriculture and industry has been destroyed for the sake of world trade. The cry is raised for a rural policy which will make the cultivation of corn profitable for the farmer, which will bring back the labourer to the land, which will attract to the native soil the capital that now finds its way to the ends of the earth, and finally, which will diminish the extent of this island's dependence upon other countries for feeding its people.

In the age of mercantilism the agrarian situation had not assumed its present serious dimensions : nevertheless it bristled with difficulties and complications. In the first place, the passage from the mediaeval to the modern village necessarily stamped rural economy with a transitional character. A momentous change was taking place in the structure of society. The failure of the Tudor monarchy to endow the English peasantry with a clear legal title to the land facilitated the concentration of property in fewer hands, and made possible the large farms to provide raw material for an expanding industry and food for an expanding population. The result was seen in the decay of 'the yeomen of England'—the small farmers, both owners and tenants. Their decline was a continuous process originally set in motion by the disintegration of the mediaeval manor, accelerated by the growth of sheep-farming in the sixteenth century, and far advanced before the last quarter of the eighteenth century. The majority of labourers still occupied some land or at least had access to the commons, and their scanty income was supplemented by the earnings of their wives and children in spinning; yet their position, too, was precarious. In the second place, the dissolution of the monasteries meant that a considerable portion of the soil passed out of the hands of its conservative-minded owners. Their more enterprising and sometimes more unscrupulous successors exhibited a greater disposition to swim with the tide. Speculation in land became widespread, and a moneyed class enriched by trade found opportunities for profitable investment in the purchase and exploitation of the great estates which were being brought into the market. The effect was to promote the more thorough utilization of the resources of the soil and of the mineral wealth beneath its surface; but at the same time the lack of regard for local custom and tradition increased the social instability generated by rapid changes. In the third place, there already existed all the elements of a problem which have come to their maturity in the present century: already there had emerged a conflict of views between the farmer and the manufacturer: already there was the insistence that agriculture must be left to the free play of economic forces—that self-interest (and not an alleged national interest) must determine the course of its development. It was this fresh orientation, this new outlook on the land, which enhances the significance of the first planned economy in its bearing upon agriculture. The issues at stake were fundamentally those which have perplexed statesmen ever since Tudor days. We shall be the better prepared to approach the problems of our own times if some attention is devoted to these issues and to the manner in which they were handled.

For centuries it had been considered axiomatic that the primary purposes of farming were to grow corn for the nation and to support on the land as large a population as possible. These were the twin postulates of agrarian economics in the light of which all rural questions were discussed and all rural changes approved or condemned. During the middle ages there was no serious challenge to these postulates. Feudal military obligations and the economic requirements of his estate combined to give the lord of the manor a motive for maintaining a numerous peasantry. In so far as there was a population problem, it arose from the shortage not from the superfluity of labour—at any rate, in the years which followed the Black Death ; and even at other times the waste or uncultivated land was always at hand to provide an outlet for any natural increase of the country stock. It is true that corn was not the only product of the soil : wool was in regular demand abroad, for down to the nineteenth century wool (and not cotton) was king. However the Cistercians, who were notable producers of wool, established themselves in remote and sparsely-inhabited regions. There was, until the fifteenth century, no marked encroachment of pasture-farming upon corn-growing and the traditional balance in husbandry remained unimpaired.

The growth of a native textile industry in the later middle ages created a new situation. The home market for raw materials expanded rapidly, and it had a profound repercussion on the fortunes of English agriculture. It drove a wedge between the two branches of corn production and wool production. The sheep-farmer no longer kept to remote regions or to the waste that was no man's property.

He now invaded the corn-fields. The foot of the sheep turned sand into gold ; but where the foot of the sheep passed, farmsteads were pulled down, cultivators of the soil were sent adrift, the open fields [1] with their maze of strips were enclosed—and the landscape, economic, social and physical, was transformed. The successful wool merchant proudly displayed on the portal of his mansion the ' posie ' :

> " I thanke God, and ever shall,
> It is the Sheepe hath payed for all ".

The fate of the victims of economic progress was inscribed in the lines of Oliver Goldsmith :

> " The mournful peasant leads his humble band,
> And while he sinks, without one arm to save,
> The country blooms—a garden and a grave ".

The conversion of cultivated land into grass land at the present day raises an economic and a social problem. On the one hand, a diminished amount of corn is grown ; on the other, a diminished amount of labour is employed. The sixteenth and seventeenth centuries were concerned only with the social problem. The supply of corn does not seem to have been adversely affected in this period by the extension of sheep-farming. The reason is that, side by side with the curtailment of the arable in certain areas, there was in progress a vital improvement in husbandry due to technical discoveries and more economical methods. This improvement, combined with the cultivation of the commons and the drainage of the Fens, resulted in an increase of crops which compensated for the loss sustained when arable was turned into pasture. Yet the social problem remained—the problem of the rural exodus. And it was the more serious in an age when the poor laws laid restraints on the mobility of labour, and when gild restrictions and the insistence on

[1] The open fields were so called because they had no permanent hedges. The temporary hedges erected to protect the growing crops were removed after the harvest, and the fields then lay open. A farmer's holding in the open fields was not a compact area, but consisted of strips intermixed with those of other farmers.

apprenticeship hindered access to urban occupations. The injury inflicted upon the occupiers of the soil involved an ethical question whether a landowner was morally justified in putting his estate to whatever use he considered best for his own interests. Sixteenth-century moralists were quick to perceive that the older conceptions of right and wrong were breaking down: in their stead was growing up the conviction that a man might do with his own as he would. More stress came to be laid on the rights of ownership than on its duties; and when land was thus treated primarily as a source of income to its owner, its real relation to the community was obscured.

It was one of the objects of the first planned economy to maintain the English peasantry on the land, to check the rural exodus, to prevent the displacement of the population from its traditional mode of life. Apart from the desire to avoid social unrest, considerations of national security reinforced the argument for official intervention because from the ranks of the husbandmen were recruited the defenders of the realm. "Whosoever doth not maintain the plough", said Cecil, "destroys this kingdom", for when military levies are raised "we find the greatest part of them to be ploughmen". Accordingly the government set its face against the commercialization of agriculture, that is, against the exploitation of the soil purely for purposes of profit without regard to the social consequences which might ensue. The urgency of the occasion was brought home by 'riotous and tumultuous' assemblies. Near the end of Elizabeth's reign a rising was planned in Oxfordshire, where it was rumoured that "the commons long since in Spain did rise and kill all the gentlemen and sithence have lived merrily there. It was but a month's work to overrun England". In the next reign occurred the Midland revolt. The insurgents called themselves 'Levellers'; and they issued a manifesto in which they protested against encroaching tyrants who would "grind our flesh upon the whetstone of poverty so that they may dwell by themselves in the midst of their herds of fat wethers".

The ministers of Charles I. made a more determined effort to stem the agrarian movement, to preserve the cornfields, and keep the villages intact. The era of ' prerogative government ', when Charles I. ruled without a Parliament, is stigmatized by constitutional historians as the Eleven Years' Tyranny. In these days, when the working of parliamentary institutions is closely scrutinized—often with eyes none too friendly—we are perhaps less ready to look upon them as an end in themselves. We are more prepared to recognize that, like other institutions, they work badly when they become a cloak for self-seeking and the pursuit of personal ends. To men like Strafford and Archbishop Laud the English Parliament, as it was then constituted, appeared to be a barrier to the realization of the social commonwealth of which they dreamt. Its members were largely drawn from the rural gentry or the urban *bourgeoisie*, that is, from the very classes which were seeking to profit by the economic opportunities of a stirring age. It was the rural gentry who, in the words of Isaiah, laid field to field : it was they who pulled down farmsteads and employed a shepherd and his dog on land where hitherto a score of families had worked and lived. It was the urban *bourgeoisie* who were displacing the independent craftsmen and creating a capitalist system with its appanage of dependent wage-earners. From a legislature composed of representatives of these classes, it might well seem hopeless to expect the social reforms on which some of the contemporary idealists had set their hearts. It is not surprising that the latter were out of sympathy with an assembly which appeared in their eyes to serve as a vehicle for the satisfaction of private interests. We can at any rate understand how many reformers in the seventeenth century might find in the conception of patriot princes ' indulgent nursing fathers to their people '—which Bacon and Strafford advocated—a better promise for the nation's welfare than in the political ascendancy of landed proprietors and industrial magnates.

The famous decade 1630 to 1640 was marked by an unwonted vigour in all spheres of social policy, and a new spirit was breathed into the administration of the laws which were probably more stringently executed than in any other period in the sixteenth or seventeenth century. The Privy Council was engaged during these years in a sustained effort to cope with the problem of destitution, but it was not content merely to relieve poverty ; and it sought to strike at the very root of unemployment in so far as this was due to the conversion of arable into pasture. Unfortunately the fiscal taint sullied the monarchy's handling of economic affairs, and debased the pursuit of social justice into an ignoble lust for pecuniary penalties displayed with a zeal that recalled the evil practices of Empson and Dudley under Henry VII. The levying of fines offered a temptation to the official tribunals to seek opportunities for extortion ; and the whole reforming programme was discredited when individuals were prosecuted for offences of which they were innocent. Even to-day historians find some difficulty in believing that proceedings, which served so conveniently to replenish the royal coffers, had any other motive behind them than that of turning breaches of the law into a source of revenue. However this may be, the agrarian policy of the Tudors and Early Stuarts proved a failure. The period during which it was seriously enforced was too short for any permanent results to be achieved. Doubtless, in any event, the economic forces set in motion by the overwhelming impact of industry on agriculture were too strong ; and henceforth the energies of the rural community were to be diverted into channels which might best satisfy the needs and requirements of the urban population. When the authority of the Privy Council waned, no further attempt was made to stem the current of economic change. After the Civil War there were issued neither statutes nor proclamations against enclosures of the open fields ; and once the landed aristocracy was placed firmly in the saddle by the Revolution of 1688, enclosures — so far from being condemned—began to be encouraged by parliamentary sanctions.

The significant thing for our purpose here is to observe

that no sooner did the Great Rebellion curb the power of the monarchy, than the new outlook on the land was clearly articulated. The plea of economic freedom—tentatively urged by Sir Walter Raleigh in the last Parliament of Elizabeth when he said : " I think the best course is to leave every man free, which is the desire of a true Englishman "—now found open expression in its widest implications. More than a century before Adam Smith published *The Wealth of Nations*, the gospel of self-interest was proclaimed. The ethical standpoint, from which economic questions had been discussed in the sixteenth century by men like Tyndale and Latimer, was definitely discarded. Another era, for good or evil, dawned when Lee, ' minister of the Gospel ', demanded to know whether landowners might not with good conscience put their lands to the best advantage. Lee was not opposed to sheep-farming, since he was prepared to trust to the profit-making instinct to promote the public good. If there were a shortage of corn, he wrote, " men will plough up their enclosed land for their own profit ; it's an undeniable maxim that everyone will do that which makes for his greatest advantage ". The argument disclosed how far men's opinions had travelled, when they were ready to accept self-interest and economic freedom as the natural basis of human society. The displaced rural population was bidden to migrate to other districts, where " they might better benefit themselves and profit the public ". Formerly the social mischief attendant upon economic changes had dominated the whole discussion. Now it was thrust into the background : it was, somewhat cursorily, dismissed with the suggestion that the victims should find something else to do. And it was not only in this appeal to self-interest that the trend of opinion was revealed, and a challenge was thrown down to the orthodox canons upheld by the state. The revolutionary notion was also beginning to prevail that the crux of the agrarian problem was the best mode of investing capital in the land and not the best method of supporting people on the land.

The new standpoint completely triumphed. Henceforth

the use of land was to be determined by considerations of what was most profitable. The owner was encouraged to give free reins to the promptings of personal gain. The social injury which resulted from selfish indulgence no longer carried its former weight. Impressive consequences flowed from the inability of the early mercantilist state to check the movement which treated agriculture purely as an economic category, and ignored its other aspect as a way of life conducted on a traditional basis. They came to a head in the eighteenth century when the rapid increase of parliamentary enclosures—a procedure stigmatized by Arthur Young as " a composition of public folly and private knavery "—gave full scope to commercial forces with little regard to their ultimate reactions.

Hitherto I have been concerned with the rivalry between the two branches of husbandry—corn production and wool production. The age of mercantilism witnessed another struggle which was even more significant for the future development of the English people. This was the conflict of interests between agriculture and industry—between agriculturalists as primary producers and industrialists as consumers of food and raw material—a conflict which in one form or another has lasted down to the present day [1]. Here both corn-growers and wool-growers found themselves united in their opposition to the claims of industry. The manufacturers wanted cheap food and cheap raw material. They therefore demanded that native corn and wool should not be exported abroad, in order that they might be plentiful and low-priced ; while at the same time they demanded that foreign corn and wool should be admitted freely into England, where they naturally entered into competition with home-grown produce. Owing to this divergence of interests the vision of an ordered commonwealth—in which the farmer and the manufacturer, the plough and the spinning wheel, co-operated harmoniously,

[1] " The landed and trading interests are eternally jarring ", exclaimed an old writer ; and the acrimony still persists.

the one to feed and the other to clothe the nation—remained unfulfilled. The problem which here confronted the statesmen of the day was of a more complicated kind than that which affected the relations between the two branches of farming. When they had to make a choice between arable and pasture, the grave social issues at stake left them almost with no alternative but to support the growing of corn and to discourage the growing of wool. When they had to choose between the claims of industry and those of agriculture, social issues appeared to be less seriously involved; and the economic issues could therefore be isolated and weighed on their own merits. It is noteworthy that the policy upon which the later mercantilist state eventually embarked in the course of the seventeenth century continued in operation until about a hundred years ago: its general tenor was to afford protection to the producer of food but not to the producer of raw material. I shall consider the solution adopted in regard to corn: of wool something has already been said.

Tillage was one of the pillars of a planned economy. It maintained people on the land in healthy employment, and freed the nation from dependence upon other countries for its food supply—"The realm doth more stand upon itself". In harmony with this broad conception of the place of agriculture in the national economy, corn producers were encouraged to raise grain sufficient to satisfy the nation's requirements and furnish a surplus for sale abroad. The agrarian policy pursued under the early mercantilist state professed to provide the requisite stimulus by permitting the export of corn and prohibiting its importation, except when prices became excessive at home. "It hath always been the care of the state", announced the Privy Council, "to keep the price of corn in times of plenty at such reasonable rates as may afford encouragement and livelihood to the farmer and husbandman". Actually the enactments made on their behalf were largely illusory. While the national destinies hung upon the will of the sovereign, the legislation which was nominally framed to protect the producer veiled a consistent determination to favour the consumer. The statutory price limit, at which the transportation of corn was allowed, was almost invariably below the price in the home market, so that legally no shipment was permissible. The main reason is doubtless that the government sought to keep the price of corn low for the sake of the poor, partly from humanitarian motives and partly to prevent disturbances. The export of corn when it was scarce and dear at home was bound to provoke resentment ; and the monarchy was sensitive to every breath of popular discontent. If its economic policy eventually alienated the middle class, as will be seen later, its social policy was intended to conciliate ' the poorer sort '. Even in the letter just quoted the Privy Council manifested its concern " to moderate [the price of corn] in time of scarcity for the relief of the poorer sort ". Moreover an illuminating debate in the House of Commons during the reign of James I. affords clear evidence that the preference shown to the consumer was approved by public opinion.

After the Restoration there was a complete reversal of the corn policy which had been followed in earlier times : genuine protection was now accorded to the English farmer. The change was due primarily to the ascendancy of the landowning class, which was no longer held in check by the coercive authority of the Privy Council. It was intended to promote the interests of the landowner whose rents would benefit, and to give the farmer an assured market for his corn. It must be noticed, however, that the adoption of a new corn policy was facilitated by the progress which was taking place in agriculture. In the later seventeenth century there came into existence a race of spirited landowners and farmers—the counterpart of the entrepreneurs in manufacturing—whose improvements set a standard to the rest of the farming community. Their exertions were attributed to the Civil War when landed proprietors, in order to repair their ruined fortunes, " fell to such an industry [to quote a contemporary writer, Houghton] and caused such an improvement as England never knew before ". The ' good husbandries ', which revolutionized English agriculture, included in particular the use of turnips (among other roots), artificial grasses, and the reclamation of the land by drainage and irrigation. The significance of roots and artificial grasses proved far-reaching. They made it unnecessary to leave a large portion of the land fallow every year, and they enabled the cattle to be kept alive in the winter. Fresh meat was rendered available throughout the year, and its substitution for salted meat in winter-time led to a decline in the death-rate and a consequent increase of population. Although partial and imperfect, the developments of the seventeenth century paved the way for the ' Agrarian Revolution ' associated with the names of Jethro Tull, Townshend, Bakewell and Coke.

Owing to the advance in agricultural technique the standard of husbandry was raised and the apprehensions of famine were allayed. From this time onwards, for a hundred years, it was believed that English agriculture could be relied upon to fulfil the national requirements. The change of policy was enunciated in the act of 1670, which permitted the export of native corn whatever its price might be in the home market. Not less important was the principle laid down in regard to foreign corn. A high duty was imposed by the act of 1670 on imported grain when prices in England were low, and a low duty was imposed when prices were high. In other words, foreign corn could only be imported when native corn was dear. The result of these measures was to yield the corn-grower almost complete protection. He could freely export his own grain, and he was protected from alien competition except when prices here soared to famine heights. The corn law of the Restoration thus gave effect to the fundamental maxim of the first planned economy that a country should aim at being self-supporting. It embodied the view expressed in the last Parliament of Elizabeth : " If corn is too cheap the husbandman is undone whom we must provide for, for he is the staple man of the kingdom ".

The encouragement bestowed on the English farmer under the Later Stuarts went further, for the system of bounties on the export of corn—which Adam Smith vigorously assailed though his criticisms were based on assumptions that were historically not well-founded—was also inaugurated after the Restoration. It was then laid down that a bounty should be paid on different kinds of grain when shipped abroad, so long as the prices at home did not exceed a stated figure. The purpose of the bounty was to ensure stability of prices, which would remove the farmers' apprehension of loss in the event of the market being glutted with a surplus of grain. It expressed the idea that the state should determine the nature of the economic activities of the community, encouraging some forms of enterprise by means of subsidies or bounties and discouraging others by the imposition of duties.

I may now sum up the general conclusions. Throughout the sixteenth, seventeenth and eighteenth centuries the course of English rural life was profoundly disturbed by the conflict between those who wished to preserve, and those who sought to disrupt, the traditional basis of agriculture. On behalf of the innovators the claim was openly made that land was to be regarded like any other commodity and converted to any use that its owner thought fit. The early mercantilist state endeavoured to uphold the maxim that land stood in a separate category, but it was unable to place any effective limits upon the commercializing of agriculture; and when the monarchy ceased to exert its former control in economic affairs, the new outlook became almost universal. The ground was thus prepared for the rapid acceleration of parliamentary enclosures, which started as a tiny rivulet and in the second half of the eighteenth century were swollen into a torrent. In another direction the economic statesmanship of the mercantilist epoch proved less impotent to influence the agrarian movement. After the Restoration was inaugurated the historic policy of encouraging tillage by means of duties on imports and bounties on exports. Whether the achievement must be placed to the credit of the later mercantilist state or ascribed, partially at least, to favourable seasons and the progress of husbandry stimulated by the needs of an urban population, England became ' a famous kingdom for corn '. She had emerged from the stage in which the Venetian envoy could write home : " In some places grain abounds, and there would be much more did not the natives shun fatigue ". Nor did she feed her own people alone. The statistics of the export trade register its growth and lend colour to the claim that England did " feed other countries ". Even in the early years of George III.'s reign Arthur Young still clung to the belief that foreign nations might be induced " to buy their corn of us than to cultivate it themselves ". In the last quarter of the eighteenth century, when the foundations of the mercantile system began to crumble, the increase of population led to the abandonment of the attempt to make England a self-supporting country. Nevertheless the protection of agriculture survived to the middle of the nineteenth century when the corn laws were at length repealed, and it has been again reinstated in our own day.

CHAPTER THREE

THE GROWTH OF FREE ENTERPRISE

MY purpose in this chapter is to trace the growth of free enterprise and to show how it transformed the economic structure as it had existed for several centuries ; while in the next chapter I shall describe its influence upon the shaping of economic statecraft. I begin with a brief sketch of the traditional organization of English society as a preliminary to a more detailed review of the forces which were responsible for its disruption.

§ 1. *The Evolution of a Capitalist System of Industry*

The village community of the middle ages constituted an agrarian partnership. The occupiers of the soil were shareholders in an agricultural concern, and their ' shares ' consisted of scattered strips of arable land together with rights of usage over the waste and meadow. When the sixteenth century had run its turbulent course, individualism had made great inroads upon the communal system ; and in many localities the partnership had been dissolved. Nevertheless a considerable part of the realm was covered with open fields, where no man was ' truly master of his own ' and the control was vested in an association of shareholders : the routine of husbandry, the rotation of crops, the seasons of ploughing, were settled by common agreement : the whole rhythm of village life was determined by joint decisions. Until the enclosure movement was accelerated under the Hanoverians a large section of the English nation formed a co-operative commonwealth, in which a detailed code of by-laws was laid down for its guidance by the village courts.

Upon the development of town life in England it was natural that the rural elements—who usually comprised the nucleus of the embryonic municipal bodies in the capacity of artisans and traders—should enter into the same relationship with each other as they and their forebears had been accustomed to in an agrarian environment. The instinct of the mediaeval Englishman was to act in concert with his fellows in his undertakings, and its strength was fortified by the conditions under which the early towns grew up. Exclusive franchises were conferred upon the boroughs, and for its grant of concessions the Crown exacted a price: it was therefore inevitable that the townsmen should seek to confine participation in their privileged position to those who were willing to bear their share of the fiscal burdens. The corporate functions of the urban community found a vehicle in the historic gilds—the merchant gilds and craft gilds; and the latter governed trade and industry just as the village courts directed the affairs of the rural community. Even after the close of the middle ages the craft gilds survived as a force with which to be reckoned. Their power and prestige had diminished but they embodied a living tradition of co-operation, and they continued to exercise a very real though limited degree of authority. In the sphere of foreign commerce similar influences made themselves felt. The Englishman conducted his business abroad not as an individual but as the member of a semi-official body whether Merchant Staplers or Merchant Adventurers. While the members of a company 'adventuring' overseas traded each on his own, they were subjected to a common discipline. They were bound by ordinances of an all-pervasive kind, which dictated to them in what centres they might market their goods, in what quantities, and with what stipulations.

When the invention of printing and the discovery of America combined with the Renaissance and the Reformation to usher in the modern era, the corporate character of mediaeval society still persisted. The traditional fabric could not readily be discarded; and to the naked eye England in the opening decades of the age of mercantilism, as in the middle ages, seemed to be a land whose economic life was organized on a communal basis. Her agriculture was regulated by the village courts and her industry by the craft gilds; moreover the principle of association was extended to new branches of foreign commerce, so that Bacon even concluded that "trading in companies is most agreeable to the English nature". Actually this corporate system had been undermined by the subtle penetration of the spirit of individualism.

The progress of individualism was for a long period so unobtrusive that it has largely escaped the attention of historians altogether. The conventional view, which is widely held, portrays a primitive economy functioning for a local market. England almost down to the nineteenth century is represented as a country of peasant cultivators where there was little industry and less trade, though it had a network of independent artisans whose chief interests were agricultural. The industrial community, according to the current impression, was composed of small producers —handicraftsmen who worked under their own roof on their own materials and with their own tools, assisted by their families or a hired journeyman and apprentices, dividing their time between their cottage workshops and their farms, and supplying the neighbourhood with rude and unspecialized wares. A sprinkling of capitalists lurked obscurely in the background but they were not considered an integral, and much less an important, element in the older structure. An article in a standard *Dictionary of Political Economy* explains how until near the end of the eighteenth century "the general character of industry in England presented broadly the same features as those which it had exhibited during the greater part of the middle ages. . . . Manufacturing industry was carried on with few exceptions by craftsmen working with their own hands in their own homes, although . . . some capitalist employers existed. . . . Employment, such as it was, was regular; fashions varied slowly and slightly; and men produced in the main, though not exclusively, for a market which was close at hand". Corresponding to this account of an immature industry is the picture drawn of English foreign trade in a book written by an economist of distinction : " [Before the nineteenth century] there were very limited manufactures in our present sense of the term, no ships to carry our superfluous goods, no foreign demand for them, no admission to other countries. . . . In fact, in the eighteenth century foreign trade was of so little importance to the majority of the inhabitants of England that, but for some importation of wheat, the whole might have been destroyed without making any appreciable change in the habits or wealth of the people ; the rich would have been deprived of some luxuries, the poor of very few, a small class of traders would have been affected, and an unimportant branch of revenue destroyed ; but no other result would have followed " [1].

In the state of knowledge implied by these quotations, it is not surprising that the introduction of machinery is generally viewed as the beginning of modern economic life. According to the common belief the inventions constitute the starting-point of our present industrial society. It is usual to trace to them all the phenomena that appear to be most characteristic of the prevailing economic and social order. Capitalism, factories, large-scale production, world-wide markets, trusts, cartels, credit instruments, trade cycles, unemployment, the industrial proletariat and trade unions—these are supposed to have come into existence with the adoption of power-driven machinery not very much more than a hundred years ago. Beyond the 'Industrial Revolution' the historians depicted centuries of slow and imperceptible growth during which the face of England remained almost unchanged. A static society slumbered in blissful unconsciousness of the dynamic forces which the invention of the steam engine was destined to let loose upon it. A fanciful picture, which has long passed for authentic history, of a backward community suddenly convulsed by uncontrollable

[1] It is often stated that foreign trade was confined to 'rare and costly objects'. Actually England exported grain, wool (until it was prohibited), coal, cloth, tin, etc. and she imported timber, iron, naval stores, etc.

economic impulses and upon which there descended, like a bolt from the blue, a whirlwind of inventions bringing in their train the capitalist system, the factory system, the wage system, exploitation of labour and social strife.

One difficulty in accepting the popular interpretation of England before the 'Industrial Revolution' lies in the astonishing contrast, which it presents, between an arrested state of social development and the outstanding achievements in the domain of literature, of politics, of exploration and colonization. It raises the natural question why the energetic qualities of the English genius found scope in every sphere except one. The answer can only be that the implied antithesis of a vigorous national movement in thought and action on the one hand, and economic stagnation on the other, is false. Already in mediaeval times spirited pioneers were finding opportunities for enterprise in agriculture as well as in industry and commerce. The break-up of the manor, the modifications in the customary routine of husbandry, the expansion of textile production and the foundation of trading companies, all bear witness to the influence of progressive tendencies. When we turn to the sixteenth, seventeenth and eighteenth centuries nothing more remote from historical truth than the stereotyped descriptions can well be imagined. There is a wealth of material to demonstrate that the age of mercantilism had a vigorous manufacturing and mercantile life of its own, in which striking economic resemblances to the modern pattern may be fairly set against the social dissimilarities born of the factory system. The predominant form of industrial organization—the domestic system (where the work was carried on in the home)—was essentially a capitalist system; and this supremely important fact must deeply colour our interpretation of the 'Industrial Revolution'. The latter involved no violent breach with the past. It produced consequences of profound significance arising from the application of steam power to industry and transport, and from the concentration of workers in factories; but it did not give birth to an entirely different regime based on the cleavage between capitalist employers and proletarian wage-earners. Much that is reputed novel in our economic structure is in reality old. Hence, to present a more correct picture of what England was like before the nineteenth century, I must describe the revolutionary changes brought about by the dissolving influences of individualism.

Individualism as a force in English society is almost as old as the corporate system itself. Yet for centuries it remained the weaker force, and it sought to express itself inside the communal shell and not apart from it. In the village it manifested itself in the husbandman who added acre to acre in the open fields, or carved a holding out of the waste land, or accumulated a stock of corn for sale in the urban market, or purchased his emancipation from labour services. The notion that mediaeval rural economy was unprogressive is a travesty of the actual conditions which prevailed. The permeation of a commercial outlook had relaxed its rigid lines and created an atmosphere favourable to more elastic arrangements. The increasing mobility of real property gave rise to a land market in which holdings or fractions of holdings exchanged hands freely : an incipient capitalism began to undermine the basis of the village community by shattering the primitive equality of the original shareholders in the common fields : the customary system of tillage, responding to the growing demand for wool and corn, revealed signs of breaking down with the gradual spread of piecemeal enclosures and profit-making husbandry. There are, indeed, abundant signs that a more vigorous peasantry was springing up under the spur of a restless individualism. In the towns the spirit of initiative was revealed in the enterprise of those who outstripped their fellows in the race, who raised themselves to wealth and honour, who developed the woollen manufacture, who opened up markets abroad, all the while retaining their status as members of the merchant gilds and craft gilds. Alike in agriculture, industry and trade there were pioneers of a brave new world and opportunities for the penetration of a capitalist mentality.

However the great transformation was brought about when individualism was no longer content to play a subordinate part, when it strove to free itself from the tangled network of communal regulations, and to become an independent and even the predominating element in the life of the nation. The far-reaching consequences exerted by this development upon the national economy and public policy were momentous. To contemporaries they sometimes appeared like a convulsion of nature. In agriculture the conflict came to a head between those who wished to retain, and those who aspired to destroy, the historic field systems. As the result of an immense acceleration of pasture-farming, the open fields with their intricate pattern of proprietary rights and antiquated practices were swept away in a torrent of commercialism. Even when their survival preserved in an attenuated form the control of the village community, the latter was only a vestige of the powers once enjoyed by the agrarian courts. In the boroughs the craft gilds, whose regime was consecrated to the principle of stability, vainly endeavoured to discourage the growth of capitalism among their members by limiting the number of apprentices and prohibiting excess of competition. When opportunity came knocking at the door the more enterprising gild-brethren, ambitious to pass their rivals in the race and become large employers of labour, were able to set authority at defiance by moving to outlying districts where the writ of the craft gilds did not run. Thus in agriculture and industry an insurgent individualism was in revolt against the cramping restrictions of a communal society. Alone in foreign commerce the corporate system persisted in its old strength and actually extended its province in new directions, owing to the unique circumstances in which oversea trade was carried on, though the independent traders—or interlopers as they were called—were growing in numbers and self-assertion.

The sphere of industrial organization furnishes the most

signal example of individualism emancipating itself from the traditional checks and restraints of an environment hide-bound by custom. It is doubtless true that seventeenth and eighteenth-century England counted numerous small producers wedded to the antiquated methods inherited from their forebears. They also exist in twentieth-century England, for it is erroneous to suppose that large producers employing hundreds or thousands of men monopolize the whole field. In many occupations at the present day the average number of operatives employed by a firm is remarkably few, and in France it is still fewer. None the less it was not the small producer who, before the middle ages had run their course, converted England into an industrial country of which the staple export was no longer raw materials but manufactured goods. It was not the small producer whose highly specialized fabrics displaced the products of Flanders, once a workshop of the mediaeval world, and found a market in every known quarter of the globe. It was not the small producer who transformed English towns from squalid and sparsely inhabited villages into prosperous urban communities with fine gild halls, hospitals, market crosses and ' bar gates ', or whose piety covered the countryside with the magnificent churches which excite our admiration. These changes were wrought by the ' adventuring ' spirit of the ' captains of industry ' —such as the fifteenth-century Tame of Fairford, who as a sheep-master raised his own material and as a manufacturer worked it up into cloth.

The advent of the large producer, in the premier industry of the country, dates as far back as the fourteenth century ; and by the end of the middle ages the great body of workers engaged in cloth-making depended upon the discretion and foresight of a capitalist class. Even a factory system emerges into the light of day in the sixteenth century. John Winchcombe of Newbury—pronounced by Fuller, the church historian, to be " the most considerable clothier (without fancy and fiction) England ever beheld " —gathered weavers, spinners and carders under one roof.

" Within one room being large and long
There stood two hundred looms full strong ".

William Stumpe took over Osney Abbey and Malmesbury Abbey, where (wrote the antiquarian Leland) " every corner of the vast houses of office that belonged to the abbey be full of looms ". Tuckar of Burford, who " daily employs five hundred of the king's subjects ", sought to gain possession of Abingdon Abbey. Other great industrialists whose names have come down to us include Humphrey Chetham of Manchester, Peter Blundell founder of the famous Free Grammar School at Tiverton, the Springs of Lavenham and Thomas Dolman of Newbury. Indeed innumerable indications testify that the capitalist spirit, as evinced in the conception and execution of speculative undertakings, is older than the 'Industrial Revolution'. In addition to the 'captains of industry' just mentioned, there were far-sighted merchants such as Sir Edward Osborne who played a leading part in establishing trade with the Levant, and financiers such as Sir Thomas Gresham who negotiated public loans and manipulated the monetary exchanges.

In the seventeenth century many notable men rose into prominence—among them Sir Edwin Sandys a principal member of the Virginia Company, Sir Josiah Child the chairman of the East India Company, and Sir Ambrose Crowley the famous ironmaster. One example of capitalist enterprise in the reign of William III. discloses a type which is often viewed as the creation of modern finance. This was Alderman Sir Joseph Herne—a financier through whom the English government subsidized its allies in the war against France, an army contractor, a company promoter, a merchant and a shipowner. Ambitious men pushed themselves up from the ranks, carved out a career, and acquired a controlling interest in capitalist concerns. The history of a peasant family in Northumbria furnishes an illustration. The founder, James Cole, lived in the reign of Elizabeth : he was a blacksmith who developed into a tradesman selling fish and grindstones. His son, Thomas, extended his operations by laying out his money at interest and he bequeathed much of his fortune to his nephew, Ralph, a grandson of James. Ralph migrated to Newcastle, invested his wealth in collieries, and became one of the chief coal-owners on the Tyne. The careers of the 'captains of industry' and merchant princes, whose names are here recorded, reveal the heights which men of commanding ability could scale either by their natural gifts or by their seizure of opportunities. The rank and file of the business world did not win the glittering prizes that are reserved for the chosen few, though upon their shoulders was reared the broad structure of industry and commerce. The important role of the shopkeeper—the indispensable link in the chain which connects the producer with the final consumer—still awaits its historian, but the autobiography of William Stout (1665–1752) allows us to follow step by step the course of one successful shopkeeper in a provincial town. It indicates how diligence and thrift enabled retailers to build up a substantial competence, and to pass into the higher grade of wholesale dealers and sometimes of merchants 'adventuring' abroad.

Abundant evidence is now available to prove that mercantilist England possessed a complex society, which functioned in an increasing measure under business leadership and bore many of the hall-marks of a capitalist system. The entrepreneur had emerged as the outstanding figure, and his activities were writ large over the whole field of economic endeavour, alike in the staple industries of the realm (cloth, coal and iron), in oversea trade and in the domain of public policy. His influence gradually permeated every branch of the national economy. The mediaeval fabric was profoundly modified in order to afford scope for his enterprise: the chartered boroughs were forced to surrender their monopolistic claims so that he might draw upon cheaper supplies of labour in rural areas: the official regulation of industry was discredited by the steady advance of *laissez-faire* principles. The entrepreneur was the powerful dissolvent of a communal regime which had been organized on the basis of craft gilds and village courts : he was equally the architect of the new England which rose upon the ruins of the old order. For good or evil it was the forces of individualism which marked out the path of progress, and won for this country the distinctive status which it enjoyed long before the nineteenth century. When the steam engine was harnessed to industry and transport it found an environment prepared for its reception—above all, a class of entrepreneurs accustomed to large-scale production, the handling of labour, the utilization of credit instruments, the dependence on imported materials and the requirements of distant and varied markets. The 'Industrial Revolution' came first to England primarily because she already had a rich and diversified economic life, and—more than any other nation—had developed her industrial, commercial and banking institutions on lines which facilitated an extensive outlay on machinery and buildings. In short the inventions were not the product of a primitive community absorbed in agricultural pursuits, but the mature achievement of an advanced community in which industry and commerce had become fruitful sources of wealth. If we destroy the legend that the inventions abruptly revolutionized the character and structure of English society, we can at least put in its place a more rational interpretation in which the mechanical changes appear as a natural phenomenon in harmony with the historical setting and as the climax of centuries of steady growth.

I do not share the view that the rise of individualism and the advent of capitalism can be explained alone in terms of self-interest, although the acquisitive instinct has been in all ages a potent influence in shaping economic conduct. Moreover the existence of capitalism before the Reformation forbids us to regard the capitalist spirit as the product of Puritanism. I believe that the explanation must be sought primarily in the impersonal and imponderable forces which govern the affairs of men. Three main factors have contributed to the evolution of a capitalist society ; and they enable us to understand why it was inevitable for capitalism to establish so complete an ascendancy in the industrial system. These factors are the extent of the market, the division of labour, and the nature of the processes. In the first place, a local market may easily be supplied by independent bodies of craftsmen. In the second place, where the division of labour is small, co-operation may be possible between the various groups of artisans without bringing them under unified direction. In the third place, when the processes require only a negligible amount of fixed capital in the form of appliances, it may be provided by the workers themselves. In the light of these factors we can best account for the development of industry on capitalist lines. An ever-widening market and a corresponding advance in production called for an intricate organization, while it also made the investment of capital a profitable venture ; the division of labour in the textile manufacture seemed to necessitate a closer cohesion of its interdependent branches ; and in certain occupations the capital expenditure increased as the processes grew more difficult, for instance, in coal-mining and glass-making. The decisive influence was the first. It was the disintegrating tendencies of an expanding market that sapped the foundations of the older industrial system based on the co-operation of independent craftsmen. The transformation of a local market into a national and international market raised problems affecting the buying of raw materials and the disposal of the finished products, which could only be handled by capitalist enterprise. In the face of the rising demand at home and abroad, it was found impracticable to maintain a procedure under which the market was supplied by small producers working on their own. Hence it was inevitable for the latter to be superseded by the entrepreneur as the master builder of the new economic order, in which the control of industry was transferred to employers of labour who stood outside the ranks of the manual workers.

I may glance first at the home market. The myth that in former centuries England was a land of self-sufficing communities—where each locality, isolated from its neighbours, subsisted on its own produce—dies hard. Even in the middle ages there existed a national demand for the specialized wares of particular districts, and the cultivators of the soil found the means to purchase them by raising a surplus of corn for sale in the towns. The fairs were the channels through which native commodities were distributed throughout the realm. Here were bought the best grades of wool from Shropshire and Leominster and the Cotswolds, textiles of innumerable varieties—of which one, made in Stamford, was imitated in Italy in the thirteenth century under the name of 'Milanese Stamfords'—tin from Cornwall, salt from the Worcestershire springs, lead from the Derbyshire mines, iron from the Sussex forges. Here also forgathered the alien traders who flocked to these shores from many parts of Europe—merchants from Venice and Genoa with costly spices from the East and silks and velvets and 'things of complacence', the Flemings with linen cloth, the Spaniards with iron, the Norwegians with tar, the Gascons with wine, and the Teutons with furs and amber. And if the oft-repeated generalizations as to the local range of the mediaeval market are misleading, still less are they applicable at a subsequent period. In the Jacobean age London drew its supplies of broadcloth from the west country, worsted cloth from East Anglia, kersies from Yorkshire, coal from Newcastle, cheese from Cheshire, butter from Suffolk, wheat from the home counties; and the metropolis was unique only in the size, not in the nature, of its requirements.

Native produce was not limited to a national market: it furnished also the needs of an international market. It included wool, England's golden fleece and the most highly-prized of her raw materials, which formerly occupied the place in our economic system now held by coal; cloth of which it was said in later days that almost half of Europe wore England's 'livery'; and a miscellany of other articles

—corn, tin, coal, pewter, metal wares, leather goods, meat, cheese, butter, honey, herrings and salmon. The growth of the international market constituted one of the epoch-making developments which give a distinctive character to the age of mercantilism. After the discovery of America and of a fresh sea route to India, the products of this country ceased to be confined to 'a very small part of the earth'—Europe and Asia Minor: henceforth they found their way to the hemisphere in the West and to the Empire of the Mogul in the East. Two new worlds, as Adam Smith justly said, were rendered accessible to the industry of Europe. The consequences made themselves felt both in respect of the volume of production and the increased trend towards industrial specialization. Near the end of the seventeenth century Davenant calculated that the annual addition to the national wealth made by the colonial and Indian trades was no less than three times that accruing from the European trade.

In opening up an unlimited field of enterprise, the extension of the market abroad was at once a challenge and a stimulus to the skill and ingenuity of the entrepreneur. The Indian trade gave a marked impulse to the art of navigation, since distant voyages necessitated the building of "goodly ships of such burthen as never were formerly used in merchandise". This benefited the ship-building and carrying trades, while in addition woollen goods were exported in exchange for silks. Moreover the industry of calico-printing was established here by "some of Britain's unnatural children, whom we call drapers", who "set all their arts to work to mimic the more ingenious Indians". The prospect that the upstart cotton manufacture might displace the old-established woollen manufacture provoked acute dissensions, which have repeatedly recurred down to the present day whenever a vested interest is menaced by some new development in industry or transport. "I question not", said one writer, "but we shall have cotton cloth, and knaves to make it a fashion, and fools enough to wear it". The fashion soon spread, and—

"Our Ladies all were set a gadding,
After these Toys they ran a madding . . .
And like gay Peacocks proudly strut it,
When in our Streets along they foot it".

The American colonies—another 'main branch' of England's wealth, described by the customs officials after the Restoration as 'his majesty's Indies'—demanded a wide sweep of commodities, and they fulfilled the anticipations that the New World would 'create a new commerce'. At their first foundation they needed cattle and foodstuffs, arms and ammunition: subsequently their growing population took from England textiles, iron wares, shoes, hats, horses, household furniture and provisions such as flour, beer, cheese and butter. And while the plantations opened up a fresh demand for the products of the parent state, they also developed into fresh sources of supply. On the eve of the War of Independence they accounted for as much as one-third of the oversea trade of the mother country. Apart from the beneficial reaction upon English industry and shipping, the obstacles to trade in Europe served (as in our own times) to accentuate the importance of the colonial market. Indeed England may be said to have called in the New World to offset the tariffs of the Old. In America trade followed the flag: in India, as also in Africa, the flag followed trade.

I may observe, at this point, that the discovery of America exerted a profound influence on England not only by extending the range of her markets but also in the sphere of monetary prices. The influx of precious metals from the New World served to promote the growth of a class of entrepreneurs, partly because it made the national wealth more liquid, and partly because the rise in prices swelled profits and so encouraged investments in industrial and commercial enterprises. In the middle of Elizabeth's reign men spoke of "the great store and plenty of treasure, which is walking in these parts of the world, far more in these our days than ever our forefathers have seen in times past".

Notwithstanding Spain's persistent efforts to keep intact the treasure which she drew from the Peruvian mines, it was drained away by the Dutch War of Independence, the English privateering expeditions and an adverse balance of trade. The precious metals in consequence were distributed over Europe. A large portion reached these shores. " How many millions we have taken from the Spaniard ", exclaimed an Elizabethan writer, " is a thing notorious ". The circulation of American silver produced an abrupt rise in the general level of prices, which caused an economic revolution in the sixteenth century and foreshadowed a political revolution in the seventeenth century. Owing to the fall in the value of money, rents rose sharply but rates of wages did not keep pace with prices. In so far as the employers of labour, whether in agriculture or industry, intercepted the surplus value—arising from the fact that the prices of their products moved upwards while labour costs remained comparatively stationary—they enjoyed an increment of profits which was doubtless a stimulus to invest capital and increase production.

A recital of the factors responsible for the rise of individualism must include the institution of a more flexible system of finance, which helped to create the requisite conditions for its proper functioning. Five significant developments facilitated the accumulation and employment of capital. The first was the growth of wealth, derived from the gains of those who produced raw materials and those who traded in them. The second was the influx of foreign investments, which were attracted to this country at a much earlier date than historians have hitherto recognized. In the early seventeenth century Dutch capitalists financed English merchants and provided the money for schemes of land drainage. The third was the universal use of credit, which enabled the fabric of commerce to rest upon an infinitely wider foundation. It is a common misconception about the older economy that the credit system was almost non-existent. It is evident that if every transaction had to take place on a cash basis, and if every entrepreneur had to rely upon his own resources to supply him with the requisite capital, the economic mechanism would have operated only in a very contracted field. It is true that the Bank of England was not founded until after the Revolution of 1688, and it is true that provincial bankers barely numbered a dozen in the middle of the eighteenth century. None the less the economic apparatus need not necessarily conform to a given pattern in order to achieve a given set of results. The railway is not a *sine qua non* of a national market nor the steamship of an international market : the cable and the telegraph are not essential for making a corner in commodities and for 'rigging' markets. Similarly a credit system can exist whether or not banks of the modern type act as intermediaries between lenders and borrowers. The remarkable extent to which credit facilities prevailed in the middle ages is evinced both by the wool trade of which every stage was financed by credit dealings, and by the abundance of mercantile debts relating to all kinds of business matters. The importance of credit grew enormously in the age of mercantilism. It was officially stated in the seventeenth century that a great part of English trade was conducted on a credit basis. Book-credit was, in fact, a normal practice and it was often extended for long periods and large amounts—no less than £20,000 was owed by one merchant in the reign of James I. The instrument of credit transactions was the bill of exchange, whose usefulness is reflected in the measures taken to invest it with legal sanction and a negotiable character.

The fourth development was the advent of banking in its modern form : of the Bank of England, in particular, it may be said that its history is an epitome of the financial history of England since the Revolution. The banks created yet another form of credit instrument through the issue of paper money, which for large payments became current in lieu of specie. The various kinds of paper credit—bills of debt and bank notes—enlarged the currency and broadened the basis of the credit structure : consequently they served in the nature of new resources and thereby quickened trade and industry. An important service rendered by the banks was the advance of loans, though even prior to the growth of banks moneyed men found no lack of suitable openings for profitable investment. Thus the entrepreneur was enabled to buy goods ' at time ' (that is, on credit), and also to buy money ' at time ' (that is, raise loans). In this way he was not precluded from extending the range of his operations, and embarking on fresh enterprises, by any inability to borrow the capital which he might require. The use of borrowed capital on a considerable scale was made possible by the abandonment of the mediaeval attitude towards the ' damnable sin ' of usury. The legal toleration of interest marked a revolutionary change in public opinion, and it gave a clear indication of the decay of the traditional ethics under the pressure of an expanding economic system.

The fifth development in the sphere of finance merits particular attention because it registered another stage in the evolution of enterprise. This was the employment of the methods of a joint-stock. Industry was financed not only by independent entrepreneurs employing their own or borrowed capital but also by joint-stock companies and partnerships. From the sixteenth century onwards these institutions afforded an important means of obtaining capital since they enabled an undertaking to derive support from a circle of investors. Hence, as at the present day, the financial organization of industry assumed a simple or complex form accordingly as it was reared on individual or associated enterprise : in the former case capital and management were vested in the same hands, and in the latter they were separated. The adoption of one or other of these forms was determined by the amount of capital required in a business, which in turn depended upon the nature of the concern and its size. Fixed capital was needed for buildings and plant, circulating capital for materials and wages. Under the factory system—interpreting the term to include work in any industrial establishment—the employer owns both the fixed and the circulating capital. Under the domestic system, where the work was done in the homes of the artisans, the ownership of capital was divided: the manual workers furnished the fixed capital in the shape of tools and workrooms, and the employer supplied the circulating capital to purchase materials and pay wages. Thus the capital invested in a domestic industry was drawn from a wide area. Its principal source was the entrepreneur himself, but in addition it was provided by innumerable artisans in their instruments of production—spinning and weaving appliances, cutlery tools, and the like.

A few illustrations may be given of the varied forms of industrial finance. In the textile industries the entrepreneurs or clothiers as a rule expended only circulating capital apart from warehouses, yet the amount was often considerable, and they were ' generally men of substance and good stocks ' (that is, capital). Indeed the fortunes raised in the woollen manufacture compel us to modify our impressions of the opportunities offered by a business career [1]. One clothier born in the late sixteenth century, Peter Blundell, left £40,000: a seventeenth-century clothier died worth near £100,000: in the eighteenth century Wiltshire clothiers possessed ten to forty thousand pounds a man. When these figures are related to current values, it will be seen that they represented immense amounts. Other types of businesses in which the entrepreneurs were responsible both for the circulating and fixed capital might necessitate an outlay beyond the resources of individuals. The beginnings of joint-stock companies are connected with enterprises of this kind, for instance, the copper industry, coal-mining, the iron industry, glass-making, etc. Hence the modern methods of financing industry were being widely practised as early as the seventeenth century; and as a corollary two vital features of the present industrial system were already known in former ages. The first was the diffusion of the ownership of capital consequent upon the system of joint-stocks and the

[1] Sir Ambrose Crowley the ironmaster, who died in 1713, left a fortune of £200,000.

workers' property in their instruments of production. The second was the separation of the ownership of capital and the functions of management—a divorce which occurs in joint-stock companies when the capitalist who invests money in a business ceases to be identical with the entrepreneur who is entrusted with the conduct of the business.

The growth of joint-stock companies gave rise, as early as the seventeenth century, to a phenomenon similar to that which we are apt to consider peculiar to modern times—namely, " that new mistery we call stock-jobbing ". The following is an example of fluctuations in the price of stock in the East India Company—it was £60 in 1664; £500 in 1685; £33¼ in 1698. One of the most memorable episodes in the history of the stock market was the South Sea Bubble, which affords a parallel to the crash on the American stock exchange in 1929. The national excitement found vent in an outburst of frantic speculation. Men hastened to borrow money to buy shares, and women sold their jewels. On January 30, 1720, £100 stock in the South Sea Company could be bought for £129: on June 24, 1720, the price reached £1050. The projects for which subscriptions were invited numbered over two hundred, and included one with a large capital for an undertaking which was to be revealed in due course! The Bubble was soon pricked; shares fell even more rapidly than they had risen; and all who had bought beyond their means were ruined. " There never was such distraction and undoing in any country ", wrote a contemporary:

> " All the riches that we boast
> Consist in scraps of paper ".

It must be noticed that the capitalists themselves were not of purely native origin. Alien entrepreneurs introduced numerous 'useful trades' and helped to establish the industrial supremacy of England. The successive waves of foreign settlers, both 'captains of industry' and craftsmen, are therefore notable landmarks in English history. Many of them were exiled from their own land through religious persecution which, like racial persecution in the twentieth century, enriched the state where they found an asylum ; and they were welcomed by the government as religious refugees and as invaluable assets. Their immigration takes rank as one of the major influences in England's economic development. Every branch of economy was stimulated by the inestimable services which they rendered. The infusion of new blood enriched and strengthened the national fibre, while their technical skill and expert knowledge of the industrial arts enabled this country to wrest from its rivals the secrets of important industries and become a workshop of the world. Moreover the fact that the strangers within the gates were not born in the English way of life meant that they could not be fitted easily into the framework of a communal society. In the eyes of their native competitors, " obedient subjects to the laws and customs of this land ", they seemed " a most obstinate and perverse kind of people ; the customs and privileges of incorporated cities they respect not ". Hence their presence was a disruptive element which served to reinforce the prevailing trend towards individualism.

The counterpart of mobility of capital is mobility of labour. The growth of an industrial system is likely to be greatly retarded in a country where the population tends to immobility. The United States affords the outstanding example of a highly mobile society ; and the future place of Great Britain in the world's economy will largely depend upon the facility with which the working community adjusts itself to changing conditions. On this account it may yield a measure of guidance to ascertain the extent to which mobility of labour prevailed in former ages. We need to revise our notions of the immobility of the older English society : the practice of internal migration was a common phenomenon in earlier times. The stability of agrarian life was often apparent rather than real, and its conservatism was impotent to prevent massive changes. In the fourteenth century, after the Black Death, the discontent of the peasantry with the burdens of villeinage spurred on their ambition for better things, and the flight of serfs from the manor dispersed a considerable portion of the rural stock. In the next century industry began to prove more attractive than husbandry. It offered a wider scope to men of initiative and enterprise who craved for new opportunities of advancement and profitable sources of livelihood: it afforded fresh openings to restless spirits impelled to wander from their homes and fields to seek their fortunes in the towns, within whose walls a fugitive villein could secure his emancipation by residence for a year and a day. The cry went up that tillage was decaying from the scarcity of agricultural workers, and the efforts of the government to check the rural exodus and maintain labour on the land led Oxford to complain that scholars had withdrawn from the University, "saying that they may not have artificers to serve them". Although in some districts peasant families have clung to one locality for hundreds of years, we have learnt from manorial rolls and Tudor subsidy rolls that in other districts the inhabitants shifted from generation to generation—clear evidence of the mobile state of the countryside. Another factor was the expansion of the woollen manufacture, which caused a reverse trend from the corporate boroughs to the 'townlets'. Artisans flocked into the country influenced by the easy access to water mills, the cheapness of provisions, and the desire to escape the financial oppression and industrial supervision of the craft gilds. Mobility of labour also became a marked feature of the iron and coal industries. It was the necessary outcome of the dependence of the former upon charcoal and water-power, and of the latter upon the location of the coal measures. They drew their workmen from every part of the kingdom, and agents were sent out to seek them. An industry itself, for instance iron or glass, might move to other centres as the supplies of timber became exhausted. The migratory movement was not confined to the lower ranges of the industrial hierarchy, for manufacturers and merchants alike recruited their apprentices from a wide area. Nor was it confined to the natives of England. Irishmen helped to build and work the furnaces and forges at Furness, and hundreds of them crossed over to England to render assistance at harvest-time ; while Scotsmen came southwards to man the keels at Newcastle.

The position of labour in the new economic order, which by easy stages dissolved the fabric of mediaeval society, attests the early growth of capitalism and affords perhaps the most convincing testimony to the emergence of the entrepreneur. The structure of industry was being reconstituted on lines which were incompatible with the survival of the craftsman in an independent capacity.

We can best account for the rise of a wage-earning class if we bear in mind that the advent of capitalism, in the sense in which the term is here defined, implies a phase in industrial evolution where the ownership of the raw material is transferred from the manual producer to an employer, who hires labour to work it up and sells the finished product. In consequence the manual producer is transformed from an independent craftsman owning the material on which he worked into a wage-labourer engaged on material supplied by the capitalist, even though he may continue to own the instruments of production. Hence the fundamental feature of capitalism is the wage-system under which the worker has no right of ownership in the wares which he manufactures : he sells not the fruits of his labour but the labour itself—a distinction of vital economic significance. The genesis of the wage-system is not connected with the introduction of machinery : its criterion is whether the worker has any property in the goods which he makes. If the goods do not belong to him because the material is provided by another person, then he is a wage-earner whether the instruments of production belong to him or not. So long as the artisan purchased his material (as in the 'gild' stage), he was independent : he could dispose freely of the finished product : he worked for a price, not for a wage. When, however, the artisan worked on material furnished by an employer (as in the 'domestic' stage), he had to hand back the finished product, and what he received in exchange was only the earnings of the labour expended on the material. The work might still be performed in the home, but a wage-earner was none the less a wage-earner because he toiled under his own roof. Accordingly the contrast between the domestic worker who carries on the work at home, and the factory worker engaged in an employer's establishment, has a social rather than an economic significance. It follows that Engels's famous assertion—" the proletariat was called into existence by the introduction of machinery "—betrayed ignorance of the fact that a wage-earning class possessing no resources but its technical skill and a few tools existed in England for several centuries prior to the factory age. Neither the use of machinery (involving as it does capitalist ownership of the instruments of production and the assemblage of workers in factories), nor the division of labour, comprises the essence of the capitalist system. This lies in the capitalist ownership of the material and the consequent power of disposal over the manufactured article.

The process of evolution was already far advanced towards the close of the middle ages when the tide of industrial capitalism began to submerge the defences erected by the craft gilds, and the skilled artisan was reduced to dependence upon an employer. The oldest and most widespread of English manufactures (the woollen industry) was conducted on a capitalist basis, and by the sixteenth century the majority of textile workers were wage-earners. The entrepreneur or clothier supplied the carders, combers and spinners with their wool, the weavers with their yarn, the fullers and dyers with their cloth. At every stage of production he owned the material, directed the processes, and disposed of the finished product. Even the most rapid survey of the industrial scene in the age of mercantilism discloses numerous other manufactures, besides the woollen, which were managed on capitalist lines. I draw attention to them here because they may serve to dispel some prevalent misconceptions as to the economic condition of England in former times.

In the cotton industry, as is indicated by the career of Humphrey Chetham one of the architects of Manchester's greatness, prominent makers carried on substantial operations early in the seventeenth century. In the silk industry 'workmasters' or silkmen were the employers of the silk weavers, and here the modern factory system had its beginnings early in the eighteenth century. Capital for the development of a native linen industry was provided by joint-stock companies. In the hosiery industry frame-work knitters often worked on an employer's material and sometimes on an employer's frame. Nor was the capitalist system limited to the textile industries. Coal-mining was essentially a capitalist undertaking in which not only the hewers but the transport workers were wage-earners. Inasmuch as it was impossible to forecast the expenditure involved owing to the costly hazards of water and fire, it was peculiarly a field for capitalist speculation, and it presents the most striking examples of the sinking of capital in industrial ventures. In tin-mining the appearance of the capitalist producer was revealed as far back as the fourteenth century, when 'Abraham the Tinner' had in his employment over three hundred workers; and as in other industries there were early complaints of the exploitation of labour. In lead-mining in the same century all the elements of a capitalist concern may be discerned in the absentee owner, foremen and hired workmen. In the iron industry every stage of the extractive and manufacturing processes was, with a few exceptions, organized on a capitalist footing. The foundry and the forge were capitalist enterprises in which the raw material and fuel were owned and the product marketed by an entrepreneur, while capital was also invested in extracting the mineral as well as in the conversion of the metal into finished products. The copper and brass industries furnish the earliest instances of the formation of joint-stock companies to run a business which demanded buildings and expensive plant. The glass industry involved the disbursement of large sums for furnaces. The manufacture of salt, soap, paper, alum and a variety of other commodities was capitalist in type. The building industry conformed to the character of a capitalist business : building operations often required a great number of masons who were mostly wage-earners and worked under the direction of experts. Similarly ship-building called for the employment of carpenters and other artificers on a considerable scale.

All these concurrent indications of the prevalence of capitalism in English industry, prior to the introduction of machinery, justify the conclusion that a capitalist society was no new creation when the great inventions inaugurated its second phase, that of power-driven machinery. Side by side with the small independent producer, working under his own roof on his own materials and with his own tools, there already ranged the large producer of the modern pattern. Long before the advent of the factory age the capitalist employer had become the pivotal figure in industry, whose organization he controlled and dominated.

The effects of the changed status of the workers, now transformed into a wage-earning class, were momentous. The strained relations, which at once developed between employers and employed, provoked an acute conflict of capital and labour protracted over many centuries. The fundamental divergence of interests was manifested in chronic disputes over wages. The employer treats wages primarily as the price paid for a commodity, while to the workman they are the means of subsistence ; and this clash of concepts produces the bitter fruit of industrial strife. The argument which passed for current coin in the nineteenth century was familiar in former times : " Cheapness of labour, and consequently the cheapness of goods, is the only means to increase their consumption either at home or abroad ", and so stimulate the demand for labour. Moreover it is significant to observe that, as in later ages, the cause of industrial unrest was not low wages alone but also unemployment, for insecurity with its unsettling reaction on the standard of life is more demoralizing than poverty. Even in normal times, apart from commercial crises, irregularity of work was a recognized trait of the industrial order at least from the sixteenth century. It was due partly to the ebb and flow of trade and partly to technical difficulties —the intermittent supply of yarn in the woollen industry, the deficiency of water-power in the iron industry, the seasonal demand for fuel in the coal industry. In short there existed a working class often poorly remunerated, exposed to the hazards of unemployment, already largely divorced from the soil, and frequently working away from their homes. It is therefore not surprising to find that Dean Tucker, who wrote in the reign of George II., considered that the relations of master and man " approach much nearer to that of a planter and slave in our American colonies than might be expected in such a country as England ". The employer is " tempted by his situation to be overbearing " and to consider that he " has a right to squeeze [his workfolk] whenever he can ". The men are equally tempted " to get as much wages and to do as little for it as they possibly can ", and to look upon their employer as " their common enemy ". His observations serve as a further reminder that the realities of industrial life anterior to the ' Industrial Revolution ' did not correspond to the idyllic picture which is apt to be drawn. Disraeli's description in *Sybil* of two nations warring with each other within the confines of a single state was true not only of his own age but of an older England.

The tangible sign of the cleavage between capital and labour, and of the friction engendered by it, was the growth of trade unionism which preceded the introduction of machinery. Indeed trade unionism was so far from being the outcome of machinery that the invention and adoption of machines were, partly at any rate, inspired by the hope of liberating employers from their dependence upon labour. As early as the fourteenth century there were formed associations of wage-earners, but it was the collapse of the benevolent autocracy which did much to stimulate the self-assertion of the working class and to awaken the latent instinct of self-preservation. The workers were driven by the abandonment of the industrial code, instituted by the state with some measure of regard for their interests and protection, to depend upon their own efforts. Manifestations of trade-union activity are to be found in the manufactures of wool, cotton, silk, linen, iron and leather, among others ; and they register the degree to which capitalism had permeated English industries. During the eighteenth century repeated laws were enacted against associations of working-men in various occupations, and the combinations laws of 1799 and 1800 were only the climax of a series of measures dating back to the opening decades of the century. They were, however, powerless to repress a widespread trade-union movement which persisted throughout the eighteenth century and bequeathed its traditions to later generations. It is instructive to notice the reasons why the older combinations among wage-earners—the forerunners of the unions of our own day—proved largely ephemeral. One was that the energetic members were more easily absorbed into the ranks of the employing class. Another was that trade unionism did not attain its present stability until the 'Industrial Revolution' achieved the final victory of capitalism by taking from the workers the ownership of the instruments of production ; while at the same time it evoked a more continuous resistance to capitalism by concentrating the workers in large factories, where a sense of security was instilled in them by the confidence born of numbers.

An analysis of the industrial structure provides ample indications of capitalist phenomena, and reveals the extent to which the entrepreneur had assumed direction of the economic mechanism. At every stage of production and marketing we have evidence that men endowed with organizing abilities were finding a wider field for the exercise of their talents than lay within the four walls of their town.

Observe, first, that there had already developed an elaborate machinery for the distribution of raw materials.

The kingdom was treated as a single economic unit upon which any locality could draw for the satisfaction of its own special requirements. Thus the numerous industries which consumed large quantities of coal were able to obtain their fuel even when they were situated remote from the coal mines, and the wool merchants linked up the manufacturing districts with distant sources of supply. Moreover the importation of cotton, silk, flax, Spanish wool and Swedish iron shows that manufacturers of cotton in Lancashire, Cheshire, Derbyshire and Dorsetshire, manufacturers of silk in London, Derby, Coventry, Norwich and Macclesfield, manufacturers of linen in a dozen English counties, manufacturers of 'Spanish cloth' in the west country, and Sheffield cutlers famed in the days of Chaucer for their knives, were not precluded from utilizing materials produced in Europe and Asia on the one hand and in the New World on the other. And just as there was a national and an international market for the supply of raw materials, so there was a national and an international market for the disposal of the finished products.

Observe, next, the scale of production since it measures the degree to which an industry is managed by a class of entrepreneurs. It is usual to associate the capitalist system with great undertakings—and with good reason. Small-scale production does not afford scope for the faculty of organization which is displayed in co-ordinating the various technical processes, in combining division of labour with supervision from a common centre, and in seeking out new markets both to provide raw materials and to absorb the manufactured articles. It is important, therefore, to ascertain what traces exist of large-scale production in the seventeenth and eighteenth centuries. Our evidence demonstrates that it is no recent development. In the woollen and worsted industries makers of cloth were engaged in a substantial way of business—it was not unknown for clothiers to employ a thousand workfolk, although not everyone on the clothier's books worked for him alone: in the silk industry master throwers kept 500 to 700 operatives and subsequently even 1500 : makers of sail cloth hired 5000 or 6000 persons : a salt-maker had 1000 workers : a manufacturer of small metal wares ('toys') 600 : a lace-maker and a calico printer 200 or 300 : a hat-maker and a glass-maker 100 apiece. These examples could be multiplied, but they are sufficient to refute the assertion that "the class of capitalist employers was as yet but in its infancy". Large undertakings constituted, in fact, a recognized feature of the extractive and manufacturing industries in earlier centuries, and they are an unmistakable proof of the functioning of the entrepreneur.

The size of the business unit might yield opportunities for the emergence of integrated concerns—this discloses an aspect of capitalism which is often looked upon as new. Thus in the iron industry it was normal for the owner of the foundry and forge to control part, at any rate, of the sources of his raw materials (iron ore, wood and coal), and he even extended his activities to the metal trades and worked up the iron into finished goods. The seventeenth-century establishment of Ambrose Crowley presents a notable instance of an integrated business : it carried on all operations from the production of bar iron to the making of iron wares. In the copper industry there existed companies which owned copper mines, smelting works, rolling mills, manufacturing shops, together with ships for the transportation of materials. In the woollen industry the west country clothier concentrated in his hands every process of cloth-making from the time the wool was carded and spun until it was woven, fulled and 'finished' : a clothier might possess the flock from which he obtained his supply of raw material, and he might be a merchant exporter. In the coal industry the coal-fitters, who became the link between the sellers of coal and the shipowners, sometimes owned the ships ; the hostmen, who were the sole coal merchants at Newcastle, sometimes owned the mines ; and the London dealers sometimes had a financial interest in the ships which conveyed the coal from Newcastle to the metropolis.

In certain respects the most striking manifestation of an

entrepreneur regime is the creation of cartels, for the attempt to set up a controlled market presupposes an advanced phase in industrial evolution. A German economist distinguishes between two stages of capitalism, the individualist or personal and the federated or impersonal. He regards the first as typical of England ; and the second, the disciplined form of capitalism, as the product of German organizing ability. The ' private employer of the old style '—that is, the individualist entrepreneur who ploughs a lonely furrow and shrinks from co-operation with other entrepreneurs—characterizes the first stage. The ' disciplined industrial community ', in which the employer becomes a ' federated employer ' and merges his individuality into an ' economic co-operative existence ', characterizes the second stage. Yet though modern Germany has furnished the classic examples of cartels, she was not the original home of the system which can be traced back far beyond nineteenth-century capitalism. A cartel in the English coal industry came into being at the close of the middle ages and survived intermittently into the last century. It was a highly-organized type of trade association which exhibited all the principal devices of a controlled market and a rigid monopoly : it restricted membership, fixed prices, limited output, assigned each member a percentage of the output, and exacted contributions to a ' pool ' to penalize those who exceeded their allotted quota and to subsidize those who fell short of it. At the distributing end of the coal trade the London market was exploited by combinations in every grade of middlemen through whose hands the commodity passed. Nor did the difficulties of communication, on which historians are apt to lay undue stress, daunt the London coal merchants ; they instituted a system of intelligence by which they knew whether supplies at Newcastle were plentiful or scarce, and whether a coal fleet was at sea or held back by contrary winds ; and they used their knowledge to ' rig ' the market and manipulate prices.

The prevalence of ' rings ' which determined prices and

regulated supplies was a feature of other industries besides coal, for example, iron and copper. Ironmasters in the seventeenth and eighteenth centuries entered into price agreements which eliminated competition in the purchase of raw materials or in the sale of their products : these compacts sometimes included a 'pool'. Similarly the companies engaged in the copper industry avoided competition in the buying of copper ore as well as in the price and quantity of goods which they placed on the market. Merchant importers themselves were not always in a position to shift the import duties on to the buyers, since the latter collaborated to beat down their prices. Those who traded in provisions furnish parallel instances of tacit or overt understandings : thus the mealmen who dealt in meal and flour seized the opportunity afforded by their key position in the corn trade to "fix the price of corn on the farmers and the measure too". Even the device of the 'boycott' is found among a 'ring' of London butter merchants, which at the end of the seventeenth century practically monopolized the butter trade with Suffolk by the threat to boycott local warehouse-keepers and carriers who acted for those outside the 'ring'. Another method of suppressing competition, practised by alien importers in the early seventeenth century, was doubtless not unknown among native manufacturers : this consisted of 'dumping' wares on the market at low prices and of 'cornering' supplies of the raw material. These noteworthy examples of what is generally considered a modern development—the tendency to make combinations and 'rings' among producers and distributors—serve to show that the fertile genius of the entrepreneur had already impressed its stamp upon a society which was fast assuming many of the traits usually identified with the most highly-developed form of capitalist organization.

A seventeenth-century illustration of capitalist enterprise in the sphere of industry is the remarkable establishment erected in the North of England by the greatest ironmaster of the age, Sir Ambrose Crowley. It was conducted on a large scale, for several hundred men were employed, but its signal feature was the autocracy which ruled it. Crowley created a 'model village' which anticipated Robert Owen's experiment at New Lanark. His iron works still retained some of their characteristic features in the early nineteenth century; and if they were known to Owen they may prove to be an unsuspected source from which the Father of English Socialism derived inspiration. Crowley laid down a code for the welfare of the workmen, made provision for the poor and sick through a contributory insurance scheme, instituted a school for the children (the schoolmaster was enjoined not to dismiss his scholars or absent himself "upon any account of races, cock-fightings, rope-dancers or stage players"), and set up a body of arbitrators on which the workmen were represented. He displayed marked consideration for the self-respect of his workmen, instructing the 'surveyor' to "have a great regard to what the workmen say and especially in hearing their allegations and reasons where they are rational". Thus Crowley foreshadowed the leading principles of social reform in the nineteenth century together with the idea of devolution of control in industry. We have no reason to suppose that the Crowley regime, however exceptional it might have been, was in every respect unique: the survival of records is so purely a matter of chance that we must be careful not to draw misleading inferences from the paucity of evidence. We certainly get glimpses of other industrial establishments which drew labour from remote parts of the country, built houses, made loans to the workmen, and provided schools for their children[1]. "Business", stated the *Report of the Balfour Committee on Industry and Trade*, "is not exempt from laws which regulate other forms of human association, and requires for its success good intelligent leadership". There are grounds for thinking that this doctrine did not go entirely unheeded in the seventeenth and eighteenth centuries. Doubtless employers of the

[1] Even schemes of profit-sharing were not unknown in the seventeenth century. The East India Company began by crediting each sailor with a share in the enterprise 'for the better advancement of his salary'.

advanced type here visualized were not numerous, but neither are they especially numerous at the present day. Yet the survival of private enterprise is likely in the long run to depend less upon its claims to superior economic efficiency than upon its success in humanizing industry.

The influence of the entrepreneur is evinced, not only in the intricate pattern of the production and marketing organizations of which he was the pivot, but in the variety and range of his industrial pursuits. " The sort of men we call Undertakers "[1], it was said near the end of the seventeenth century, " are very instrumental in the public by advancing manufactures ". The introduction of a new branch of industry is generally a speculative undertaking which attracts those who are prepared to risk their capital in the hope of substantial returns. It was, therefore, owing to the exertions and sacrifices of the entrepreneurs that England was enabled to develop fresh industrial arts and attain a position of supremacy in world trade. Indeed the initiative in economic matters had perforce to come from the entrepreneurs because all proposals for an experiment in state socialism were still-born, such as the suggestions that the state should carry out improvements in transport by making rivers navigable, that it should take over the coal trade, that it should provide cheap bread for the poor.

In enumerating the industrial arts which were discovered or adopted after the middle ages, one thing needs saying at the outset—namely, that they are not to be conceived as the manifestation of a newly-born spirit of capitalism created by the forces which the Reformation set in motion. It is a common view that England remained throughout the middle ages economically in a backwater, and that industrial capitalism commences after the Reformation ; yet it is contradicted both by the growth of commerce and by authentic evidence of industrial proficiency, which

[1] In the seventeenth century the word ' undertaker ' was used in the present sense of ' entrepreneur '. We still speak of an ' undertaking '.

warns us against the erroneous assumption that English craftsmanship in the middle ages was barren of technical achievements. The notable number of craft gilds bears eloquent testimony to the diversified character of the manual arts in Early England ; moreover the remarkable expansion of the woollen manufacture and its conduct on a capitalist basis were in the nature of an industrial revolution. An emperor of the Byzantine empire, who visited these shores in the year 1400, commented upon the flourishing state of the country. " In populousness and power, in riches and luxury, London the metropolis of the isle may claim a pre-eminence over all the cities of the West ". At the end of the fifteenth century a Venetian wrote in a similar strain. " In one single street named the Strand leading to St Paul's there are fifty-two goldsmiths' shops so rich and full of silver vessels great and small, that in all the shops in Milan, Rome, Venice and Florence put together I do not think there would be found so many of the magnificence that are to be seen in London ". In fact, the study of mediaeval records has in store for the unbiassed investigator as many surprises as the study of the age of mercantilism has for those who come to it with minds freed from current clichés about the ' Industrial Revolution '.

Let us take a bird's-eye view of the striking industrial progress which England had achieved prior to the ' Industrial Revolution '.

The making of cloth—described by chief justice Coke as ' the worthiest and richest commodity of this kingdom ', and by Camden the antiquarian as ' one of the pillars of the state '—enjoyed pre-eminence over all other manufactures from the twelfth to the nineteenth century. In the second half of the sixteenth century a fresh branch of the woollen industry, known as the ' new drapery ', was established : it consisted of the finer worsted fabrics. An old English rhyme ran :

" Hops, Reformation, *Bays*, and Beer
Came into England all in a year ".

The same era witnessed the beginnings of machine-wrought hosiery, which resulted from the invention of the knitting frame by William Lee ; and the history of the cotton industry can now be carried back to the year 1586. Silk, a mediaeval industry, grew into " one of the most considerable branches of the manufactures of this kingdom " as a consequence of the improvements effected in the seventeenth century ; and in the next century the linen industry was widely distributed.

Outside this group of textiles a vital place in the national economy came to be occupied by coal and iron. Originally wood was not only the fuel for household consumption and manufactures of every kind but also the material for buildings, ships, carts, looms and tools. The growth of population and the expansion of industry (especially iron works) put an excessive strain upon native timber resources. The ' general destruction ' of ' goodly trees ' aroused national anxiety. ' No wood ', the warning was uttered, ' no kingdom '. The lament of the poet Drayton evinces that the ruthless exploitation of natural resources is an old phenomenon :

" These iron times breed none that mind posterity . . .
Jove's Oak, the warlike Ash, vein'd Elm, the softer Beech,
Short Hazel, Maple plain, light Aspe, the bending Wych,
Tough Holly, and smoother Birch, must altogether burn :
What should the builder serve, supplies the forger's turn ;
When under public good, base private gain takes hold,
And we poor woeful Woods to ruin lastly sold.
This utter'd they with grief. . . ."

Hence arose the need for extracting the subterranean mineral fuel in order to provide ' new fire ' for the domestic hearth and for industrial requirements. The need was met principally by the rapid exploitation of the northern coal-beds. Newcastle was enthusiastically acclaimed :

" England's a perfect World ! has Indies too !
Correct your Maps : Newcastle is Peru ".

The importance of the coal industry in the nineteenth and twentieth centuries is universally recognized. Its prominence in earlier ages has been obscured by focussing attention upon the use of coal for smelting iron ore and neglecting its relation to other fields of economic activities. In mercantilist England coal had grown into general usage as the indispensable fuel of the householder, and it was extensively consumed in a great variety of industries. Confined in mediaeval times mainly to workers in metal (smiths) and lime-burners, it was subsequently adopted by others—bakers, brewers, brick-makers, calico-printers, casters of brass and copper, coopers, distillers, dyers, founders, glass-makers, pottery manufacturers, salt-makers, soap-boilers and sugar-refiners. It was employed in making iron wares though it was not suitable, on account of the sulphur in it, for smelting iron ore. A French traveller in 1738 termed coal 'one of the greatest sources of English wealth and plenty' and 'the soul of English manufactures'; and he expressly mentioned that lime which was burned with coal was widely applied as a fertilizer of the soil, and not merely for mortar in building, thus making coal an accessory of agriculture. In this way coal-mining was closely linked with the progress of numerous industries and with improved methods in farming. Its historical significance is reflected further in the contribution which it made to the evolution of a capitalist society, and in the influence exerted on public policy (especially as regards price regulation) in the interests of the consumer. In addition the transport of coal along the coast or to the Continent was an immense stimulus to shipping, since it accounted for a large proportion of the mercantile marine and nourished a 'nursery for seamen'; its conveyance from the pits to the river-side led to the invention of 'railways' in the sixteenth century; and the drainage of the mines gave birth to the steam engine in the seventeenth century.

The economic importance of coal in the age of mercantilism was matched by the great advance in the metal industries. Even in the middle ages metal workers had achieved renown for the high quality of their wares which found a market abroad. The tribute which William of Poitiers, the chaplain of William the Conqueror, paid to the proficiency of English artificers in the eleventh century [1] shows that a long tradition lay behind the skill which continued to extort the admiration of foreigners in later centuries. The extensive use of metals for industrial and domestic purposes was revealed in a notable expansion of the iron industry. "No particular manufacture can be named", asserted Defoe, "which has increased like this of the hardware"; and Burke described Birmingham as 'the toy-shop of Europe' because of its variety of small metal wares. A native industry of copper and brass was established in the sixteenth century as a result of the discovery of calamine. Other industries which were started or developed in the sixteenth and seventeenth centuries included alum, breweries, brick-making, glass, paper, salt, saltpetre, soap and sugar-refineries. Ship-building was stimulated by commercial intercourse with the Continent, the American plantations and India, as well as by the coasting trade in coal and other commodities; and the growth of a mercantile marine laid the basis for an empire which rested on sea power.

All these industrial changes came to maturity in the age of mercantilism; and their effects worked themselves out in many directions. They enlarged the sphere within which the entrepreneur could find scope for his talents and the capitalist could enjoy opportunities for investment. They fostered the insistent plea for economic freedom. They caused the abandonment of the traditional belief that the kingdom was over-populated—after the Civil War it was held that the increase of population failed to keep pace with the expansion of trade and industry. The fact that enclosures of the open fields were no longer attacked on the ground of unemployment indicates that manufactures were absorb-

[1] He praises the skill displayed by the women in working cloths of gold, and the distinction attained by the men in all manner of craftsmanship. On this account, he adds, German experts in the industrial arts were accustomed to reside in this country.

ing many more hands. The diversion of the national energies into industrial channels was made possible by technical improvements in agriculture : the export of grain after the Restoration and the substitution of wheat for rye imply that corn production was adequate to meet the demands of a growing population and a rising standard of life. Thus England in the age of mercantilism was a busy hive of industry, in which specialization was pursued in a marked degree to serve a wide range of markets with varying tastes and fashions. Her mature status is evinced in the testimony of a correspondent who wrote in 1672 : " The English through all the world are counted the most ingenious in all manner of manufactures as cloth, serge, woollen stockings, silk stockings, both woven and knitted, . . . all sort of leather, scarlet cloth, gloves, watches, knives, etc." Long before the ' Industrial Revolution ' the reputation of her wares had made England a workshop of the world.

The manifold developments, which I have related, bear witness to the fertile activities of the entrepreneur. They were born of the restless spirit of the age—but inasmuch as the motive spring of human progress is intellectual curiosity, they had their counterpart in the domain of scientific inquiry, namely, in the foundation of the Royal Society. This body in its beginnings had close associations with the economic movements of the day. It was formed by a group of thinkers " who had begun a free way of reasoning ", and about the year 1645 commenced to hold meetings to investigate the ' new and experimental philosophy '. Its first historian, Thomas Sprat the eloquent Bishop of Rochester, described in 1667 how " the late times of Civil War and confusion, to make recompense for their infinite calamities, brought this advantage with them that they stirred up men's minds from long ease and a lazy rest, and made them active, industrious and inquisitive. . . . Now men are generally weary of the relics of antiquity and satiated with religious disputes. . . . Now there is a universal desire and appetite after knowledge ". The practical trend of the members' interests bore fruit in scientific discoveries, which led Voltaire to pronounce that " in this respect they entitle the age to be called the age of the English as well as that of Louis XIV ".

In its early stages the Royal Society did not keep aloof from the economic ferment of the seventeenth century, for it had the co-operation of many merchants who " assisted it with their presence and thereby have added the industrious, punctual and active genius of men of traffic to the quiet, sedentary and reserved temper of men of learning ". And the ' men of learning ' did not disdain to " consider the purpose of the Royal Society in respect of all the manual trades ". Sprat raised the significant question " whether the mechanic arts are still improvable by human industry " ; and he answered in the affirmative " that it is not a vain or impossible design to endeavour the increase of mechanic contrivances ". He maintained that recent mechanic inventions " cannot but convince us that many more are still to come ". At the same time he recognized the difficulties which were to delay for a century the advent of the ' Industrial Revolution '. He explained that invention " requires an active, a bold, a nimble, a restless mind ; a thousand difficulties must be contemned. . . . Many attempts must be made to no purpose ; much treasure must sometimes be scattered without any return ". He commented upon the popular aversion to new inventions and the hostility to aliens, adding ironically—" for the sake of the poor whom we thereby do certainly make the poorer ". He defended the adoption of ' shorter ways of labour ' on the ground : " That country is still the richest and most powerful which entertains most manufactures. The hands of men employed are true riches. The saving of those hands by inventions of art and applying them to other works will increase those riches ". In this conviction the Royal Society set itself the task of gathering descriptions of mines and ores, iron-making, salt-making, cloth-making, paper-making and many other industrial arts. The institution of a lecture on mechanics was acclaimed as " the first lecture that has been founded of this kind ", the want of which " has chiefly caused the slow progress of manual arts ". A questionnaire was issued to agriculturalists in order to obtain information on the technique of husbandry ; and Houghton claimed that " the whole land hath been fermented and stirred up by the profitable hints it hath received from the Royal Society ". In these scientific inquiries into the actual workings of the economic mechanism was mirrored an England that had grown conscious of a boundless horizon and an illimitable field of new discoveries.

I have endeavoured to indicate the salient features of the structure of industry which existed before the introduction of machinery, and to draw attention to some of the prevalent misconceptions about its nature. Perhaps the most common of all is the idealized picture often presented of the domestic system. It has been depicted almost in the light of a golden age where the artisan was his own master working as he pleased at his loom or bench, and where no rift between capital and labour marred as yet the social harmony. The current impression of the ' Industrial Revolution ' owes much to the fact that its antecedents are viewed through rosy-tinted glasses. In reality the notion that English society passed from an age of gold to an age of iron is a poetical illusion. The domestic system had one outstanding merit, the wide dispersion of the manufacturing community which contrasted favourably with the concentration in towns produced by the factory system, but it also had many drawbacks.

First : there was no harmonious grouping of the industrial forces since employers and employees were separated by the barrier of wealth and status, and their relations were embittered by chronic disputes over wages. The domestic artisan might seem to enjoy greater social independence than the factory operative in the arrangement of his working day—though an independence which was purchased with twelve hours' labour a day was more nominal than real. Yet he was as economically dependent as the factory operative, despite the advantage that he might own his instruments of production, for both alike were wage-earners. Second: the embezzlement of the raw material was a frequent practice—this was the principal defect in the eyes of the employer. Third: the long hours of labour worked under the early factory system were no novelty but a legacy of the domestic system when twelve hours constituted a normal working day. One writer (1700) remarked: "No country but Great Britain can boast that after twelve hours' hard work its natives will in the evening go to football, stool-ball, cricket, prison-base, wrestling, cudgel-playing, or some such vehement exercise in their recreations". The state regulated the hours of labour in the reign of Queen Elizabeth; and it instituted a monthly holiday during the Civil War—every second Tuesday in the month was to be a day of 'recreation and relaxation' for scholars, apprentices and other servants, and shops and warehouses were to be closed. Saturday evening was also a closed time for spinning. A legend tells of a woman who appeared after her death to a fellow-culprit, displaying her burning hand with the words:

> "See what I in Hell have won
> Because on Saturday I spun".

Fourth: the factory system inherited another evil tradition, namely, that of infant slavery. The exploitation of child labour was no new practice but an integral feature of industrial life which met with general approval. The example of Germany—where "every child, though but seven or eight years old, is put to work and is enabled thereby to get his own livelihood"—was held up to England. There, it was said, "a man that has most children lives best whereas here he that has most is poorest. There the children enrich the father but here beggar him". In so far as the relations of parents and children were softened by feelings of natural affection, the evils of child labour might be mitigated. But one who was brought up under the domestic system declared that children "were set to work as soon as they could crawl, and their parents were the hardest of taskmasters ". Fifth: the domestic worker, broadly speaking, was assured of less continuous employment than the modern factory operative. Sixth: the connexion between agriculture and industry has been unduly stressed. The development of a proletarian class —that is, a class divorced from the soil, possessing no property, and living entirely upon wages—had made a considerable headway prior to the advent of the factory system, which completed the process by extending it to the spinning population composed of women and children, whose earnings had supplemented the wages of agricultural labourers. The opportunities for rural employment, available for men who were out of work, were not so frequent as is usually represented: all the indications are that the typical artisan was a landless artisan restricted solely to manufacturing. In any event men engaged in a sedentary occupation were unlikely to possess the physical qualities needed for farming operations—a fact overlooked by those who lay emphasis upon the combination of rural and industrial pursuits. Seventh: the invention of machinery did not destroy craftsmanship in the textile industries, where the monotonous routine of the work done by hand was already mechanical in character even before the adoption of mechanical devices.

This review of the economic conditions which prevailed under the domestic system applies more particularly to the west country—once the principal seat of England's greatest industry—as well as to East Anglia. In these areas capitalism had gained a footing from the earliest times, and there existed a highly-developed capitalist organization. In the north country (where nineteenth-century capitalism achieved its most signal triumphs) the traditional structure of society maintained its ground more successfully: here the industrial mechanism was not so sensitive as in the west to the free play of economic forces, and it succumbed less readily to the dissolving influences of the new order. The 'domestic manufacturers' or working clothiers of Yorkshire, the counterpart of the yeomanry in agriculture, were themselves manual craftsmen ; and they enlisted the unstinted praise of contemporaries because of the friendly relations which subsisted between masters and men, combined with equality of opportunity—the chance afforded to the workers of rising in the world.

It is the fashion to speak as though all industrial processes before the great inventions were performed in the homes of the artisans. Actually this was far from being the case since the domestic system was not universal. Apart from the extractive industries—agriculture and the mining of coal, iron, copper, tin, lead and alum—where the labourers naturally worked away from their dwellings, there were numerous occupations in which the operatives were concentrated under an employer's roof—in the woollen industry at the finishing processes, in the silk industry at the mills for throwing, in the linen industry at the factory for cambrics and lawns, in the iron industry at the foundry and forge, in the glass industry with its glass-houses, in the copper and brass industries with their smelting and battery works, in brewing, in brick-making, in building, in calico-printing, in net-making, in paper-making, in the pottery manufacture, in rope-making, in salt-making, in ship-building, in soap-boiling, in sugar-refining, in the tailoring industry, and in tapestry-making. This comprehensive list, which in the aggregate embraced the greater part of the working population (when the extractive industries are included), furnishes decisive proof that the 'Industrial Revolution' introduced no new form of industrial organization. In addition we occasionally find large industrial establishments in other occupations which were normally conducted on a domestic basis—in the spinning and weaving branches of the woollen, silk and linen industries or in the production of metal wares. In all instances where the labour was done at the master's 'works', the operations would be carried on under the immediate inspection of the entrepreneur ; and the general conditions in respect of discipline and regularity would not be essentially different from those of a modern factory—except that the dependence on water-power would result in spells of enforced idleness, which might be compared with the present-day practice of ' short-time ' working in periods of slack trade.

In the light of a fuller knowledge English industrial society in the age of mercantilism wears a different aspect from that generally portrayed. The key to its character must be sought not in a network of small producers but in the crucial position occupied by the entrepreneur. The latter found scope for his organizing ability in the enlarged scale of production based on a division of labour which was often minute. He found scope for his speculative instincts in sinking capital (whether his own, or borrowed, or provided by partners) in new industrial arts. He found scope for his technical insight in lowering the costs of production through an improved technique—the early utilization of coal, the erection of blast furnaces, and the adoption of innumerable mechanical devices. We shall find fresh evidence of his creative powers in the domain of foreign commerce.

§ 2. *The Evolution of an International Market*

The foundations of an international trade had been laid in the middle ages when connexions were established with most European countries. In the sixteenth century it grew considerably in volume and began to assume a world-wide character. The exports of England penetrated into nearly every part of the globe : her imports comprised the products of four continents. A large portion of her population was mainly dependent for its livelihood upon oversea markets. Her commercial organization was highly developed on the basis of companies, while the working of her credit system and monetary exchanges reproduced in its essentials the mechanism of modern business life. In short her economic destiny appeared closely interwoven with that of other nations, and in the age of mercantilism it was a commonplace that her "prosperity and power depend on trade". As a seventeenth-century writer exclaimed: "Trade is now become the Lady which in this present age is more courted and celebrated than in any former". Two outstanding developments stimulated the expansion of commerce and opened up wider fields of opportunity to the entrepreneur. One was the discovery of America and of a new sea route to India, which created a fresh outlet for the energies of the mercantile class. The other was the sense of nationalism, which became a driving force to preserve economic independence by instituting direct trading connexions with countries hitherto monopolized by actual or potential enemies. In fact the efforts of Elizabethan merchants to devise new channels of commercial intercourse contributed not less to the security of England than the exploits of Elizabethan seamen and the diplomacy of Elizabethan statesmen. The success which crowned these efforts is measured by the observation of the Venetian ambassador in the reign of James I. that "the English trade in all parts of the world with large capital"; and at the end of the seventeenth century England and Holland were coupled together as the two states which "drive the greatest trades of all European nations". England's foreign commerce was remarkable not only for the extent of her markets abroad but also for the variety of her exports and imports. This is convincingly demonstrated in a striking survey compiled by an Elizabethan merchant.

We live in an age when politics and economics are inextricably interwoven. It is therefore of interest to observe that mercantilist England had attained an economic status which required her rulers to devote considerable attention to the problems arising out of her intercourse with other countries. Although foreign policy was not as yet dominated by economics, the latter entered more largely into international politics than political historians are wont to recognize. It is true that during the middle ages consistency in economic statecraft was rarely achieved owing to counteracting influences. English sovereigns were preoccupied with futile schemes of territorial aggrandizement on the Continent, and sheer political considerations cut athwart the pursuit of a systematic economic policy. The native wool supply or the location of the staple abroad served as counters in a game of diplomacy which sacrificed economic realities to dreams of conquest. Indeed fifteenth-century ' tracts for the times ' advanced the claim that her industrial resources in wool and cloth, combined with her geographical situation, endowed England with an instrument of diplomacy which must make the whole world seek her friendship and good will. Tudor voyages of discovery enlarged the vision of Englishmen ; and they revealed to the nation its true element, the sea—as well as its true destiny, the expansion of the English people. Nevertheless the process of enlightenment was only gradual, for in consequence of the Reformation religion emerged as a potent factor in determining the attitude of states towards one another, though eventually it was completely superseded by the economic factor. Thus the sixteenth and seventeenth centuries may be viewed as the battleground in which religious and economic issues contended for the mastery. The Thirty Years' War is usually regarded as the last of the religious wars ; and certainly after the middle of the seventeenth century the play of economic forces was less distracted by religious feuds. Still, much earlier it is manifest that the underlying purposes of statesmanship were being related to the achievement of economic objects. Admittedly there are cross-currents which make the picture often appear blurred and confused. England's foreign policy was in reality a mosaic, and its many-patterned texture disproves the notion that English governments have pursued a consistent design of economic aggrandizement abroad. Territorial security, traditional relationships, religious antipathies, trade jealousies, the personal predilections of the sovereign, all might deflect the course of external policy ; but the economic issues ultimately proved paramount, and only the resolution to tolerate no military hegemony in Europe took precedence over them.

Even a cursory glance at England's relations with the Continent shows that the tidal forces of national self-interest were fast asserting themselves, and that these forces were fundamentally economic. In the sixteenth century Spain occupied the foreground of the picture, in the seventeenth Holland, and in the eighteenth France. The first, Spain, was formerly one of the props of the English commercial system because she controlled or influenced the chief European markets for cloth ; yet she was also the buttress of the Counter-Reformation, and this—together with her claim to appropriate the wealth harvested in South America, into which " no other man ought to thrust his sickle "—produced a state of tension and then open war which was detrimental to trade. Holland was linked with England by close religious ties, and they shared a common aspiration in stemming the advance of the Counter-Reformation. Moreover Holland, the pattern of the nations, was constantly held up as a model to the English people and no other country has exercised a more profound influence on their economic development. Nevertheless these considerations did not prevent a succession of wars, since they were overridden by jealousies. The interests of the two states were everywhere in conflict. They were competitors in northern and south-eastern Europe, in the East Indies, in America and in Africa ; the wealth garnered by the Dutch from fishing off the English coasts was a perpetual irritant ; and the tariffs which they laid on English cloth in order to protect their own textile industry nourished the embittered feeling. The antagonism fostered by these grievances was reinforced when Holland seized the opportunity furnished by the Civil War to establish an undisputed ascendancy in the world's carrying trade, and it bore fruit in the acts of navigation and the three Dutch Wars. In the eighteenth century the French supplanted the Dutch in public estimation as 'our greatest and most dangerous rivals in trade'. Economic friction served to sharpen the edge of the national animosities which drew England and France apart, thus providing a conspicuous example of the interaction of politics and economics. The nature of the traffic, it was declared, enriched France "whose power England ought not to increase", and a tariff war paved the way for the second Hundred Years' War. In addition the belief that French imports exceeded English exports set the stage for a concrete application of the theory of the balance of trade, and it inaugurated what came to be looked upon as 'a remarkable era of English commerce'. The world was afforded the classic spectacle of protective tariffs carried to the point where they resulted in the almost complete eclipse of normal commercial relations between the two leading countries of Europe. After the Restoration a parliamentary enactment excluded the principal French products; and during most of the eighteenth century Anglo-French trade was mainly in the hands of smugglers. To this impasse futile economic jealousies and the logic of protection inexorably led.

The unique prestige accorded to the merchants engaged in oversea trade reflects the exceptional appreciation in which this class of entrepreneurs was held. The public esteem was traditional, for in Anglo-Saxon times the merchant who thrice fared over the seas by his own means was rewarded with the rank of nobility. He was eulogized as the 'master workman' and 'the steward of the kingdom's stock'; and it was declared that "all other callings received their vigour, life, strength and increase from the merchant", to whose hazardous as well as prudent undertakings "this nation chiefly owes all its wealth and glory". It is significant that it was the normal practice in England, in marked contrast with the Continent, for the younger sons of gentlemen and 'sometimes of the nobility' to be 'bred' to trade 'without prejudice to their gentility'. High premiums, occasionally no less than one thousand pounds, were exacted from apprentices who received a training in "the excellent qualities which are required in a perfect merchant"; and as a consequence they were largely recruited from the wealthier sections of the community. Individual merchants were often in command of considerable capital. The Venetian ambassador wrote home in 1557 that among the Merchant Adventurers and Staplers "there are many individuals possessed of from fifty to sixty thousand pounds sterling": in terms of modern currency they were almost millionaires. The fact that merchants were commonly men of substance and credit meant that they were in a position to embark upon speculative undertakings, which is at once the hall-mark of and the primary justification for a capitalist system. The American plantations provided an extensive field for investment, in which moneyed men sank and often lost their capital. The foundations of an empire in India were laid by a group of merchants at a meeting held in London in September 1599, presided over by the lord mayor, when it was decided to form an association to establish direct intercourse with India. English capitalists promoted other new trading corporations such as the Eastland, Levant and Russia Companies; they financed voyages to Africa which bore fruit in an immense accession of territory; and their efforts to capture the traffic in furs from the French resulted in the acquisition of Canada.

The growth of commerce, as evinced in the discovery of new markets and in the rapidly-expanding statistics of exports and imports, testifies to the existence of a vigorous and enterprising merchant class. "The merchants of England", it was affirmed in the seventeenth century, "are an industrious people and lovers of trade. They do not upon small—no, not upon great—discouragements give it over". None the less the communal system survived longer in the domain of foreign trade than elsewhere. The many difficulties attendant on 'adventuring' abroad help to explain the success with which the companies engaged in 'feats of merchandise' asserted their exclusive rights long after individualism had emancipated itself in other directions. The circumstances of the age impelled merchants to assume the functions which are now the province of the state—guarding against the dangers of piracy at sea and robbery on land, presenting a united front against oppression and exploitation by alien potentates, maintaining embassies, and erecting forts. Thus the natural instinct of Englishmen to act in a corporate capacity, while it lapsed in the spheres of industry and agriculture, was powerfully reinforced in the sphere of oversea trade. Two types of companies were evolved—the regulated and the joint-stock. The broad distinction between them lay in the degree to which individual enterprise was tolerated. The regulated company was the older form of association ; and its looser cohesion made it suitable for trafficking with countries where conditions were more settled. The joint-stock company was adapted for remoter lands where the normal risks of commerce were enhanced by political hazards. The posture of affairs might dictate an alternation of type—a company was sometimes regulated and at other times joint-stock. Every company had a territorial area assigned to it, in which the right of trading was restricted to its members.

There is a strong movement at the present day for the erection of trade associations which in principle, and sometimes even in their actual practice, bear a resemblance to the regulated company—thus demonstrating the persistence of traditional elements in our economic system. The regulated company was an association of merchants, each of whom transacted his business separately but was subject to the ‘ old trade principles ’ laid down by the fellowship to which he belonged. Even the briefest survey of the ‘ common rules ’ of the Merchant Adventurers, the greatest of the regulated companies, discloses the narrow limits within which a merchant was confined in his operations. The by-laws covered all the aspects of trade. They stipulated that no member should sell his wares in any place inside the company's territory other than the ‘ mart ’ or ‘ staple ’ towns. Merchandise had to be shipped abroad in vessels chartered by the company, which sailed together at set times of the year. The continental market was held in appointed seasons during which commodities were offered for sale on certain days only in the week. A code of trading etiquette was prescribed—for instance, the enticing of customers was prohibited. More important still, a 'stint' fixed the volume of exports which a member might handle. The idea of a 'stint' was in accordance with mediaeval gild principles, it existed in the coal industry in the seventeenth century, and it is a feature of the modern cartel: hence it furnishes a remarkable illustration of the continuity of economic practice through centuries of growth and change. The market was further controlled by the expedient of a restraint of shipping whenever the company wished to prevent a glut or produce a scarcity. Other regulations limited the maximum period of credit, imposed penalties on recalcitrant debtors, and endeavoured to maintain a high grade of quality by the exaction of penalties for defective wares.

Although the chartered companies were entrenched in the stronghold of privilege and sheltered behind the prerogative of the Crown, they were destined one by one to succumb to the pertinacity of those who assailed the traditional structure of commerce in the name of economic liberty. The conflict between the companies and the interlopers or 'free traders' raised a thorny subject of controversy. It involved the crucial question whether communal discipline or individualism should gain the upper hand, or (as it was expressed in the seventeenth century) whether trafficking overseas could be "possibly managed to the public and assured advantage of the commonwealth better by all English pretending merchants in a loose (which they call a frank and free) trade, than by merchants bred up in the mistery of this trade and associated together under order and government". On behalf of the regulated companies it was claimed that they enjoyed 'ancient privileges' in foreign countries, which ensured them inviolability of person and property, speedy justice against natives, immunity from taxes and the right of self-government. In addition they rendered public services by building 'many tall warlike ships', by making loans to the government, by preventing frauds in the customs, and by continuing to buy goods when there was a stoppage of trade abroad. Above all, they established ' politic government ' based on the ideal of a ' well-ordered and ruled trade '. This ideal, inherited from the middle ages and maintained down to the Revolution of 1688, embodied a philosophy of commerce in which ' adventuring ' abroad was deemed a profession requiring training and experience, prices were kept at a high level, the standard of quality was guaranteed, and production was restricted. Upon these four fundamentals rested the communal organization of commerce.

The arguments in favour of an open trade show how the traditional outlook, embodied in the basic concepts, was being modified under the inexorable pressure of economic realities. The practice of endowing a company with exclusive privileges was bound to evoke the jealousy of those shut out from its limited membership. Freedom of trade, it was declared in the House of Commons in the reign of James I., " is every man's inheritance and birthright ". Its denial infringed the ' Englishman's liberty '—a phrase which (it is worth while to notice) occurs in a fifteenth-century statute, although in the economic sphere the ' liberty ' of Englishmen was scarcely more than a convenient myth. And those who hammered at the gates of the company—vociferating that " all free subjects are born inheritable to the free exercise of their industry "—were supported by the testimony of facts, since behind the façade of a communal system which stood for equality of opportunity the forces of individualism were already in possession of the citadel. The bulk of the company's business was actually handled by a coterie of large traders who had managed to squeeze out the ' young beginners ' and men of ' lower estates ', despite the ' order of stint ' which was nominally designed to curb ' the overgrown and great-pursed merchant '. Moreover hostility to the competitive instinct, which was enshrined in the communal system, had considerably weakened with the passage of time. The growth of competition, " all the world striving to engross all the trade they can ", gradually forced upon English merchants the conviction that they must make it the interest of other nations to deal with them by discarding the policy of high prices. The doctrine that nothing "conduceth more to the enlargement of selling any commodity than cheapness" was a challenge to the mediaeval commercial concepts, and its eventual acceptance marked a fresh stage in the evolution of international trade. Thus against the regulated companies—the enemies of excessive competition, which flooded the market with goods and lowered prices to the benefit of foreign buyers—were pitted the unlicensed traders, the 'active and industrious spirits', opposed to the staple system, insistent that commerce should be left free to find its own channel, eager to seek out fresh places of traffic, and ready to reduce prices for the sake of quicker returns.

The triumph of individualism in its conflict with the regulated companies was delayed—as in the parallel case of industry—until after the Restoration, when Parliament inaugurated the policy of throwing open by stages the oversea markets which had hitherto been the close preserve of these companies. Under the spur of provincial jealousy of the metropolis—which sought to make itself the focus of the economic activities of the kingdom, "as if God had no sons to whom He gave the benefit of the earth but in London" —coupled with dislike of the companies' financial proceedings, the legislature had become converted to the view that the communal organization of England's trade with European countries was no longer appropriate in an age when commerce had attained its present 'height of perfection'.

The joint-stock company was a corporate body whose capital was provided by a number of shareholders who participated in the profits. The possibility of individual trading was not excluded, for private transactions might be permitted to the members in proportion to the amount of their stock. In the same way a regulated company was not incompatible with corporate trading because groups of partners were sometimes formed. There was a rapid increase of the joint-stock system in the second half of the sixteenth century. Its merit was that it enabled capital to be drawn from a wide area : anyone was free to hold shares in the company whether ‘ skilled in trade ’ or not. The drawback of a joint-stock was that a member could not, with certain exceptions, carry on business as an independent merchant : he merely drew dividends on his investment as a shareholder. Hence it did not afford the same scope for individual enterprise as did the regulated company in spite of the restrictions imposed on its members. The joint-stock companies played an important part in the development of English oversea trade by opening up new branches of commerce in India, Africa and Canada, but they encountered the hostility of those who opposed the confinement of a lucrative traffic to exclusive corporations. The case for the protraction of their monopoly beyond a limited period rested on political rather than economic considerations, namely, the peculiarities of the situation which existed in non-European countries. This was notably the position with the East India Company, the greatest of the joint-stock companies, which originated as a mercantile body and grew into a sovereign power.

I may conclude this account of the trading companies by remarking that the present century has witnessed the nominal survival of one of the two oldest trading companies (the Company of the Merchants of the Staple which down to the early seventeenth century exported wool), and the active survival of one of the two youngest (the Hudson's Bay Company whose sphere of trade lies in Canada).

§ 3. *The ‘ Industrial Revolution ’*

The foregoing description of England in the age of mercantilism points to the conclusion that in the seventeenth and eighteenth centuries the entrepreneur was recognized as the mainspring of the economic mechanism, and that belief in freedom of enterprise had crystallized into a dogma. The historical significance of these developments lies in the fact that they completely destroy the general notion that the inventions of the late eighteenth century involved an abrupt revolution in the tenor and rhythm of the national life. There is a natural temptation to dramatize great events : we picture them as thunderbolts emerging out of a clear blue sky which in an instant convulse human society : our minds are impressed by their apparent unexpectedness. Yet to the historian this attitude is profoundly untrue to historical realities. Where the popular imagination visualizes a swift transformation of the social or political landscape, the historian is conscious of a process of gradual change in which the old is blended almost imperceptibly with the new. Hence to view the ' Industrial Revolution ' in its proper perspective we must first discard the current clichés, which embody the traditional account of the inventions and serve to distort their real meaning.

The events which are designated as the ' Industrial Revolution ' constituted no sudden breach with the existing order but were part of a continuous movement which had already achieved marked advance. The famous inventions associated with the names of Arkwright, Watt, Stephenson and many others, were the climax of a long series of experiments extending over two centuries, in which progress seemed tardy because the initial stages are necessarily the slowest and most arduous. The idea of an invention may be grasped but decades may elapse before it can be made to work. Another impediment which discouraged inventive talent was the hostility displayed by the workers to labour-saving devices. Their aversion sprang from an inherited dislike of innovations, coupled with the fear that they would lose their means of livelihood. From the thirteenth century the introduction of machinery was a fruitful source of dissension, and the government frowned upon the ' abridgement ' of labour in order to avoid social unrest. To disarm the popular opposition the apologists of machinery were learning to use the familiar argument that cheapness stimulates the demand for commodities, which in turn stimulates the demand for labour. Mainly owing to these causes, success in vital things eluded the grasp of the seventeenth century ; but without the barren enterprises in which experience was painfully and dearly bought, the discoveries of a later age would have been impossible. The eager search for technical improvements —reflected in an astonishing list of industrial patents—led Miege (1691) to claim that "no nation has been more industrious than the English in mechanic arts, and the world to this day is obliged to them for many of their useful inventions and discoveries". And Cary (1695) depicted a community in which "new projections are every day set on foot".

It was as a result of the persistent efforts of innumerable pioneers that a generation before the accession of George III. —the customary date assigned to the commencement of the 'Industrial Revolution'—there had already dawned the 'new world of experiments' which had been confidently predicted in the previous century. In industry the new order was foreshadowed in a galaxy of great technical achievements—the steam engine to drain water from the coal mines, the fly shuttle in weaving, spinning by rollers, the carding machine for preparing wool, the smelting of iron ore with coke, and the production of steel by the crucible process. It is not surprising, then, to find this picture of the industrial state of England in the middle of the eighteenth century drawn by Dean Tucker: "Few countries are equal, perhaps none excel the English in the numbers and contrivance of their machines to abridge labour. The English are uncommonly dexterous in their contrivance of the mechanic powers". In agriculture the ground was similarly prepared for the important changes known as the 'Agrarian Revolution'. Thus in spite of the obstacles which retarded progress in the invention of machinery—imperfect technical knowledge and the antagonism of labour—economic society in the age of mercantilism did not remain stagnant. It was continually evolving, and the stage was being set for the coming of the factory age with its concomitants of power-driven machinery, mass production and the assemblage of workers under one roof.

The question has often been asked why the 'Industrial

Revolution' came first to England. The explanation is commonly found in the growth of her oversea trade with a far-flung commercial empire in America, India and Africa, which together with the Continent of Europe furnished markets for her manufactures. Admittedly the existence of markets abroad provided an incentive for the adoption of inventions. However it is only a part of the explanation, since France also made notable commercial strides in the eighteenth century but was outstripped in the race for industrial supremacy. Nor would it be correct to infer that the French people were lacking in inventive talent: on the contrary, at one period they led the way in many of the industrial arts. We must take other essential factors into account.

In the first place, prior to the inventions English industry, commerce and banking were organized on lines which served to make a large outlay on machinery and buildings a practicable as well as a profitable venture. Manufacturers were enabled to utilize the inventions because England had accumulated sufficient capital for investment in productive enterprises. In the second place, there existed a class of entrepreneurs equipped with the requisite technical qualities and organizing abilities, accustomed to latitude in the conduct of their business, and infused with the spirit of enterprise to which Dean Tucker bore testimony when he declared (1757) that "almost every master manufacturer hath a new invention of his own and is daily improving on those of others". In the third place, the growth of population in the hundred years following the Restoration failed to keep pace with the expansion of trade and industry: in the eighteenth century it was but one-third of that in France. The shortage of hands in the textile manufactures, combined with the comparatively high standard of wages, furnished English producers with an inducement to avail themselves of mechanical methods which would economize in the use of labour—a similar motive was not present in the same degree on the Continent. They had further incentives for the introduction of machinery in the shortcomings of the old hand-yarn products because manual spinning had many defects, and in the rise of trade unionism which strengthened the desire of employers to be liberated from their dependence upon labour.

In the fourth place, the home market catered for a population among whom property was widely diffused, and whose standard of comfort was substantial without being luxurious. Side by side with a widespread middle class which consisted of manufacturers, traders and farmers, there ranged the better-paid sections of artisans and peasants. Voltaire on his visit to our country in the early eighteenth century was struck by the fact that "the feet of the peasants are not bruised by wooden shoes; they eat white bread, are well-clothed"; and he could have added that they were learning to drink tea. Hume, who considered that "a too great disproportion [of wealth] among the citizens weakens any state", drew attention to "the great advantage of England above any nation" in this respect, and he spoke of the 'riches' of her artisans. Unlike France, the fabric of English society was composed of numerous layers which bridged the gulf between rich and poor, and made it relatively easy to move up in the social scale into a higher grade. A writer in 1767 remarked that "in England the several ranks of men slide into each other almost imperceptibly; and a spirit of equality runs through every part of the constitution. Hence arises a strong emulation in all the several stations and conditions to vie with each other; and a perpetual restless ambition in each of the inferior ranks to raise themselves to the level of those immediately above them. In such a state as this fashion must have an uncontrolled sway. And a fashionable luxury must spread through it like a contagion", since "our luxury keeps full pace with our opulence". This eighteenth-century picture of a fluid and progressive society throws a strong reflected light upon the conditions which were current in earlier times. The ability to rise from lowly beginnings is seen in the careers of two seventeenth-century entrepreneurs—Ambrose Crowley the greatest ironmaster of the Stuart age, who started life as a working blacksmith, and Peter Blundell one of its greatest clothiers, who also sprang from the ranks. The strength of the movement to overcome class barriers is attested by the complaints that servants aped their superiors in luxury in dress, which put " all degrees and orders of woman-kind into disorder and confusion ", while the master could not be known from his man except that the latter " wears better clothes ". The more even distribution of wealth in England, as compared with the Continent, reacted upon the sphere of production. The nature of the market determines the nature of the productive processes, and the prevailing demand of the English people was for commodities which were sound and useful rather than flimsy and artistic. Such commodities could be manufactured by machinery without the loss of their essential qualities. Not only did the character of English wares lend itself to *machine* production, but the flexible trend of national consumption was responsive to *mass* production in a country where the population was expanding, wages were increasing and wants were elastic. The history of the United States demonstrates how a rapidly-growing nation with a rising standard of life affords encouragement for the introduction of new industrial methods.

In the fifth place, the early exploitation of the coal measures stimulated the expansion of industry, for coal served as the fuel of numerous manufactures and as the motive power of machinery. In the sixth place, all the varied influences (enumerated above[1]) which contributed to England's economic growth played their part in paving the way for the achievements of the factory age. To sum up—the ' Industrial Revolution ' came first to England because she had expanding markets at home as well as abroad for her wares ; because the nature of these wares was suitable for mechanical production ; because the shortage, frequent inefficiency, relatively high price and organized power of labour made it desirable and profitable to expend capital on plant and buildings ; because the

[1] See above, pages 58-59.

necessary resources were available for investment ; because there existed men of enterprise with the energy to exploit novel methods ; because it lay in the logic of centuries of development as moulded by a variety of contributory influences.

There are many aspects of the ‘ Industrial Revolution ’ concerning which scholarly opinion is moving in another direction. For one thing, the expression is apt to convey an erroneous idea of the rapidity with which the industrial changes proceeded. It is now recognized that technical and other difficulties made the adoption of machinery and the extension of the factory system a much slower movement than was formerly supposed : even in Yorkshire only half the workers in the woollen industry were engaged in the factories in the middle of the nineteenth century. This naturally raises the question whether the term ‘ revolution ’ can be appropriately used when it is applied, not to violent political changes, but to an economic process for which the ground had been long prepared and which in its actual operation was more evolutionary than catastrophic. For another thing, the evils attributed to the inventions were not wholly due to the introduction of machinery. They were caused in part by the circumstances of the period. The inevitable evils of the transition were aggravated by a succession of wars which involved serious dislocation of markets, monetary inflation, and an unparalleled growth of the national debt coupled with a fantastical fiscal system —and which also induced the conviction that in the life-and-death struggle with France the production of wealth must over-ride all humanitarian considerations. But here I am concerned alone to urge that the study of the ‘ Industrial Revolution ’ must be carried back far beyond the decades with which it is traditionally associated. Certainly, any history of the ‘ Industrial Revolution ’ which does not take due account of the facts that in England the industrial regime was already largely capitalist in character, and that the ‘ inventions ’ were the creation, not the creators, of a capitalist society—or which teaches that the English artisan was transformed by the introduction of machinery from an independent producer into a wage-earner—can only yield a fresh lease of life to an historical myth.

It must be added that the interpretation of the 'Industrial Revolution' which I have put forward does not imply any desire to minimize the epoch-making status of the features comprehended in the term. Among the great events that have shaped the destiny of mankind, a distinctive place will always be assigned to the series of inventions which have subjected the forces of nature to the service of mankind, and substituted for human energy the machine working under human guidance. The stimulus given to the productive agencies by the application of motive power to industry and transport is a commonplace; and the increased command which man has acquired over the resources of nature merits the stress which is rightly laid upon it. The effects are writ large over the whole face of modern society. They shifted the centre of gravity from agriculture to industry: they made the factory system the predominant form of industrial organization: they enlarged the unit of production: they provided the means for the employment and maintenance of a much vaster population: they promoted the rapid growth of a class-conscious proletariat with its attendant fruits both social and political. These are effects whose importance no one will be tempted to belittle—but neither ought we to be tempted to magnify and distort their meaning by a false perspective which under-estimates the degree of economic development attained prior to the inventions. We must not let our minds be dazzled by the glamour of statistics. The true gauge of economic progress lies less in the scale of operations than in the fundamental adjustments which man makes in his efforts to satisfy his wants. From this standpoint the rise of individualism, and the far-reaching consequences which flowed from it, have an immense significance. For they show that the 'Industrial Revolution' was not a watershed, nor was it the genesis of a new industrial society composed of capitalist employers and proletarian wage-earners.

CHAPTER FOUR

THE TRIUMPH OF FREE ENTERPRISE

THE growth of free enterprise was attended by practical consequences of the first magnitude. It not only bore massive fruit in the new economic structure of society which I have just described, but it also had a decisive influence in the domain of public policy. From the first the standpoint of the entrepreneurs was clearly defined : they claimed a free hand in the conduct of their business. As a result of the pressure which they successfully exerted, the industrial system began to be liberated from state control as early as the seventeenth century, although the commercial system was not released from the stranglehold of tariffs until the nineteenth century. The one development emancipated the manufacturing class, the other the mercantile class[1]. These historic manifestations of the power of individualism set the stage for a trial of strength between the state and free enterprise, which constitutes the motif of the present chapter. In the sequel free enterprise was destined to submerge England's first planned economy so completely that even the memory of it has vanished from our minds almost as completely as the open fields have vanished from our countryside.

§ 1. *Stability versus Progress (1558–1660)*

The age of mercantilism was the battle-ground in which was fought out the issue whether individualism should be allowed a free hand or kept rigorously under control—whether the dissolving forces of commercialism should ruthlessly destroy the corporate fabric of society or remain subject to the traditional checks and balances. The issue

[1] The emancipation of the mercantile class from the control of the trading companies came much earlier, as was shown in the previous chapter.

was a momentous one for the future destiny of the English people. Every economic regime prescribes its own standards of conduct, and there was a fundamental difference in the basic concepts of the old order and of the new.

The old order did not divorce economics from ethics, but judged economic behaviour by an ethical standard which took account of the social reactions. In subordinating sectional claims to the common good it reflected the current precepts of morality. Hence the insistence on righteous dealing between landlord and tenant; hence the view of commerce as the means to promote the welfare of the community and provide a 'sufficient' recompense to the trader; hence the doctrine of a 'just price' that was fair alike to producer and consumer; hence the efforts to extirpate the 'corrupt practices', as they were styled, of commercial speculation which manipulated supplies with the object of forcing up prices; and hence the unsparing denunciation of enclosures for sheep-farming. The new order judged economic behaviour by the standard of enlightened self-interest; and the frank recognition of the latter as the dominant motive force registered a stage in the evolution of economic thought. The author of a famous *Discourse of the Common Weal* in the reign of Edward VI. rested his arguments on the promptings of self-interest, since he believed that every man seeks "where most advantage is"; and a seventeenth-century writer categorically affirmed that "everyone will do that which makes for his greatest advantage". These quotations indicate that the classical economists did not discover the 'economic man', who pursues his personal gain. Indeed in the middle of the seventeenth century he had already inspired the bitter reflection: "What does the merchant care, so that he be rich, how poor the public is?" Nor was there any novelty in Adam Smith's famous dictum which became the accepted postulate of his school of thought—"Man's self-love is God's providence". The contention that public and private interests are ultimately identical had been anticipated nearly a century earlier by Sir Dudley North (1691), when he claimed that "wherever the traders thrive the public of which they are a part thrives also ". And Dean Tucker—of whom it was said by Bishop Warburton that he " makes Trade his Religion "[1] —wrote in 1757 : " The self-love and self-interest of each individual will prompt him to seek such ways of gain as, by serving himself, will promote the public welfare at the same time ". The trend of opinion voiced in these utterances created the setting in which an insurgent individualism could work out its destiny unhampered by the older standards of morality.

This revolution in economic ideas was not only a crucial departure from orthodox principles but it involved a choice of two opposing ideals — stability and progress. For a century (1558–1660) England was distracted by the conflict between these rival concepts. It is not, perhaps, the province of the historian to consider whether she would have been a happier country if she had retained some, at least, of the fetters which clogged individualism : wisely or unwisely she sacrificed them on the altar of progress. The ' Industrial Revolution ' was enabled to come first to England because the entrepreneur had already been set free from the prison-house of tradition and authority.

In the light of these considerations we can measure the significance of the problem as it presented itself to the statesmen of the sixteenth and seventeenth centuries. It raised the fundamental question whether the state could successfully control the rising tide of individualism ; whether it could give scope to the free play of capitalist enterprise while ensuring that the pursuit of private gain did not involve social loss to the community. In its handling of the situation the monarchy stood unmistakably for the preservation of the old order—in the economic sphere not less than in the spheres of religion and politics. Without attempting to check the development of a capitalist class,

[1] And of another Dean Bishop Warburton said that he " makes Religion his Trade ".

it endeavoured to define its activities: to this end, it applied on a national scale the principles by which in the middle ages the corporate institutions—urban gilds and village courts—had sought to regulate industry and agriculture. Statute law came to the rescue of local law: it reinforced a decaying custom which was breaking down under the pressure of economic forces. The position taken up by the Crown was one of the main reasons for the alienation of the middle class whose political self-assertion, born of a sense of economic power, was nourished and inflamed by specific grievances. By the side of the religious and constitutional struggles proceeded another struggle—a duel between the monarchy seeking to preserve the traditional framework of society, and an aggressive and progressive middle class bent on establishing its ascendancy. The issues at stake in the Civil War were not only those of the Crown versus Parliament and of the Established Church versus Nonconformity, but of a community conducting its economic functions on a disciplined if confined basis versus the entrepreneur following a lonely furrow. In all ages the collision between authority and individualism has been a symbol of human progress and unrest; and the significance of the Great Rebellion lies in the all-important fact that it was a revolt against authority—not alone political and religious but also economic. The triumph of the Roundheads destroyed 'prerogative government' and a national church; and simultaneously it destroyed a society in which enterprise and initiative were fettered by a network of restrictions. The eclipse of the Tudor and Early Stuart regime was destined to usher in an era of economic freedom not less than an era of constitutional and religious freedom.

Whatever may be our view of the religious and constitutional issues which set at variance the monarchy and the nation, it is difficult to avoid the conclusion that in economic affairs the former was constrained to adopt a conservative attitude. Particular features of its policy may be condemned, but in so far as it aimed at the conservation of the social fabric it was in harmony with tradition. Much of the criticism levelled against the earlier mercantilist statesmen is vitiated by the implied assumption that they were presented with a blank sheet, on which they could inscribe any kind of programme in disregard of the psychology and immemorial practices of the community for which they legislated : in a word, it lacks the sense of historical realities. A violent breach with the usages of an ordered economic life was inconceivable on the part of the early mercantilist state, which pursued the consistent aim of protecting the existing structure from the corroding influence of the commercial spirit. Drawn irresistibly into the struggle between the conflicting ideals of stability and progress, the Tudors and Early Stuarts ranged themselves uncompromisingly on the side of stability, because they inherited the traditional outlook of their predecessors and stood for the maintenance of a society based on communal discipline and authority. Moreover it must be remembered that the armed forces at the disposal of the Crown were negligible ; the shadow of insurrection hung over it like the sword of Damocles ; and it had an inducement to discourage activities which threatened to stir up the masses. Economic progress might seem to be bound up with individualism but a heavy price had to be paid in social welfare. Sheep-farming involved the displacement of the tenantry from their ancestral holdings, and flooded the peaceful countryside with swarms of beggars who were a menace to public order and private security. The growth of capitalism in industry degraded the status of the independent craftsman and created the wage-system. The expansion of commerce exposed England to the vicissitudes of a world economy, with its concomitants of commercial crises and unemployment. In short, economic change meant a loss of social stability which was repugnant to the traditional morality, and which no government could afford to ignore.

We are confronted with the question : why did the monarchy fail to control the dynamic forces which shattered an obsolescent society? Ultimately the explanation lies in the fact that the forces which animate a progressive community are too strong to be held in check by governmental agencies. Their triumph lay in the logic of evolution. Whether or not, capitalism in its present form proves to be a historical category suited to a particular stage of man's development, it appears that in the past at all events economic progress has been largely dependent upon individualism, upon personality, upon the concentration of capital and the marshalling of labour groups under unified direction. The communal organization of society had for the time being exhausted its vitality. Its slower-moving mechanism was not sufficiently flexible to adjust itself spontaneously to the ever-changing needs of a people in whom the adventuring spirit of enterprise was never wholly quiescent. None the less subsidiary causes were in operation, and they help to explain why the government found itself powerless to halt the process of disintegration.

The personal character of the monarchs and the difficulties of their position have an important bearing in this connexion. Queen Elizabeth inaugurated an elaborate code which turned local law (the custom of the locality) into national law (the custom of the country) by extending the scope of the age-old principles of wage assessment, technical training, a balanced economy and relief of the poor; and the code remained on the statute-book for two hundred and fifty years. Her successors were signally unfitted for the planning and execution of a coherent policy or for the management of any public undertaking. James I. lacked dignity: Charles I. aroused mistrust by his tortuous methods. It is not impossible that if the Early Stuarts had been cast in a different mould, and if their statecraft had been more disinterested and single-minded, the breach between the old and the new, between mediaeval society and modern, might have been less irreparable. At a critical phase in England's development, those in whose hands lay her destinies proved unequal to the greatness of their opportunities. The ministers of Charles I.—Strafford and

Laud—were men of another stamp, with greater vision, courage and resolution than their royal master ; and they gave to the so-called Eleven Years' Tyranny its impress as one of the most remarkable decades in English social history. Yet both allowed themselves to be carried away by their zeal for what they believed to be a righteous cause, and their arbitrary methods helped to deepen the cleavage between the monarchy and the middle class.

Apart from the personality of the rulers who were placed at the helm in these momentous years, there were problems of another kind, religious and constitutional, which the Tudors had bequeathed to their successors. The economic question became inextricably entangled with questions which excited even more passionate feeling. This is the peculiar feature of the situation which has served to obscure the trend of events. The issue between the monarchy as the champion of the established economic order, and the rising middle class as its assailant, became involved with a widely different issue between the monarchy as the champion of the established religious order and the Puritan opposition. And yet a third issue was created when the monarchy, seeking to maintain its traditional position in the state, came into collision with the legislature which was encroaching upon the royal prerogative. Thus on one side was ranged the historic monarchy, defender of the national church and a communal society ; on the other side a representative assembly voicing the demand of the pioneers of individualism for religious and economic freedom. In the circumstances an open breach between Crown and Parliament was inevitable whatever the particular causes of friction, for they represented irreconcilable principles of national development. And in this confused medley of issues the fate of one determined the fate of all. The interaction of religious and economic factors provided the mainspring of a constitutional movement which resulted in consolidating the ascendancy of Parliament and in freeing the capitalist class from control by the Crown.

The authority of the monarchy in the economic arena

was impaired not only by its conflict with the religious and parliamentary forces arrayed against it but also by its alienation of the law courts. The common law of England was not unfavourable towards restraints on individualism when they were definitely sanctioned by immemorial usage; but it was opposed to any fresh restrictions upon enterprise, and it disliked the exercise of the royal prerogative in economic affairs. "The common law", declared chief justice Coke in a memorable passage, "hath so admeasured the prerogatives of the king that they should not take away nor prejudice the inheritance of any; and the best inheritance that the subject hath is the law of the realm". The Crown, therefore, could not look to the law courts for support of its economic policy. Accordingly it found itself at variance both with the legislature and the judicature.

The fiscal problem brought its own quota of difficulties. The monarchy lacked the resources for experiments in state socialism, and this was a potent cause of its failure to stem the encroaching tide of capitalism. Moreover the price revolution which occurred in the sixteenth century seriously aggravated the plight of the royal exchequer. It grew impossible for the king to manage on the normal sources of income—to 'live of his own', as the expression went—even in respect of the ordinary expenditure. In default of parliamentary subsidies he was driven to gather money by all kinds of shifts and devices, for instance, by exacting penalties for the breach of obsolete laws, by grants of monopolies and by other dubious expedients. The financial embarrassment of the Crown both stimulated its interest in economic affairs and threw doubts upon the sincerity of the motives which prompted its designs. Everything done by the Early Stuarts betrayed complex motives. A genuine desire to promote the national interests was combined with proposals of a fiscal nature. We see the mixture of motives in the incorporation of crafts, in the bestowal of patents, in the penalizing of enclosures, and in the manipulation of the industrial code which was laid open to grave abuses. It is not surprising, then, that some historians have discerned in the policy of the Early Stuarts nothing but the pursuit of sordid aims—the raising of revenue without parliamentary sanction. Yet to adopt such a view, unless it is considerably modified, is to miss the significance of the whole economic trend of the seventeenth century. It was a coincidence that the maintenance of the traditional system became mixed up with purely fiscal measures.

Another defect of economic statesmanship in the first half of the seventeenth century was its lack of coherence and consistency. (This is a defect which tends to beset modern economic policy.) The struggle for mastery between the contending principles of co-operation and individualism became lost in what seemed like a chaotic welter of petty projects, ill-conceived and worse executed. Every interest in the land was in turn attacked and alienated. The gentry were irritated by commissions of depopulation sent to inquire into enclosures. The farmers were alarmed by plans for public granaries and angered by the ruthless repression of tobacco-growing for the sake of Virginia. The manufacturers had innumerable grievances in patents of monopoly, which " entrenched upon the freedom of the subjects ", in schemes for textile corporations, in the complexity of the laws prescribing the processes of industry, in the prohibition of labour-saving devices, in the assessment of wages, in the pressure put on employers to keep their men at work in bad times and to employ none but those who had served an apprenticeship. The retail traders found their existence menaced by efforts to suppress speculation in grain and wool and coal. The merchants engaged in oversea commerce were rendered hostile by attacks upon the trading companies, by interference with the monetary exchanges, by the seizure of the bullion stored for safety in the Mint, by intervention between creditors and debtors, and above all by the exaction of increased customs duties —" In no part of the world [are traders] so screwed and wrung as in England " ; " Our estates are squeezed from us, and we now become only to have the name to be rich ".

All these elements of disaffection combined to widen the breach between the monarchy and the industrial and trading classes.

Richard Baxter's analysis of " the quality of the persons which adhered to the king and to the Parliament " implies that economic causes had a conspicuous share in determining the alignment of parties in the Civil War. He rightly held that it was " principally the differences about religious matters that filled up the Parliament's armies " ; yet the cleavage between Puritans and non-Puritans reflected, in a degree which was scarcely a coincidence, a division between conflicting economic interests. " A great part of the lords came to the king. A very great part of the knights and gentlemen adhered to the king except in [the eastern counties]. And most of the tenants of these gentlemen and also most of the poorest of the people did follow the gentry and were for the king ". On the side of Parliament were ranged the smaller part of the gentry in most counties, " and the greatest part of the tradesmen and freeholders, and the middle sort of men ; especially in those corporations and counties which depend on clothing and such manufactures ". If, proceeds Baxter, " you ask the reasons of this difference—the reasons which the [Parliament's] party themselves gave was because (say they) the tradesmen have a correspondency with London and so are grown to be a far more intelligent sort of men than the ignorant peasants. And the freeholders, say they, were not enslaved to their landlords as the tenants are. The gentry (say they) are wholly by their estates and ambition more dependent on the king. The other side said that the reason was because the gentry did better understand affairs of state than half-witted tradesmen and freeholders do ". It is evident that potent economic influences were at work, though they might be veiled or unsuspected.

We must not, in fairness, overlook the fact that the monarchy was gravely handicapped by the absence of a trained civil service, which would have made it more practicable to curtail the field of capitalist enterprise. The attempt to focus the economic life of the community at a single point, and to bring its varied activities under control, broke down inevitably owing to the shortcomings of the administrative machinery. Ambitious economic programmes remained largely paper programmes, because adequate resources were lacking to give them substance. The strict regimentation of the economic system was viewed as the province of the state at a time when the machinery of government was primitive and a civil service of the modern pattern hardly existed. The progress of legislation outran executive efficiency, and many laws became a dead letter owing to the disinclination of the unpaid magistracy to enforce them. There was a marked contrast between the zeal displayed by the central authority and the lukewarmness of its local agents upon whose shoulders were piled the stacks of statutes. In all ages the execution of laws has lagged behind the good intentions with which they have been framed. The successful functioning of a legal system must depend upon the willing co-operation of the people ; and the monarchy, in spite of an imposing appearance of strength, was powerless to carry out an economic policy which was unacceptable to the middle class. The lesson handed down from the days of antiquity was taught once again—not walls but laws make a city : not laws but their administration make a government.

In this enumeration of the reasons for the failure of the monarchy, we reach the final consideration. Even if the Crown had been supported by a staff of trained administrators, it could not have averted, though it might have modified, the establishment of a capitalist society. For while it was fortified by the prestige of centuries and by the innate loyalty and conservatism of the English people, it was impotent to check the insidious advance of individualism. Alike in industry, commerce and agriculture the foundations of the old order had been sapped by the subtle penetration of the spirit of capitalism. The mediaeval fabric still retained much of its old aspect yet its vitality had been largely drained away until there often remained little more than an empty shell. However the struggle between the monarchy and the middle class might have proved more protracted, and the issue might have continued longer in suspense, but for the outbreak of the Civil War. The revolt against authority in the constitutional and religious spheres swept away the obstacles which had hitherto stifled the protests against authority in the economic sphere. The dissolution of the bonds which held society together had abiding consequences. A violent shock was given to institutions which had regulated the workings of the economic system; and although the process of change had begun, it was immensely accelerated by the decay of the legal sanctions. When a settled government was at length established, it was unable to revive in their fullness the authoritarian traditions which had enabled the monarchy to destroy or penalize enclosures; to bring pressure to bear on employers; to require local magistrates to provide work for the poor; to insist on technical training for artisans; to assess wages; to place individuals or corporations in charge of a branch of industry; and in other ways to superintend the economic life of the community. As the outcome of the Great Rebellion the movement towards *laissez-faire* acquired increasing momentum. In the relaxation of state control lies the untold economic significance of the Civil War.

§ 2. *The Trend towards Laissez-Faire (1660–1800)*

After the Restoration, more than a century before the 'Industrial Revolution' or the publication of *The Wealth of Nations*, the doctrine of economic freedom began to gain an increasing hold over the minds of the governing body. A number of factors were working in this direction.

In the first place, the development of capitalism and the stimulus of expanding trade had fostered and brought to maturity the nascent individualism of the middle class: already released from the jurisdiction of the craft gilds, it was grown ripe for the assertion of industrial liberty against the state itself. Even under the Tudors and Early Stuarts the entrepreneurs had displayed an inflexible determination to break loose from restrictions which did not accord with their own interests. To all attempts to put into execution laws which kept them in swaddling-clothes and hindered the conduct of their business, they responded by passive resistance. Their opposition to paternal legislation, and the repeated but futile admonitions of the government, remind us once again that economic practice cannot be interpreted from the pages of the statute-book ; and they warn us not to date the beginnings of *laissez-faire* in industry from the belated repeal of laws, which in actual fact had always been honoured more in the breach than in the observance. In the second place, the new political system which prevailed now favoured economic emancipation since the monarchy could no longer exercise a restraining influence. The collapse of the authoritarian regime proved to be the turning-point in the evolution of capitalism in England. It eliminated the one barrier which obstructed the path of the entrepreneur who was allowed henceforth a freer hand in industry. The constitutional order established at the Restoration and consolidated by the Revolution of 1688 created the framework within which a capitalist society could work out its destiny, unhampered by the control that the Crown had endeavoured to enforce. If the constitutional changes were themselves mainly the result of the growth of the middle class, they in turn stimulated its political instincts and commercial progress. Voltaire penetratingly observed that " as trade enriched the citizens in London, so it contributed to their freedom ; and this freedom on the other side extended their commerce ".

In the third place, the Civil War proved a powerful dissolvent of traditional ways of thought. The reaction against constituted authority extended inevitably to the economic field and encouraged a critical attitude towards state interference. The vigorous attack made by a group of Restoration writers upon restraints in internal trade and industry revealed the extent to which a growing body of public opinion had emancipated itself from many of the dogmas enshrined in the outlook of the age. In the fourth place, the trend of the judicial decisions given in courts of law was in favour of industrial freedom, and the judges were particularly potent in circumscribing the scope of the Statute of Apprentices and in undermining the legal position of the craft gilds. In the fifth place, the waning power of the Privy Council—whose multifarious activities, mirrored in its records, had pervaded every branch of the national economy—weakened irreparably the existing mechanism of administration. Once the government ceased to wield its former authority, the structure of which it had been the pivot began to disintegrate, and the economic functions of the local bodies in consequence largely lapsed.

The combined weight of all these factors produced an orientation of policy, which found expression in a definite advance towards *laissez-faire*. Owing to the movement which culminated in the Revolution of 1688, Parliament came directly under the influence of a capitalist regime which had successfully challenged the right of the Crown to limit its power, and proceeded to demand its liberation from the shackles laid upon it by the legislature. Nothing was to be allowed to stand in the path of the entrepreneur : even the case for religious toleration was based on the plea that persecution was a bar to prosperity in view of the prominence of the Dissenters in the business world. Henceforth Parliament concentrated its energies upon commercial policy, which was now systematically designed to protect the interests of the producer and ensure him the undisputed possession of the home market : it grew less concerned to control industry, regulate labour conditions, and promote social stability. In accordance with the change of attitude, the old industrial code was allowed gradually to fall into desuetude. The whole economic outlook of the eighteenth century was permeated by an encroaching individualism which insisted upon unfettered freedom of action, and imposed upon the government the course that it must pursue. Owing to this reversal of roles, the state renounced the right to dictate to entrepreneurs the terms on which they should employ their workfolk, and exhibited an increasing disposition to tolerate their claims to make their own contract regarding the rates of remuneration, the length of service, the quality and supply of labour, and the nature of the products. Parliament pronounced the maxim in 1702 which was to mould its policy throughout the century —" Trade ought to be free and not restrained ". Fifty years later a parliamentary committee was appointed to inquire into ' the laws relating to trade and manufactures '. Its report, which constitutes a landmark in the progress of economic thought, indicated how drastic was the alteration in sentiment towards the enactments of a by-gone age, " perhaps well calculated for the times in which they were made, yet now become prejudicial to Trade in its present state ". In the traditional spirit of English institutional development piecemeal legislation, combined with the process of natural decay, sapped the foundations of the old order. Once the state abdicated its authority the relations of capital and labour entered on a fresh stage and ceased to be subject to the rule of law. Instead of the general conditions of employment being controlled by a superior power, they were determined according to the respective strength of the opposing sides—and the consequences are manifest in every facet of the national economy of our own times.

I may indicate, first, the position as it affected wages. The reign of Charles II. has been regarded as ' the posterior limit ' of the system of wage regulation : actually it survived the transformation of the political landscape as numerous assessments abundantly testify. Yet in the main it was kept alive not by official pressure but by its own inherent vitality born of custom and usage. In one form or another the institution went back three hundred years, and so we should not expect a sudden cessation but rather a gradual lapse—with the result that in the eighteenth century there was local and intermittent action on the part of the magistrates, but wage assessment was not in national operation as a regular function of the economic organism though it did not die out completely. The change of front on the part of the state was signally displayed in the year 1756, a landmark in the history of *laissez-faire*, when the case was fought out between the advocates and opponents of legal minimum wages. The weavers in the west of England had appealed to the legislature to revive the system of wage regulation which had passed out of living memory in the textile industry of the west country. In response to their petitions Parliament re-enacted the Elizabethan statute. The employers who had been taken by surprise fought strenuously against the act. They based their opposition on the technical difficulties of drafting complicated piece-lists and on the doctrine of industrial freedom. "We think it repugnant", they declared, "to the liberties of a free people and the interest of trade that any law should supersede a private contract honourably made between a master and his workman. Trade is a tender plant that can only be nursed up by liberty". These arguments prevailed on Parliament to annul the measure which it had enacted in the previous year. The action of the state in stripping itself of the right to fix wages was almost in the nature of an economic revolution. For centuries this right had been recognized as a cardinal principle of industrial regulation; and though in practice it had fallen into disuse its survival on the statute-book had vested in the authorities a reserve of power to which they could always turn. The repeal of the act of 1756 signified that the system of wage control was now definitely abandoned in the premier industry of the country. The principles of *laissez-faire* had thus received their first legislative sanction.

In the case of unemployment the effect produced by the new outlook on industrial problems was more immediate. The Civil War brought to an end the practice by which employers were required by the state to keep their men at work in times of depression. Their right to expand or contract their business freely in response to the market for their goods was no longer questioned. The attempt to secure continuity of employment was relinquished : instead the machinery of the poor law was utilized to relieve the distress created by unemployment. The fact that the workers had no safeguard against dismissal threw them upon their own resources. They were forced to shoulder responsibilities which had hitherto been the province of the state, and to rely upon their own efforts for the maintenance of their standard of life. It is therefore significant that the change in public policy was shortly followed by the rapid growth of trade unions, which sprang into prominence as soon as the state relaxed its control over economic life.

In another direction we observe how the Civil War loosened social ties and weakened the respect for economic usages. During many centuries the institution of apprenticeship was the basis of organized industrial society. Nominally it remained obligatory, but a process of disintegration set in owing to a marked disinclination to administer the system. Parliament steadfastly refused to lend its support to the old Elizabethan code, and apprenticeship was deprived of its legal guarantees—although some of the local authorities intermittently put the machinery of the law into operation against those who took up a trade to which they had not served an apprenticeship. While the system of technical training held its ground successfully in normal times, its survival was a matter of custom rather than compulsion. An increasing volume of public opinion, responding to the needs of an expanding trade, advocated the removal of restraints of which many were now clearly antiquated. Sir Josiah Child, one of the leaders of the business world in the seventeenth century, announced the gospel of economic freedom. " To improve and advance trade [we must] begin the right way, casting off some of our old mistaken principles in trade which we inherit from our ancestors ". Among the ' common errors ' of the day he included the notions that " none shall use any manual occupation except he has been apprentice to the same ", and that " to suffer artificers to have as many apprentices as they will is to destroy trade ". As a consequence of the change in the attitude of the state towards the institution of apprenticeship, the moral sanction alone remained and its weakness manifested itself in the early decades of the nineteenth century. Trained workmen were then unable to resist the invasion of unskilled and ill-paid labourers, who swamped the textile industries and dragged down with fatal results the handicraft worker's standard of life. The disintegration of the apprenticeship system in its legal form paved the way for its dissolution in its economic form when the factory owners, indifferent to the claims of technical workmanship, sought only to buy their labour in the cheapest market.

And finally the national regulation of industry, which was intended to standardize the production of staple wares, fell into disfavour. In actual practice it was found impossible to coerce the manufacturers into managing their business on the lines laid down for them. The revolt against industrial legislation was due primarily to the irksome restrictions which it imposed on the entrepreneurs, but it was seconded by other causes. One was its complexity : the elaborate code of restrictive legislation served to defeat its own ends. The government itself confessed that manufacturers were ' perplexed and entangled ' by the multitude and contradictions of the laws in force. " It were better ", observed a contemporary, " to have fewer laws with better execution ". Another defect was the lack of a satisfactory method of enforcement ; and in the absence of an efficient administrative machinery the system of inspection was casual and abuses flourished. Acts of Parliament became discredited when they were turned into vehicles for extortion and the inspection of commodities degenerated into a tax on commodities, or when their purpose was perverted by bringing indictments against those who " excelled in their own trades by force of their own genius and not against such as have been ignorant in their

interpretation of any future planned economy. It was expressed in a series of decisions of which the practical effect was that trade associations were left in a general uncertainty as to their real powers. Long before the Municipal Corporations Act (1835) authorized " every person in any borough " to " use every lawful trade and handicraft ", the freedom which it conferred as a legal right had actually been in practice largely attained. The weight of judicial decisions also evinced openly the desire of the law courts to give the utmost latitude to the interpretation of the Statute of Apprentices, in order to diminish as much as possible the scope of a law which was looked upon by the judges as " inconvenient to trade and to the increase of inventions ". We may sum up by saying that as a rule the common law favoured the removal of restraints on economic enterprise. It still continued to pay nominal respect to the age-old principle of industrial regulation, and did not mingle privileges and monopolies in a sweeping condemnation as ' unreasonable and unwarrantable '. It was prepared to bestow its approval and protection on patents and gild by-laws provided they were intended to promote the ' well-ordering of trade '. None the less it tended to disallow any extension of restrictive practices to the new conditions which were developing on every side. As a consequence the main current of economic life swept by the traditional framework of a corporate society, unimpeded in its onward movement by any serious legal obstacles.

The foregoing account will have served to show that there are no adequate grounds for assuming that Adam Smith converted England to the doctrine of industrial freedom, any more than that he converted England to the doctrine of the free exchange of goods. A shallow presentation of the facts might bring into relation with each other the two salient considerations that *The Wealth of Nations* was published in 1776, and that within a generation the great Elizabethan code embodied in the Statute of Apprentices had been expunged from the statute-book—leaving employers freed from all legal restrictions as to the kind of labour they must employ or the rates of wages they must pay. *Post hoc ; ergo propter hoc.* A deeper analysis reveals a more composite picture than is suggested by this simple synthesis. The movement towards *laissez-faire* has a long history behind it. Even in the days when government control of industry was most active, it is difficult to determine the extent to which the manufacturing class submitted to it. In the absence of a civil service and an adequate system of inspection, it is certain that much of the industrial legislation was virtually a dead letter. The regulation of wages by the magistrates degenerated into a routine which rapidly produced a distinction between the legal rates sanctioned by authority and the market rates paid by employers. The institution of apprenticeship was undermined by the efforts of the law courts to weaken the restraints which it imposed on individual enterprise ; and in practice it was effective in those circumstances alone where it remains effective in our day, namely, when enforced by the custom of the trade. The famous assize of cloth, which fixed the dimensions of cloth, proved unworkable. It was found impossible to prevent the use of tenter-frames for stretching cloth and of gig mills for dressing cloth. Hence it is to the seventeenth century, and not to the ' Industrial Revolution ' nor to *The Wealth of Nations*, that we must look for the trend towards *laissez-faire* in industry and for the explanation of its triumph. Adam Smith only gave articulate expression to ideas in whose direction the leaders of industry had long been feeling their way. The repeal of the labour code in 1809 (in the woollen industry) and in 1813–14 (in other industries) was necessitated by the activities of informers and attorneys, who ' rummaged out ' obsolete laws in the vain hope to stem the advance of the factory system. Its importance, therefore, should not be exaggerated as though it indicated that the legislature had suddenly surrendered itself to the influence of the classical economists. The relaxation of industrial restraints was already an accomplished fact, upon which Parliament now placed the formal seal of legislative approval.

The control exercised by the state in the domain of foreign trade survived long after its control over industry had virtually lapsed. The explanation lies in the united front which the entrepreneurs presented in their demand for *laissez-faire* in industry as contrasted with the cleavage of opinion among them regarding external trade. The manufacturers insisted on protection against alien competition, and their views prevailed over those of the mercantile interests. The beginnings of free trade were delayed until the last quarter of the eighteenth century[1], when a commercial treaty with France provided for the abolition of "the prohibitions and prohibitory duties which have existed for almost a century between the two nations". It is a common assumption that the adoption of a new commercial policy was due to the influence of Adam Smith. Actually among the influences responsible for the disintegration of the mercantile system and the substitution of a policy of plenty for the policy of self-sufficiency, *The Wealth of Nations* played a much smaller part than is usually attributed to it. It served to supply an intellectual background to the forces which were transforming the outlook of eighteenth-century England: it explained or, more correctly, it provided a reasoned justification for the economic tendencies of the time: nevertheless it was not an abstract theory of international trade, nor a convincing demonstration of the fallacies of protection, that won over English industrialists to free trade.

The interaction of politics and economics had produced by the end of the seventeenth century an alignment of parties divided in their attitude towards tariffs, which has remained a conspicuous feature of the parliamentary system down to the present day. And by this time economists had found in the theory of 'the general balance' of trade (that total exports should exceed total imports) an effective weapon

[1] The climax of the free-trade movement—the repeal of the corn laws—was delayed until nearly the middle of the nineteenth century.

with which to counter the views of those who condemned the trade with any particular country from which imports exceeded exports. Moreover they had anticipated the basic arguments in favour of free trade by demonstrating that it was the means to stimulate industrial efficiency and ingenuity, foster a mercantile marine, lower the cost of living, reduce the price of materials, promote the international division of labour, and establish friendship between states. Already in the seventeenth century they taught the doctrines that " the whole world as to trade is but as one nation " ; that " trade is in its nature free, finds its own channel, and best directeth its own course " ; that " England never throve by trade but while she was an universal merchant " ; that those who seek to promote the consumption of their own native products " by an universal discouragement of foreign goods will find themselves in process of time to have little or no trade, and that their own commodities shall remain a drug upon their hands ". But neither the politicians who were eager for political reasons to break down the barriers against trade with France, nor the economists who on theoretical grounds favoured the removal of restraints, were responsible for the change in the commercial policy of the country : the pressure of vested interests was too strong. The real cause of the change was the confidence which English entrepreneurs had come to feel in their ability to meet foreign competition. The industrial interests still demanded protection, but they were content to dispense with *legal* protection once they enjoyed the *natural* protection afforded by their superior efficiency. In short the beginnings of the free trade movement in England were inspired by practical considerations ; and theoretical arguments did not carry the weight with which they are generally credited. The concept of economic freedom originated not as an abstract doctrine evolved by economic science but as the inevitable corollary to the place occupied by the entrepreneur in the national economy.

§ 3. *The Reaction from Laissez-Faire* [1] *(1800–1918)*

I have shown in the previous section that the triumph of *laissez-faire* came in the eighteenth and not, as is commonly supposed, in the nineteenth century. It was the new situation created by the introduction of machinery and the growth of the factory system which was responsible for an epoch-making departure in the national approach to economic problems. At first the state assumed an attitude of Olympian detachment, and did little or nothing to alleviate the social distress which accompanied the transition from the old order to the new. At this distance of time—as we look back upon the controversy between those who were concerned only to exploit the economic potentialities of the great inventions and those who applied a social criterion—the question springs to the mind : why did the state refrain from intervention ? When we read of the horrors of infant slavery, the long hours of work of men, women and children, and the insanitary condition of many of the early factories, we find it difficult to understand on what pretexts it was possible to offer any opposition to state control. We are driven to ask whether the 'Industrial Revolution' created a class of employers in whom all compassion was extinguished ; but even so, we have still to explain why public opinion appeared so insensitive to the sufferings of the victims of economic progress.

In order to understand the psychology of those who resisted industrial legislation, two things must be remembered. Firstly : the conditions which prevailed under the early factory system were largely inherited from the industrial society which existed before the inventions. The reason why it was so hard to arouse the public conscience was because the evils were essentially old evils, though in some cases the factory system accentuated them. Take the outstanding evil of the period, namely, the exploitation of

[1] The nineteenth century was the era of a reaction from *laissez-faire* in the sphere of industry ; but it was also, from the forties onwards, the era of *laissez-passer* in the sphere of commerce (*i.e.* free trade).

child labour. This had been a feature of the industrial system from the earliest times. The use of child labour did not commence with the introduction of machinery: on the contrary, children were often employed at an earlier age and for less wages than the majority of children in factories. The fact that child labour was an integral part of the older industrial society naturally made the task of stamping it out in factories much more arduous. In the same way the long hours of labour were a legacy of the domestic system under which a working day consisted of twelve hours' toil. Secondly: the minds of the rulers of England were in the grip of the 'dismal' philosophy of the day, which found economic salvation in the rigid dogmas of *laissez-faire*; and these dogmas were likewise an inheritance from the past. The doctrine of non-intervention had been accepted in principle by the governing classes for a century, so that it could not be discarded overnight. The reluctance to revert to the practice of state regulation measured the success with which the entrepreneurs had swayed public opinion in favour of industrial freedom.

The force of circumstances, however, proved too strong. In the early decades of the nineteenth century the whole frame of society seemed to be breaking up with the growth of a vast industrial population employed in factories, workshops and mines, which had behind it no social traditions to give it coherence and stability, and which was composed of the most diverse elements—handicraftsmen who had inherited memories of skilled labour and semi-independence, agricultural labourers divorced from the steadying influences of country life, Irish immigrants accustomed to a lower standard of living. All these elements were mingled together in the large towns, each reacting on the other, creating intense social confusion, a sense of chaos and instability, out of which emerged a militant labour movement seeking blindly to accomplish far-reaching and even revolutionary designs. The need for extensive readjustments in a period of intense unrest, when the old landmarks were being submerged in a torrent of industrialism, compelled the state to intervene once again in economic affairs. The drift towards *laissez-faire* was arrested, and the control of the state over the productive agencies was once more reasserted. As the evils created or intensified by the use of machinery attracted attention, they afforded a convincing demonstration that the accumulation of wealth in the hands of merchants or manufacturers was inadequate by itself to fulfil the requirements of national well-being. The invention of machinery had solved the problem of production, yet it still remained imperative to solve the problem of distribution —and not merely ensure that wealth was distributed over as wide a circle as possible, but also that it was produced under conditions which did not degrade the mass of the community. Under the influence of this new conception the system of *laissez-faire* began to be assailed by those who believed that the only real wealth is life itself, from which it followed that to sacrifice the health and happiness of the community in economic pursuits was to defeat the very object which the latter were intended to promote.

Other factors contributed to a change in public opinion, of which the full fruits are coming to maturity at the present day. The tentative efforts at reform were attended with a success which stimulated the activities of the social reformers, while the prophets of woe were discouraged to find that their predictions of national ruin were not verified. Experience has proved, said Lord Shaftesbury, that everything urged by the opponents of factory legislation "has issued in the very reverse. Has ruin stalked over the manufacturing districts? Has capital quitted the country? Have your wages been reduced to the minimum of subsistence? Has the produce of cotton goods been diminished?" In spite of the many restrictions imposed upon capitalists by factory and other legislation, industry and commerce—so far from languishing as was freely predicted—expanded in the nineteenth century by leaps and bounds. Moreover (a pregnant consideration) one step involved another. Once the country put its hand to the plough it could not turn back, and the movement began to develop of its own momentum.

Hence in the course of the last century the doctrine of *laissez-faire* came to be abandoned in the sphere of industry. The evils of unregulated industrialism forced the state to recognize that material progress may be purchased too dearly if human welfare is disregarded. Accordingly, while at first the state was only concerned to facilitate the march of material progress, and to remove the obstacles which impeded the free play of industrial capitalism, it had eventually to admit that something else was needed. Reluctantly the state was driven to acknowledge that it could not afford to be indifferent to an environment which went to the very roots of national life. And from this the conclusion followed that it was incumbent upon the state actively to foster the general welfare by conscious regulation instead of trusting to the operation of economic forces, such as unfettered competition, to produce satisfactory social conditions. As this conviction grew, there gradually developed the notion that it was the province of the state to legislate directly with a view to establish the foundations of social security.

The public consciousness became increasingly permeated with a new conception which replaced that of *laissez-faire*—the conception of a 'national minimum', a minimum standard of well-being to which every person was entitled irrespective of his or her position in the industrial order. This conception could be defended on the ground that it was the best method of increasing production, or on the ground of preserving the nation, or on the ground of humanitarianism; but whatever the reason for its acceptance, it has become a recognized postulate of social morality. The principle of a 'national minimum' has already found expression in factory acts designed to secure a minimum of leisure and safety, in education acts designed to secure a minimum of instruction, in trade boards acts designed to secure a minimum of remuneration, in public health acts designed to maintain and improve the health of the people, in old age pensions and insurance against unemployment, and in other measures of remedial legislation. The first world war (1914–18) also gave an increased stimulus to the movement away from *laissez-faire*, because it necessitated an immense extension of state interference in all branches of the national economy. Although the end of the war was soon followed by the abolition of many forms of control, the public had grown accustomed to state intervention in the economic sphere. In this respect the effects were the reverse of those produced by the Civil War in the seventeenth century, which accelerated the movement towards *laissez-faire*.

In the eternal flux of human affairs the cycle of the ages often brings mankind back to an earlier standpoint. The exaggerated individualism of a past age has been profoundly modified by the principle that it is the duty of the community to ensure for its members, one and all, a minimum of well-being. With an infinitely superior equipment, and a more conscious sense of purpose, this country is returning to an older tradition—the regulation of economic life in the spirit of social harmony and justice.

CHAPTER FIVE

BETWEEN THE TWO WORLD WARS (1919–39)

§ 1. *Effects of the First World War on Great Britain*

At the outbreak of the first world war in 1914 it appeared to a generation reared in the philosophy of Adam Smith that economic nationalism was extinct, that a world economy based on international specialization was within measurable distance of complete fulfilment, and that free enterprise—qualified only by the restraints arising out of social legislation—had finally triumphed. The pioneer of free trade, Great Britain, still remained faithful to her principles. Her doors were thrown wide open to the imports of both hemispheres ; and she imposed no customs on foreign commodities other than those levied for revenue purposes. She seemed to have renounced once and for all every vestige of the mercantilist doctrine of economic nationalism. By the teachings of her economists and the practice of her statesmen she upheld the rival doctrine of the international division of labour, and she offered mankind a shining example of the blessings of international trade. She stood pre-eminent as the leading commercial nation on the face of the globe, as the possessor of the largest mercantile marine, and as the world's banker and commission agent. Her population enjoyed a standard of living higher than that of any other European country. Her surplus wealth fertilized the barren places of the earth and promoted material progress in backward lands. In her hour of need she reaped in full measure the harvest of a far-sighted economic policy. During the war of 1914–18 she not only carried her own stupendous financial burdens, but she made advances to her Allies almost twice as large as her own borrowings abroad. After the war she supported an unprecedented load of taxation and the obligations of social services which sheltered their beneficiaries from the worst effects of economic adversity. All these things she owed to the energy of her people, to the mildness of her political institutions, and to the system of the free exchange of goods.

At the outbreak of the second world war in 1939 an epoch-making change had already taken place in Great Britain's economic policy, and the pendulum was swinging violently in the opposite direction. Under the influence of a blizzard which swept over the world with the force of a tornado and created a widely-different international framework, Great Britain repudiated the historic tenets of free trade and reverted once more to economic nationalism. Her commercial system, transformed within a decade, bristled with tariffs, 'quotas', subsidies, imperial preferences and bilateral treaties. A mercantilist viewpoint, long discredited, now completely eclipsed her century-old conceptions of what constituted her fundamental interests—namely, her commanding position in world trade, the highly remunerative character of her international services (investment, banking, insurance and merchant shipping), and the moral obligation to facilitate the freest access to the raw materials raised in her Empire by her willingness to purchase the products of other nations. The wheel had come full circle, and the clock of history appeared to have been put back a hundred years. In this chapter I shall review the circumstances responsible for the resurgence of economic nationalism and assess the momentous effects as they worked themselves out in Great Britain. Between the Armistice of 1918 and the abandonment of free trade in 1932 lie the fateful years in which the economic consequences of the first world war began to emerge in a clear light. The history of these years cannot but have a deep interest for all who await with anxiety—or seek to forecast and perhaps even to shape—the economic consequences of the second world war.

The dominating motif which inspired British economic policy after the war of 1914–18 was the desire to return to pre-war conditions as soon as possible, to discard the system of emergency controls which had grown up during the war, and to leave natural forces to exert an unrestrained influence on the economic situation. For a decade it appeared that the policy as a whole was justified by its fruits. The world seemed to make a rapid recovery from the effects of the war. The volume of world production of foodstuffs and raw materials was 16 per cent. greater in 1925 than in 1913 although the world population was only 5½ per cent. larger; international trade expanded; and national currencies were stabilized. In reality there were serious maladjustments in the economic structure of all countries alike. Let us look more closely at the state of affairs which prevailed in Great Britain.

After the Armistice (1918) the pressing need for commodities combined with a shortage of working capital and consumers' goods to produce a startling rise in prices. The over-hasty removal of official control gave industry a free hand; and a short-lived boom ensued which reached its peak in the early part of 1920. When the lavish expenditure of the government slackened and consumers' demands were satisfied, a recession from the abnormal prices was bound to occur and a slump in trade was the natural sequel. Great Britain took stock of her position and perceived that the economic legacies bequeathed by the war could not be liquidated so easily as she expected. To begin with, the war of 1914–18 imposed a mortgage on her resources in the shape of a debt of unparalleled magnitude which had grown from about £700 millions to nearly £8000 millions. Moreover industries such as coal-mining, iron and steel and ship-building, had been inflated in response to the imperative claims of the war, and they created the intractable problem of the 'depressed' areas which did not cease to be depressed when they were euphemistically designated as 'special' areas. Inflation of war industries was an old phenomenon, but no attempt was made to learn from past experience and to prepare for its recurrence. At the same time the inevitable changes in our oversea markets had profound repercussions on the export trade. For various reasons agricultural countries had begun to develop their own industries—the war interrupted the normal channels of supply, mechanical methods of farming required fewer people on the land, a strategic economy necessitated the building up of heavy industries which could provide armaments. In addition the improved standard of living among the masses born of the experiences of the war made them unwilling to return to low rates of wages, and the urgent need of meeting this new fact by increased efficiency in production and in methods of marketing was insufficiently recognized.

Public attention came to be focussed primarily upon the most distressing symptom of the economic malaise—unemployment. The first thing to be said about the problem of unemployment is that it is not a new problem: as I have shown in the previous chapters, it has existed for hundreds of years. Even in the seventeenth century it is probable that at least 5 per cent. of the working population was unemployed, and in a trade depression this percentage was greatly increased. And the second thing is that a certain amount of unemployment—due to variations in consumers' demand, seasonal fluctuations, improvements in industrial technique and other factors—is unavoidable [1]. Why then is our generation so deeply impressed by the gravity of the problem? One reason is that exact figures are now available owing to the system of insurance, and they have proved very disturbing. Another reason is that the war of 1914–18 expanded the volume of unemployment since it effected changes in the economic structure on account of the shrinkage of oversea markets. The third reason is that unemployment is not evenly spread over the whole country but is largely concentrated in the 'depressed'

[1] The surprising fact is revealed in the report (1943) of the Insurance Statutory Committee that after three years of war nearly £3 millions were spent on benefit—thus showing that "even in a community working as the British community has worked in 1943 at full stretch, there are intervals of not working due to changes of programme and methods and other inevitable causes". It added that the expenditure probably gave "an inadequate idea of such intervals which under war conditions are not always fully reflected in a payment of unemployment benefit".

or ' special ' areas, so that it assumes a more sombre aspect than when it is expressed as a percentage of the total number of insured. The fourth reason is that the community has grown more sensitive to the economic wastage and social misery caused by unemployment—the loss in production, the deterioration in skill, the decay of apprenticeship, the privations of poverty, and the lowering of morale. The fifth reason is that the workers are more articulate and the organs of public opinion pay more attention to the problem.

Most of us find statistics forbidding, and we are apt to avoid books equipped with a formidable array of tables and graphs. Yet their utility is incontestable because they provide the framework within which our generalizations must be fitted. Admittedly great care must be exercised in the interpretation of statistics, for they can be misleading ; and there is truth in the witticism that figures cannot lie but liars can figure. Here is a broad picture of the main essentials. In the middle of 1920, while the post-war boom was at its height, the number of unemployed was as low as 110,000 ; at the end of the year it rose to 690,000 (or 5·8 per cent. of the insured workers who numbered about twelve millions) ; at the end of 1921, when the slump was at its worst, it was nearly two millions (or 16·2 per cent. of the insured workers). Then the number of unemployed fell, and down to the thirties it averaged 11 per cent.—in other words, roughly one and a quarter million people (one in nine) were unemployed prior to the great depression of 1929–33. This does not mean that the same persons were in continuous unemployment the whole time. The personnel of the unemployed kept changing. There was a ' hard core ' of unemployment comprising those out of work for long periods, especially in the coal-mining industry, but the greater part was unemployed for short periods. How far was the war responsible for the position ? To answer this question we must look at the statistics of unemployment before the war. Unfortunately we have no precise figures until the Unemployment Insurance Act of 1920. The trade-union returns of unemployment are not strictly comparable, since they cover only the organized workers among whom the rate of unemployment was probably below the rate in general. During the decade preceding the first world war these returns show an average of 5 per cent. Allowing for their incompleteness and a different basis of calculation, the broad conclusion emerges that one of the economic consequences of the war of 1914–1918 was to double the normal percentage of unemployment in Great Britain.

Another illuminating fact is that nearly one-half of the unemployed was concentrated in the 'special' areas—South-West Scotland, the North-East coast, Lancashire and South Wales—which contained only about a quarter of the total population. In these areas were situated the staple export industries of coal, cotton and ship-building. The problem of unemployment was thus in a large measure a problem of the export or 'unsheltered' industries; and their plight is shown further in the fact that though the insured workers increased by two millions between 1920 and 1939, the numbers engaged in the export industries diminished. The benefit of the increase went to the 'sheltered' industries which catered for the home market. Coal, cotton, ship-building, iron and steel not only registered a marked decline in the numbers of their insured workers, but their percentage of unemployment was higher than the average for all industries—in ship-building it sometimes exceeded one-third, in iron and steel one-quarter.

This startling contrast between the 'sheltered' and 'unsheltered' industries posed in a dramatic fashion the question whether Great Britain should discard a system of economy exposed to the vicissitudes of international trade and which combined prosperity with instability; and whether she should return to the principles of an older economy based on national self-sufficiency. The question still lies at the root of all discussions on post-war reconstruction, in which the reconciliation of stability at home with commercial intercourse abroad still remains an unsolved enigma. It is important therefore to ascertain why our export industries failed to share in the general recovery of the world after the war of 1914–18.

There are many different opinions as to the correct answer. The prevalent view is that the depressed industries were unable to adapt themselves to the elastic conditions of a peace economy owing to the rigidity of their wage rates. It is held that the trade unions were in a stronger position after the war to keep up wages owing to state insurance, which relieved their funds of the burden of maintaining the unemployed. It is true that wages soared during the boom of 1920 (when the cost-of-living index was eventually 176 per cent. higher than in 1914). Labourers earned between three and four times as much as they did in 1914; the average rise for all grades of workers was 170-180 per cent.; and the length of the working week was reduced to 44-48 hours (as compared with 48-60 hours before the war). Then in 1921 wage rates slumped rapidly and at the end of the next year they were stabilized at about 70-75 per cent. above the pre-war level. The actual increases varied from industry to industry. Thus labourers in the building industry received double; railway porters and dock labourers more than double; cotton workers, coal miners and skilled engineers about half as much again. The cost-of-living index was 74 per cent. higher in 1923 than in 1914: this implies that wages in general had barely kept pace with the cost of living, but in the next half-dozen years the index fell ten points while nominal (that is, money) wages remained stable. Hence in these years 'real' wages rose, and those in receipt of wages and salaries enjoyed a larger share of the national income for fewer hours of labour (about 63 per cent. as compared with about 55 per cent. in 1911)[1]. The earnings of employees were augmented by the value

[1] The net national income in 1938 is estimated at £4595 millions. (Rent of land and buildings=£373 m. Profits and interest=£1351 m. Salaries=£1081 m. Wages=£1790 m.) Personal expenditure on consumption=£3467 m. Expenditure by public authorities (excluding the post office, etc.)=£807 m. Private net investment (additions to capital assets) =£321 m.

of the social services—unemployment and health insurance, old-age pensions, education, working-class housing. Rigidity of the wage structure was alleged as the reason why Great Britain could no longer compete successfully in world markets; and the refusal of the organized workers to accept a reduction of wages was considered the primary cause of unemployment [1]. Like other confident explanations of complex economic phenomena, this analysis of the situation overlooked many pertinent factors.

The costs of production are not determined by a single factor alone, the price of labour, for the efficiency of management and the efficiency of machinery are also important factors. Moreover in practice it is difficult to determine the labour cost of an article, since it is the sum of a series of wage costs at different stages of production. Nor do money wages furnish the measure of real labour cost, which depends upon the skill of the worker, the ability of the employer and the use of mechanical methods. The experience of the United States to-day—like that of a great English contractor, Thomas Brassey, over seventy years ago—shows that high wages are compatible with low prices. The establishment of trade boards in the sweated industries was followed by much-needed changes in organization: formerly employers had been wasteful of their cheap labour. The insistence of the workers on maintaining their standard of life has compelled industry to scale down costs of production by means of rationalization, labour-saving devices, lessening the fixed charges on capital, and improving the system of marketing. It must not be overlooked, also, that any attempt to force an export trade by an elastic wage level would lead to an international competition in wage reduction. To conclude: there is no reason to suppose that the position would have been improved by the general lowering of wages, while there were social and economic arguments against this course—on the one hand, the acknowledged evils of poverty; on the other hand, the decline in efficiency, the discouragement of new entrants

[1] Actually money wages had been drastically reduced in 1921.

into industry, and the falling-off in the demand for goods leading to a slump in trade.

In any event the rigidity in the price structure after the first world war cannot be attributed entirely to an inflexible wage structure. A contributory factor was a conservative banking policy. The banks made considerable advances during the boom of 1920; and they had an inducement to discourage any deflation of prices which might impair the value of the collateral deposited with them as security for their loans, and thus affect their financial stability. Their reluctance to cut their losses fortified the depressed industries in the resistance which they displayed to the requisite measures of reconstruction. This was notably the case in the cotton manufacture which opposed reorganization of the industry and revaluation of its inflated capital assets. In so far as business undertakings rely upon bank credits rather than upon reserves depleted by heavy taxation or upon the floating of fresh capital issues, their freedom of action is necessarily circumscribed by their indebtedness; and the collaboration of banks with industry may give rise to a situation (as in the twenties) in which banking policy neutralizes the efforts made by the central authorities to bring down prices with a view to support the monetary exchanges. The tendency to maintain a stable price level is strengthened by the heavy overhead charges of large-scale enterprises as well as by trade agreements.

Another factor often held responsible for unemployment in the first decade after the war of 1914–18 was the currency policy. If the prices of our exports were too high for other countries, either owing to labour costs or other causes, then (it was represented) we ought to have depreciated the exchange value of the pound, so that our foreign customers buying the pound at a cheaper rate could afford to pay high prices in terms of sterling for our commodities. Instead we restored the gold standard in 1925 at the pre-war parity, that is, we exchanged the pound for exactly the same number of dollars as before 1914. The pound was over-valued—in other words, its external value was higher than was warranted by its internal value as expressed in purchasing power : *hinc illae lacrimae!* It must be conceded that the position of some industries did deteriorate after the return to the gold standard—coal and cotton, but not ship-building nor general engineering nor iron and steel [1]. The difficulties of the coal and cotton industries were aggravated by special factors ; the former suffered from the effects of the strike of 1926, while the latter was exposed to Indian import duties and Japanese competition : a lower gold parity would not have saved the situation. It is true that the total value of our exports, as measured in sterling, declined after 1925 but this was due to the fall in prices. The important point to observe is that the total volume of our exports expanded [2]—in 1929 it was over 8 per cent. greater than in 1924. The improvement was not maintained in the thirties (in spite of the devaluation of the pound in 1931) on account of the great depression and its aftermath.

I mentioned above that one consequence of the first world war was to double the amount of normal unemploy-

[1] The average percentage of unemployment in all the insured industries declined after the return to the gold standard (down to 1930)—except in the year of the coal strike (1926).

[2] In comparing the values of British exports and imports it is necessary to avoid certain pitfalls. Imports do not show the actual amount payable abroad on merchandise account, because they include a large sum for freights due to British shipowners. Again exports do not show the full extent of our claims upon other countries because they do not include freights. Thus the one is correspondingly less, the other correspondingly higher. Again in making comparisons between different years, it must be remembered that variations may be due to changes in prices rather than in volume. It is generally believed that our return to the gold standard in 1925 handicapped British exporters owing to the high parity of exchange. It is true that the declared value of British exports (manufactures and raw materials) declined 9 per cent. in terms of sterling between 1924 and 1929, but this was due to falling prices. The value of British exports on the basis of 1924 prices was over 8 per cent. higher in 1929 than in 1924. On the same basis even the value of exported British manufactures alone was higher in 1929 than in 1924. British exports did not recover to their pre-war (1913) level, yet in the twenties they were steadily rising—in 1920 they were 30 per cent. but in 1929 only 13 per cent. below 1913—and the return to the gold standard in 1925 did not check the rise. (The comparison which has been made with Scandinavia, the Netherlands and Switzerland—all of whom re-established the pre-war value of their currency—overlooks the fact that none of these countries is highly industrialized.) In the thirties the position of the export industries deteriorated for reasons not connected with the currency.

ment in this country. The average number of unemployed was increased by more than half a million—possibly by three-quarters of a million. Why did the disparity between pre-war and post-war unemployment persist ten years after the war was ended ? I think the answer is partly to be found in another consequence of the war—the decline in emigration. In 1913 the excess of British emigrants over immigrants was roughly 300,000 : in the period 1919–30 it averaged about one-third of the figure. On this basis of comparison the net decrease of emigration during the twenties amounted to two millions, of whom male adults were approximately one-third. It is reasonable to conclude that, if the pre-war rate of emigration had been maintained, the disparity between pre-war and post-war unemployment would have diminished year by year, and perhaps it might have been largely eliminated by 1930. Either the unemployed in the depressed areas would have been numbered among the emigrants, or they would have been recruited by prosperous industries which needed a growing labour force. After 1930 there were even more British immigrants returning to the homeland than there were emigrants leaving these shores.

The checks on migration in the inter-war period (1919–1939) were partly voluntary and partly involuntary. The voluntary check was the social services which mitigated the worst effects of destitution, and so tended to immobilize labour and weaken the incentive to face the hazards of a new life abroad. It is difficult to assess the extent to which this check operated, since the arrest of emigration was not confined to Great Britain but was general throughout Europe. The involuntary check lay in the legislative restraints imposed on immigration by other countries, especially the United States. It was part of a universal restrictive system which after the first world war hindered the free movement of persons, commodities and capital. When the volume of unemployment is used as an argument to prove that the pre-war economic mechanism has ' broken down ', it is necessary to bear in mind that there formerly existed an outlet for the surplus elements in the labour market, and that we exported men as well as goods and services. Efforts were made under the Empire Settlement Act of 1922 to stimulate emigration but they were unsuccessful. One reason may have been the requirements laid down by the countries of immigration ; another reason was doubtless the fact that settlement on the land had lost much of its appeal.

We have seen that the problem of unemployment was largely a problem of the declining industries, and the latter in turn hinged on the export trade. On this something more must now be said.

When the inter-war period (1919–39), viewed as a whole[1], is compared with the opening years of the present century one outstanding feature of the national economy emerges—namely, the contraction in the export trade, with its sharp repercussions upon the prosperity of a vital group of export industries and upon the volume of unemployment. The full significance of the contraction can best be appreciated when it is set against the general position in international trade—by which is meant the total of exports and imports of all countries. To compare the value of trade at any two periods, allowance must be made for changes in prices. Adopting this standard of measurement, we find that international trade rapidly recovered from the effects of the first world war. Already in 1924 it approximated to its level in 1913, and on the eve of the great depression it was one-third higher. During the great depression (1929–33) it decreased 25 per cent. (in terms of gold the fall was 65 per cent.), yet by 1937 it had nearly reached its level in 1929. While international trade expanded, our share of it declined. Before the first world war the United Kingdom (including Ireland) accounted for one-sixth of the world's imports and one-seventh of the world's exports ; but in the two succeeding decades the percentage of imports was frequently below

[1] As already noticed, the export trade improved in the course of the twenties, though it did not reach the 1913 level.

its former level, while that of exports was always considerably below it. The depreciation of sterling (1931) and the imposition of tariffs (1932) were expected to curtail our imports and stimulate our exports. Actually we had a larger share of the world's imports in 1938 than in 1929 and a smaller share of its exports!

The statistics of the four staple industries—coal, cotton, ship-building, iron and steel—bear eloquent testimony to their depressed condition in the years 1919–39. In the coal industry the number of workers diminished by one-third (namely, four hundred thousand), and the export of coal was reduced to about three-fifths. It has been surmised that the oversea demand for British coal was affected by substitute products, electricity and oil. In reality the loss of our former markets was due to the development of coal-mining abroad (the result of a world shortage of coal during the war) and to foreign competition in neutral markets. A similar explanation covers the decay of the cotton industry, which prior to the war of 1914–18 was *par excellence* an export industry since the home market absorbed only one-seventh of its production of cloth. Here also the number of workers diminished by one-third (namely, two hundred thousand), and the export of cotton piece goods was reduced to about one-quarter. The growth of the Indian cotton industry under the protection of a tariff (3½ per cent. *ad valorem* 1914 and 25 per cent. 1933) deprived Lancashire of its largest oversea market, and the severity of Japan's competition may be gauged from the fact that eventually her exports exceeded our own by nearly 50 per cent. The consequent redundancy of spindles and looms raised an acute problem of surplus productive capacity. The protracted delay in securing agreement to schemes of reorganization was largely the sequel of financial inflation during the boom of 1920, which left a legacy of over-capitalization (in many concerns the nominal value of the share capital was trebled) and heavy debt charges.

The difficulties of the ship-building industry were created by the transition from a war to a peace economy.

Its yards had been greatly enlarged to meet war-time needs ; and also other countries, especially the United States, built ships. After the war the rise in freights led to an increase of one-third in total world tonnage : the subsequent fall in freights lessened the demand for new merchant vessels. Both the number of workers in the ship-building industry, and the tonnage of merchant vessels built in its yards, diminished ultimately by almost one-half. As a result the United Kingdom owned only 25 per cent. of world shipping instead of 40 per cent. as formerly ; it built for foreign owners only 4 per cent. of its total output instead of 20 per cent. ; it launched only one-third of the world merchant marine instead of three-fifths. In addition disarmament meant fewer warships, and these had been responsible for a considerable proportion of our pre-war tonnage. Thus the output capacity of the ship-building industry was in excess of peace-time requirements. The situation was worsened in the thirties by economic nationalism to which even this country succumbed, for it contracted the carrying trade. A report on Tramp Shipping in 1933 declared that in consequence " British tramp shipping has been brought to the edge of bankruptcy ". The iron and steel industry, whose production was greatly extended during the war of 1914–18, was confronted with a similar problem of redundant capacity. Other countries too expanded their capacity and our exports were adversely affected. In the group of export industries here surveyed not only was the total number of insured workers reduced, but unemployment among those who were retained was much above the normal percentage.

I have said that the plight of the staple export industries is one of the crucial facts of our recent economic development. We exported 30·5 per cent. of our national production in 1907, 27 per cent. in 1924, and 22 per cent. in 1930 : after the great depression the decline continued [1]. The

[1] To avoid misconception, it must be noticed that the total volume of national production had considerably increased by 1938. Thus while the percentage of exports declined, it was the percentage of a larger total.

principal cause was the growth of industry (stimulated by protective tariffs) in other countries, which lessened their dependence upon British staple commodities. The question naturally arises why British exporters did not strike out in fresh directions on a scale sufficient to compensate them for the loss of their markets in the older industries. The volume of world trade was about 25 per cent. greater in 1937 than in 1913, but during this quarter of a century our exports so far from growing had shrunk. No doubt the answer is partly that British exporters failed to adapt themselves to the altered conditions of world economy, and did not respond to alterations in demand by developing new industries and reorganizing the old ones. In some measure they moved with the times. The composition of our exports began to undergo a change : expensive consumers' goods were becoming prominent, for instance, motor vehicles, etc. A more important reason than the lack of enterprise is that British capital and energy were flowing into an expanding home market. The diversion was the outcome of a redistribution of the national income which raised the standard of living of the great mass of the people. The fall in the prices of primary products in the thirties, if it constricted the ability of the agricultural countries to buy British exports, meant cheaper food for British consumers who therefore had more money to expend on other things. Their increased purchasing power stimulated the demand for better staple commodities (houses, clothing, etc.), for the services which accompany a higher standard of living (hotels, entertainments, etc.) and for the products of the nascent industries—in particular rayon and automobiles (in 1913 there were 300,000 motor vehicles in use and in 1937 ten times as many). The general effect of this concentration upon the home market was that the export market tended to be somewhat neglected. The industrial trend due to these structural changes is reflected in the expansion of employment which catered for domestic consumption. In the years 1919–39 the distributive trades absorbed a million more insured workers ; services of all kinds (national and local government, professional, hotels, laundry, entertainments, sports) three-quarters of a million more ; the building industry a third of a million more ; motor vehicles, cycles and aircraft a quarter of a million more ; the electrical industry a quarter of a million more ; food, drink, tobacco and transport a fifth of a million more.

§ 2. *The Great Depression 1929–33*

The most dramatic episode which occurred between the two world wars was the great depression, whose unprecedented severity cast a baneful shadow upon both hemispheres from the autumn of 1929 until 1933. When the storm had passed over the earth uprooting financial institutions in its devastating course like so many trees, a completely different landscape was revealed. The leading gold currencies had been wrecked, international trade had shrunk to one-third of its value (in terms of gold), the bulwark of free trade had collapsed, and the vast structure of reparations and war debts lay buried in the ruins. The momentous consequences which attended the great depression affected every country on the face of the globe. It induced the United States, where the dying system of *laissez-faire* had found its last asylum, to throw her cherished economic dogmas to the winds and subject economic enterprise to an unwonted degree of official direction. It induced the victorious powers to renounce their claims upon the vanquished for reparations. It induced the German people to substitute an authoritarian government for the democratic regime established by the Weimar constitution, and so paved the way for a second world war. And, finally, it gave an immense impetus to the movement for economic nationalism with its concept of self-sufficiency, which replaced a world economy with its concept of international specialization. I am concerned here with the effects produced on Great Britain who was induced to dissociate her national currency from gold—her example in this being followed by the whole world—and to reverse her traditional fiscal policy by abandoning free trade. But first of all it is necessary to inquire into the causes of the ' economic blizzard '.

It is essential to understand the reasons for the great depression if we are to profit by experience, yet the difficulty arises that no single explanation will cover the whole field. To ascribe it exclusively or even primarily to the cumulative results of the war (especially reparations and war debts), or to the decline in international lending, is to overlook the fact that it began in the United States and was more protracted there than elsewhere. Speaking broadly, the great depression takes its place in the normal sequence of booms and slumps which follow each other in our productive processes with unfailing regularity. I have already pointed out that the phenomenon of the trade cycle is at least three hundred years old, for in 1620–24 England suffered from a commercial crisis that contracted her markets abroad, generated widespread unemployment at home, and led to the appointment of a royal commission—which in its analysis of the alleged causes anticipated to a remarkable degree most of the explanations (including that of an overvalued currency) adduced for the crisis of 1929–33. The enigma of the trade cycle has been the subject of much speculation ; and in the final chapter I shall allude to the various theories of its origin since they have an obvious bearing on the vexed problem of the appropriate remedies. In a general way it may be said that the volume of economic activity is not uniform and steady but expands and contracts in a sort of rhythm. This alternation, which has always characterized progressive communities, appears to follow a natural law in which an outburst of violent energy is succeeded by lassitude and recuperation. The development of civilization, however, consists in creating influences which counteract the harshness of ' nature in the raw ' ; and it is the awakening of the social conscience to the magnitude of the social evils, produced by the trade cycle, which at the present day dominates all economic discussions.

Although the great depression in its broad aspect was not a new phenomenon, its severity was aggravated by the malaise which was the legacy of the war of 1914–18. The latter left behind it a heavy mortgage upon the resources of all the belligerents. For the unparalleled destruction of wealth there was nothing to show in the material sphere beyond national debts of astronomical size. Moreover the normal economic equilibrium had been disturbed by the substitution of a war economy for a peace economy. Industries were inflated to meet the insatiable demands of the war, and when these demands ceased the process of adjustment to altered conditions proved slow and painful. In addition, the lavish expenditure both of governments and of individuals during and immediately after the war, which involved violent changes in the level of prices ; the emotional reaction which unsettled the minds of the post-war generation ; the fluctuating currencies which caused bank balances to melt away overnight ; the high rate of taxation which discouraged saving ; the swift vicissitudes of international trade which might suddenly sweep away the accumulated profits of industry ; the unsound methods of finance which were responsible for the over-capitalization of industry and agriculture, for misdirected investments abroad, and for the reliance upon fugitive short-term credits (' nervous ' money) that flitted from country to country ; the orgy of public speculation on the stock exchange markets—all these phenomena combined to produce a psychological situation in the twenties in which wasteful extravagance was rampant. While the symptoms of economic disequilibrium varied in different states, they all alike suffered from grave weaknesses in their economic structure which were ruthlessly brought to light by the great depression.

The signal for the crisis came from the United States, whose fortune it was to provide an example of unprecedented prosperity followed by an unprecedented set-back. For some years after the war of 1914–18 it was believed that she had conquered poverty, and that economic ' laws ' were suspended in her favour. Europe sent its emissaries to discover the secrets of her success—and then in the autumn of 1929 the bubble burst. The causes of the collapse are obscure. There was no inflation of commodity prices and only a moderate increase of industrial production. There is no evidence of a 'glut' of capital goods (that is, over-investment), though there was doubtless misdirection of investment in certain spheres. The arresting feature of the situation was that the industrial boom became linked with a stock exchange boom due to a wave of speculative fever. In September 1929 the index price of securities showed a rise of 125 per cent. above 1926, and the inflation stimulated industrial activity because it led consumers to spend more freely and producers to undertake capital works (new factories, etc.). The crash in stock exchange values came in October. Its effects were overwhelming. A normal recession from the peak of industrial production had already begun a few months earlier, but it was made abnormal by the shock to business confidence ; and the losses of investors severely curtailed their purchasing power and intensified the depression. The banks, which numbered about 24,000 in 1929, became involved. They had financed the speculation in industrial securities and real estate, and when the boom ended they restricted credit and so increased the deflationary pressure on prices. Another consequence was a contraction in international lending, which declined owing to the diversion of resources into the American financial market. The borrowing countries which had grown dependent upon American and British loans found themselves in an embarrassed condition when their supplies were cut off. This reinforced the trend towards a downward movement in world prices, which made the depression world-wide. The course of events served to illustrate the economic interdependence of the nations. The collapse of trade soon extended from America to Europe and early in the next year its repercussions covered the face of the globe. Nevertheless the stock exchange crisis in America, although it precipitated the great depression, was not the deep-rooted cause.

The long-term factor was in the nature of an agricultural revolution. Mechanization came later to agriculture than to industry: it was in a large measure the outcome of the war which intensified the use of mechanical methods of production and transport. The number of combine-harvesters manufactured in the United States was 270 in 1914; it was nearly 37,000 in 1929. Designed to harvest and thresh, and worked by two men, the combine-harvester accounts for fifty acres of wheat a day. The number of tractors manufactured in the United States was 30,000 in 1916; as many as 853,000 were in use in 1928. One man with a fifty horse-power tractor can plough twenty acres a day: the average for single-furrow ploughing in England with a pair of horses is under one acre a day. The instalment of these machines meant lower costs of production, while output was increased by the application of scientific research to the soil, to livestock and to the treatment of pests and diseases. In addition the curtailment of wheat-growing in Europe during the war of 1914–18, when men and horses were employed for other purposes, was responsible for a notable expansion of the arable areas overseas. Canada added (by 1931) sixteen million acres to her pre-war wheat area of ten millions, the United States eleven millions, and Argentina five millions. Moreover high prices induced the farmers to purchase costly machines and extend the scale of their operations with borrowed capital. Notwithstanding, the increase in the wheat crop was not as rapid as we might have expected: in 1928 it was 16 per cent. above the pre-war average, but the world population was 10 per cent. higher, and Russia's share in the export trade had dwindled. However the stocks of wheat and other staple commodities—for there was also a great increase of productive capacity in many primary industries—accumulated over a period of years. Between 1925 and 1930 the stocks of wheat, coffee, sugar and rubber were either doubled or trebled. Thus supplies were considerably in excess of normal demand, and the presence of large surpluses was bound to exert a marked influence on prices.

The farmers everywhere showed reluctance to accept a reduction of prices because they were burdened with heavy liabilities in the shape of fixed charges incurred during the years of prosperity. The agricultural countries also sought to stave off the evil day since they were debtor countries, and a fall in prices would augment the real weight of their monetary obligations. In carrying over surpluses from previous crops they aggravated the problem, for the existence of large world stocks must sooner or later have caused prices to crash. So long as the creditor countries continued to make loans abroad, a perplexing and even menacing situation was masked by a deceptive appearance of prosperity; but owing to a stock exchange boom in the United States (which provided an outlet for funds hitherto lent abroad), followed by a collapse of the boom (which caused a further shrinkage of oversea loans), international lending began to dry up. In 1929 the import of capital by debtor countries dwindled to one-half and in 1931 to one-third: Australasia and Latin America received practically nothing in 1931. Accordingly the debtor countries, which had hitherto based their finances on precarious foreign credits, could no longer meet their debt obligations by fresh borrowing, and were constrained to throw their stocks of foodstuffs and raw materials upon the world's markets. The artificial stimulation of exports and consequent selling pressure produced a catastrophic slump in prices which heralded the coming storm. In 1920 the farmers in the United States were demanding three dollars a bushel; in 1929 they received barely 1¼ dollars; in 1932 half a dollar.

According to the ideas of nineteenth-century economists the appropriate remedies for over-production and falling prices were two—the agricultural countries should restrict their output, while the industrial countries should throw open their doors to the flood of cheap imports; in this way the former would be enabled both to discharge their obligations and to dispose of their surpluses. The situation would then speedily right itself, since prices would rise and economic equilibrium would be restored. The dynamic of events showed that the behaviour of states is not always governed by economic reasoning. The agricultural countries met the break in world prices not by restricting output but by increasing it, in order to make good the deficiency in their income. An even more important factor came into play. The industrial countries refused to allow their own agricultural system to be submerged by a torrent of imports, partly for reasons of national security and partly to safeguard the interests of their peasant population, whose stability and even survival were menaced by the competition of machine farming. France, Germany and Italy took steps to stem the flood: as compared with 1913 the German tariff on wheat was more than fourfold and the French and Italian more than double. Besides these tariff barriers domestic production was not merely stabilized but was actually intensified—the German and Italian wheat crops were one-third more in 1932 than in 1930. Nothing revealed more clearly the break-down of international economic co-operation than this astonishing expansion of the wheat acreage of the industrial countries at a time when surplus stocks were piling up in the agricultural countries. Ultimately the non-European states decreased their production of wheat by one-quarter, while the European states increased their production by one-third. To heighten the bizarre contrast, the price of wheat in France, Germany and Italy was no less than three times the world price.

The Gilbertian situation, aggravated by the policy of the importing countries which under the influence of economic nationalism limited instead of enlarging the volume of international trade, now rapidly deteriorated. Any disturbance of the world's economic system has the same result as flinging a stone into a pool—the ripples spread until they cover the surface. The industrial nations could not escape the effects of a collapse in world prices of foodstuffs and raw materials, to which the protection of their domestic agriculture contributed. The fall in the prices of manufactured goods lagged considerably behind the fall in farm prices, among other reasons because raw materials often constitute the smallest element in the total cost of commodities. In consequence the agricultural nations, engaged in raising primary products, grew too impoverished to buy the finished products of the industrial nations—so that the latter in their turn began to suffer from over-production and unemployment. In the United States, which is both agricultural and industrial, the sharp decline in the farmer's income restricted his spending power and was largely responsible for the severity of the slump in industry. Throughout the world the intensification of the depression became unavoidable when industry was drawn with agriculture into the maelstrom, when the wheels of international commerce were clogged, and when a financial crisis following upon the contraction of foreign loans was superimposed on the agrarian and industrial crises.

On a general review of the causes of the great depression it will be seen that a variety of factors combined to bring about a drastic fall in prices, a shrinkage of world trade and widespread unemployment: their interaction makes it difficult to disentangle the confused mass of economic phenomena or to isolate the effects produced by any one factor alone. In industry there was a cyclical fluctuation: in agriculture there was a structural change due to mechanization: in finance there was a virtual cessation of international investment. Each crisis, industrial, agrarian and financial, can be traced to a separate source, and each might have happened independently of the other two; but the fact that they occurred in rapid succession was not fortuitous. The fall in the prices of foodstuffs and raw materials curtailed the demand of the agricultural communities for industrial products; while financial instability—born of unsound credits, and reflected in the avoidance of long-term lending and the rapid transferences of liquid funds—reinforced the economic malaise. Another example will illustrate the interdependence of the various elements which either originated or aggravated the great depression. The deflation of prices increased the real burden of debt, thereby decreasing the ability of the debtor states to purchase imports, which in turn discouraged enterprise in the creditor states.

Apart from the main causes there were all kinds of contributory influences in operation. (1) Rationalization designed to eliminate duplication of plant and other forms of economic wastage by the creation of 'rational' units of production, together with technology designed to replace men by machines, diminished the demand for labour at any rate temporarily. (2) It is often alleged that the rigidity of the domestic price structure in the years preceding the great depression impaired the flexibility of the economic mechanism, and so delayed the adjustments needed to bring the national economy into harmony with the downward trend of world prices. The result was that the gold standard—which (as will be seen presently) is based on the assumption that the national price system will keep in step with international price movements—became unworkable; and the confusion which ensued from its break-down had the most demoralizing impact on the structure of world prices. (3) The political situation, exacerbated by acrimonious controversy over reparations and war debts and disarmament, deepened the prevailing sense of insecurity and undermined business confidence on which enterprise in industry and trade depends. (4) Unwise international lending, which encouraged debtor countries to live beyond their income and burdened them with a load of liabilities, figured prominently in the train of events leading up to the great depression. Obligations abroad are discharged through the medium of commodities, services or gold. It was the anomaly of the inter-war years (1919–39) that creditor countries were reluctant to allow a debtor to pay its debts in the most practical way, namely, by the export of its products: they were unwilling to accept commodities on a scale which would have menaced the stability of their industries. (5) The war of 1914–18 and its manifold consequences mentioned above supplied the general background to all the factors which I have recounted.

I have surveyed the causes of the great depression: its effects, writ large over the whole decade preceding the second world war, are more unmistakable. The economic and financial chaos, for which it was responsible, may be gauged from the fact that between 1929 and 1933 the world prices of a score of staple commodities—including wheat, sugar, coffee, tea, butter, wool, cotton, silk and rubber—were halved; while the gold value of world trade shrank to one-third. The catastrophic sequel to these sweeping reductions is reflected in the statistics of unemployment. The International Labour Office's index of unemployment for the sixteen principal industrial nations showed that unemployment in 1932 was three times its volume in 1929. A more permanent consequence of the fall in prices, as I shall show later, was the stimulus given to economic nationalism by the frantic efforts of each country to protect itself from a flood of cheap imports and insulate its own domestic price level when world prices slumped to one-half.

To devise appropriate remedies a World Monetary and Economic Conference met in London, in June 1933, attended by sixty-four states. Unhappily the dilatoriness which invariably clogs international action had postponed its summons, until the swift Mercury of events had outpaced the leaden-footed and cumbrous mechanism of a world conference. If it had been held while the storm was still at its height, the governments might have consented to make the sacrifices which were needed to ensure a radical improvement—to scale down the tariff barriers and remove the other hindrances in the path of international trade. However, by the middle of 1933, the fury of the storm had abated and the natural forces of economic recovery were re-asserting themselves—the glut of commodities had been absorbed; trade was reviving; unemployment was on the decline; and economic nationalism, which had caught a glimpse of the abyss yawning beneath its feet, had regained its self-confidence. No sooner did the conference meet than a sharp and fatal cleavage of opinion manifested itself. On the one hand, the European countries were insistent that monetary stabilization should take precedence of all other problems, for it was difficult to carry out tariff abatements until an end was put to abnormal currency fluctuations. On the other hand, the United States was pursuing a reconstruction programme (the 'New Deal') intended to raise the level of domestic prices by depreciating the value of the dollar. In the absence of agreement on the fundamental question of currency stabilization, the conference was unable to arrest the trend towards economic nationalism and bring back the peoples of the earth to economic sanity. It had failed completely in its main objectives, and the only thing which it accomplished was its own adjournment. In the economic as in the political sphere it was found to be impossible to achieve any substantial measure of international co-operation on the vital issues of the day.

Apart from the toll of human misery which the great depression took in the sufferings entailed by unemployment and bankruptcies, its importance lies in the fact that it unmoored the currencies of the world from their safe anchorage and widened the circle of the protectionist countries. These massive consequences followed in the wake of the new direction given to the economic statecraft of Great Britain, whose reversal of her currency and fiscal policies had a profound influence. The one ushered in a world repudiation of the gold standard, and the other shattered the chief bulwark of the free trade movement.

I propose to examine in some detail the nature of these epoch-making changes in British policy, yet perhaps their most surprising feature is that the great depression should have produced upon this country an effect which was out of proportion to the cause. True, the volume of unemployment was doubled between 1929 (when it was 1⅓ millions) and 1932, but an evanescent influence was at work—the temporary decline in the purchasing power of our customers overseas. The determining factor in the situation was really psychological. A wave of pessimism passed over the nation and induced the belief that its economic interests were no longer bound up with those of the world at large. The opinion became general that international trade and finance were a source of danger to our national well-being, and that it was necessary to insulate ourselves against forces which were beyond our own control and threatened at any moment to bring disaster. An English economist voiced a common attitude when he wrote in 1933 : " Ideas, knowledge, science, hospitality, travel—these are the things which should of their nature be international. But let goods be home-spun whenever it is reasonably and conveniently possible, and above all let finance be primarily national ". The proposal to put back the clock of history and return to a self-sufficing economy was a counsel of despair. It reflected the opportunism which neglects the basic factors and long-term trends of national evolution. From a short-sighted view of a grave emergency proceeded events of the first magnitude, for Great Britain's abrupt abandonment of the two main pillars of her economy—the integrity of the pound sterling and the open door in commerce—was due to an atmosphere of ' defeatism ' emanating from the great depression, in which the nation blinded by panic hastily and without thought of the ulterior consequences discarded its historic policy. This startling development was aided by the fact that for a decade the existence of over a million unemployed had weighed heavily upon the national spirits and created an attitude of mind favourable to far-reaching changes. The prevailing pessimism reached its climax during the great depression, and the conviction was then almost universal that England's race was run, that her industry had been stricken with a mortal disease, and that on the national scroll of her economic achievements must now be inscribed the word ' Ichabod '.

It would be a misfortune if we were to approach the

problems of the future with the same one-sidedness displayed in the inter-war period (1919–39), when our pre-occupation with certain facets of the domestic economy was allowed to obscure other and more important facets. To avoid the misconception that the presence of a million unemployed was an indication of national decline, the following considerations may supply a useful corrective. Firstly: the excess of unemployed over the pre-war figure was only about half a million and it was connected with the aftermath of the war, the slow adjustment to altered conditions and the decline in emigration. Secondly: our general position in world trade was not in the circumstances unfavourable. Thirdly: the total number of insured workers in employment was greater in 1929 than in 1913 and their standard of life was higher. The improvement may be ascribed to several factors—the unwillingness of the masses to revert to the pre-war standard after experiencing a higher standard during the war; technical progress which not only increased the output of the older industries but also made possible newer industries such as the automobile; the reduction of costs owing to rationalization and the growth of large retail stores. Fourthly: the great depression was not occasioned by maladjustments in our own economic system but by causes which affected the world at large, and the percentage of unemployment was lower in Great Britain than in Germany or the United States. In the light of the foregoing we must inquire what was our justification for embarking upon a new currency and fiscal policy—with consequences that proved so momentous and not for ourselves alone.

§ 3. *The Suspension of the Gold Standard*

I come now to a crucial and thorny issue of the inter-war period (1919–39)—the repudiation of the gold standard. The term gold standard means that a national currency is convertible into foreign currencies at fixed rates of exchange in gold. Two views may be contrasted. One holds that

" the gold standard is a barbarous relic ". The other, expressed in a resolution adopted in 1932 by the Bank for International Settlements, declares that " the gold standard remains the best available monetary mechanism and the one best suited to make possible the free flow of world trade and of international financing ". The abandonment of the gold standard in the thirties was among the decisive facts of the decade : its revival in perhaps a modified form is among the debated questions of a reconstruction programme.

Gold formerly served two main purposes—firstly, it was the basis of the pyramid of commercial bank credit ; secondly, it was a means of international payment when there was a short-term debit balance on current account. The classical account of the normal working of the gold standard explained how it operated to keep national price levels in equilibrium. If prices rose in one country above the world level imports were attracted, exports declined, and the adverse balance on international payments was met by the drain of gold. The outflow of the precious metal was the danger signal which warned the central bank to raise the bank rate (discount rate) ; 'dear money' contracted the volume of credit because a high rate of interest reduced the demand for loans ; this curtailed expenditure which in turn caused deflation of prices ; owing to the fall in prices imports were checked and exports stimulated ; by these correctives gold flowed back, the monetary exchanges moved in our favour and the international monetary equilibrium was restored. Economists were apt to be lost in admiration when they contemplated the series of automatic adjustments brought into operation by the simple device of varying the bank rate. The flow of gold, the volume and velocity of credit, the national price level, the raising and lowering of costs (including wages), the balancing of exports and imports, and the maintenance of international monetary equilibrium—all these things were regulated by a 'most delicate and beautiful' instrument. Yet one indispensable condition had to be fulfilled : a nation must play the game according to the rules of the gold standard. The condition was not easy to satisfy. An increase in the bank rate might actually serve to attract foreign funds—which would counteract the effects produced by the outflow of gold on the price structure. And in so far as it did succeed in contracting credit and forcing down prices and wages, it involved a serious dislocation of industry accompanied by bankruptcies and unemployment. A century ago it was acknowledged by a governor of the Bank of England that raising the bank rate, in order to protect the gold reserves, was 'most prejudicial' to commerce. The economic sacrifices and social distress, which might be entailed by a strict adherence to the gold standard, presented the reverse side of the medal; and they suggested that the advantages of monetary internationalism were sometimes purchased at an excessive cost.

Accordingly the question was raised whether an expansionist monetary policy intended to maintain or raise the level of prices was not more important than stable exchanges—in other words, whether it was preferable that the volume of purchasing power should be supported at home, or that the value of the national currency should remain steady abroad at fixed rates of exchange for foreign currencies. The difficulty of reconciling the national and international factors in monetary policy was recognized by the Gold Delegation in 1928, and (as will be shown in the next chapter) we are still far removed from the solution of a vexed problem. In any event, the claim that the elimination of the gold standard had the beneficial consequence of liberating the internal price level from external influences—by removing the incubus of deflationary pressure and making it possible to expand bank credit at home without fear that an advance in prices, by attracting imports, would exhaust the monetary reserves—must be carefully scrutinized.

In the first place, it overlooks the fact that the Bank of England on occasion neutralized the effects of a drain of gold by 'open-market operations' (purchases of securities in the open market) designed to increase the supply of 'cash' and so prevent a fall in prices [1]; while the Federal Reserve System in the United States neutralized the effects of an influx of gold by sales of securities designed to diminish the supply of 'cash' and so prevent a rise in prices. Thus even in countries which were on the gold standard, the 'automatic' currency had tended to become virtually a 'managed' currency; measures were taken to support the fabric of credit and prices; and variations in the gold supply were not allowed to produce their theoretical reactions upon the domestic price level. Between the two world wars national price structures undoubtedly became more inflexible than formerly, that is, wages and other costs of production were less responsive to gold movements; and their rigidity helped to prepare the way for the general repudiation of the mechanism of the gold standard. In the second place, it must be borne in mind that credit expansion is not synonymous with trade expansion. The banks can make available an abundancy of 'cheap money', but whether it will be utilized depends on the entrepreneurs; and the violent fluctuations of exchange rates are unlikely to foster the business confidence necessary for large capital commitments. They create an atmosphere of uncertainty which is detrimental alike to oversea trade, capital investments and short-term credits.

It is often maintained that the gold standard had already ceased to function on orthodox lines before it was discarded by Great Britain in 1931. The argument runs as follows. On the one hand, the debtor countries were unwilling to deflate their price level in order to increase their exports to the creditor countries. On the other hand, the creditor countries compelled the debtor countries to discharge their

[1] The volume of credit created by the banks is about nine or ten times the volume of 'cash' which they hold in the form of bank notes, currency notes, and deposits at the Bank of England. When the Bank of England purchases securities, payment is deposited by the seller in his own bank, which now has a claim (a deposit) upon the Bank of England; this enlarges the basis of the credit structure. (The floating debt of the government is important in expanding credit. If this debt is taken up in the shape of Treasury bills by the Bank of England, it serves indirectly to increase the deposits of the banks.)

liabilities in gold instead of goods, because they checked imports by means of tariffs and a relatively low level of domestic prices. Moreover the gold which the creditor countries received was in effect 'sterilized'. This means that they were reluctant to take the monetary action which the gold standard imposed upon them of expanding credit and raising internal prices, thereby stimulating imports and causing an outflow of gold. The failure to comply with the obligations of the gold standard tended to make it unworkable, since the result was a maldistribution of gold. The world's gold supply was estimated in 1931 at about £2300 millions, of which the United States had £900 millions, France £540 millions and Great Britain £118 millions. The first two, therefore, held over one-half of the total stock of gold.

The chief creditor nation was the United States, and she has been criticized for her refusal to disturb the equilibrium of her national economy by inflating her price level for the sake of correcting her trade balance. But it is erroneous to assume that the United States "drained the gold reserves of Europe" by forcing payment of war debts and trade debts to be made in gold. The gold holdings of the United States only increased (1932) by about 8 per cent.—this was stated in a Note addressed to the British government. The additional stock of gold in her vaults represented temporary deposits by foreign bankers, which she wisely refrained from making the basis of credit inflation. There are other misconceptions about the international transactions of the United States. It is a common allegation that she failed to recognize her changed position as a creditor nation, which ought to have an excess of imports over exports. Actually in the years 1935–37 the United States did have an adverse balance on her international payments as a whole. Normally she had a debit balance on invisible items and a credit balance on visible items, whereas in Great Britain the position was reversed; and normally the two countries as creditor nations enjoyed a favourable balance on their current account as a whole.

Attention may also be drawn to a misconception relating to Anglo-American trade. It is true that Great Britain buys far more from the United States than she sells—in 1937 she bought 11 per cent. of her imports from the United States and sold 7 per cent. of her exports. What is frequently overlooked is the fact that a large part of the surplus accruing to the United States is returned to us in the form of invisible items—tourist expenditure, freights and other services. And when Great Britain and the crown colonies are reckoned together [1] there is a credit balance in their favour, for the United States purchases three times as much from the colonies as she sells to them.

Admittedly the difficulty of working the gold standard became more pronounced after the first world war, yet it would probably have continued to function though in the shape of a 'managed' rather than an 'automatic' mechanism. What then were the circumstances which led the world to abandon it and substitute monetary nationalism for monetary internationalism? The answer must be sought for in Great Britain, whose position in the world economy almost necessarily involved the alignment of other powers in their currency policy. Great Britain had suspended the gold standard during the war of 1914–18, but she restored it in 1925. Six years later she again suspended the gold standard owing to a situation which was not of her making.

One of the phenomena of international finance during the decades 1919–39 was the accumulation of immense liquid assets known as 'nervous' or 'hot' money. These floating balances, which at the beginning of 1931 were estimated at £2000 millions distributed between the different money centres, were moved from country to country

[1] They are reckoned together in the British government's *Report on Mutual Aid* (1943). The latter stated that the British government extended "reciprocal aid to raw materials and foodstuffs purchased by the government of the United States from the United Kingdom and the Colonial Empire", but not "of course" from the Dominions.

in the form of short-term credits instead of long-term investments—accordingly as they were attracted by the high rates of interest or repelled by apprehension of political or financial insecurity. They became a menace to the normal operation of the gold standard, because they involved the abrupt transfer of large amounts of gold, whereas in former days only small amounts were moved to balance trade transactions. Official circles in Great Britain, however, felt no apprehension over the existence of an unprecedented volume of international 'ready money'. The *Board of Trade Journal* wrote in 1928: "Short-term placements of foreign money in London constitute one of the most important post-war international movements of capital. [Great Britain like the United States has become] a 'great short-term debtor nation' [as well as] a great creditor nation in long-term investments. It has been suggested that the risk of the sudden withdrawal of the large sums involved constitutes a serious danger to our financial structure. The conditions appear unlikely to arise in which such danger would be serious". This official complacency was shared by the London money market. Instead of discouraging the influx of precarious and fugitive deposits of foreign money, it utilized them to make advances to German banks. Early in 1931 it found its resources seriously strained by the locking-up of substantial funds abroad under a 'stand-still' agreement, whereby its claims upon Germany were held in abeyance—that is, its assets became 'frozen'. At the same time there was foreshadowed a deficit on the British budget, which raised fears of monetary inflation. Misgivings were enhanced by the adverse balance on Great Britain's international payments. The credit balance, which she had hitherto possessed year by year, was converted in 1931 (as we shall presently see) into a debit balance.

These various factors combined to impair confidence abroad in the soundness of the country's financial position. The timidity of investors is proverbial: by an excess of anxiety they produce the panic of which they live in perpetual dread. In a race for security foreign creditors hastened to transfer their deposits in London to other money centres. The situation was aggravated by the fact that the Bank of France and other central banks, which were also unable to recall their credits from Germany and Central Europe, repatriated funds held in England in order to preserve their liquidity. After unavailing efforts to check the flight from the pound, the British government suspended the export of gold (September 1931) in order to put an end to the drain on its depleted gold reserves. Thus it was not the deficit on our international payments that compelled the Bank of England to stop payment in gold—we had enjoyed a long succession of credit surpluses and could well afford occasional deficits. Nor was it the state of the budget, which was much worse in France and the United States—and besides the budget was balanced before the suspension occurred. The real cause was the withdrawal of foreign money from London. The involuntary repudiation of the gold standard was an event of more than national significance, for it gave a profound shock to the monetary system throughout the world. Within a year over forty states had followed Great Britain's example : the United States did so in 1933 but France, Holland and Switzerland not until 1936.

When a national currency is based on gold, its external value (that is, the rates at which it can be exchanged for foreign currencies) is determined by the quantity of metal in its units. When it ceases to be convertible into gold, its external value is supposed to be determined by its internal purchasing power. In reality the exchange rates of an inconvertible paper currency may become exposed to speculative influences as well as to deliberate manipulation by a government seeking to stimulate exports. Altogether the pound depreciated 40 per cent.—this meant that it was worth only three-fifths of its former value in gold ; but its value in terms of other currencies was much less affected since they too suffered depreciation. Sharp fluctuations in exchange rates were eventually avoided by means of an 'equalization account', devised to keep exchange rates relatively stable: it operated by buying sterling when exchange rates fell, and selling sterling when they rose. Its technique, which was adopted also by other countries, made it possible to control the exchanges without having recourse to the bank rate (as was the practice under the gold standard), and without disturbing the internal price level or the credit structure.

The rejection of the gold standard snapped the link between the national price level and the world (gold) price level. It was premised that henceforth domestic prices could remain high without any need to scale them down by a contraction of credit; inasmuch as foreigners could buy our money cheaply, they would be enabled to purchase our merchandise. Actually the effects produced by the devaluation of the pound were widely different from those which were confidently anticipated. According to the orthodox account currency depreciation not only stimulates exports but it also curtails imports and raises internal prices. Instead exports declined, imports expanded and internal prices fell! One of the things which may be learnt from history is that in economics, as in war, it is the unexpected that is liable to happen. Any disturbance of the economic system sets in motion a series of changes whose reactions are difficult to measure in advance or even predict. The depreciation of sterling depressed world (gold) prices still further; moreover many countries which supplied Great Britain with foodstuffs and raw materials joined the sterling area. In consequence cheap imports—together with the slackening of business activity which lessened the demand for credit—prevented a rise in the national price level (the cost of living fell 5 per cent. 1931–33), while various factors (the rigidity of costs of production, the increase of tariffs and 'quotas' abroad, and the reduced purchasing power of agricultural countries) militated against exports. Several conclusions emerge which advocates of monetary manipulation would do well to take to heart.

The first conclusion is that lowering the external value

of a currency does not (except perhaps temporarily) stimulate exports because it starts an international competition in the rates of exchanges : the game is one in which all can participate. The second conclusion is that other countries generally impose handicaps on imports coming from a state which appears to use currency depreciation as a trade weapon to force its commodities on foreign markets. The plethora of restrictions (tariffs and 'quotas') contract the sphere of commerce, with the result that currency devaluation—so far from inflating internal prices—may exert a deflationary pressure. The third conclusion points to the unwisdom of a policy which seeks to insulate the national economy from the effects of a global depression by measures which aggravate the depression. The repudiation of the gold standard had international repercussions of the gravest significance—in a fresh collapse of world prices and constriction of world trade, in the chaos of exchange rates, in the raising of tariffs, in the institution of 'quotas', and in the impulse given to economic nationalism. These were consequences which particularly affected a country like Great Britain, who is vitally dependent upon oversea commerce and upon the income which she draws from shipping freights, investments and other financial services abroad.

§ 4. *The Balance of International Payments*

One of the main reasons advanced in favour of the suspension of the gold standard was the adverse balance of trade. This is a matter of which much more will be heard in the future, and it is therefore appropriate to say something here.

There is a widespread misconception about Great Britain's adverse balance of trade. It is popularly supposed that a surplus of exports over imports is an indication of prosperity, and a surplus of imports over exports is a premonition of disaster. But a debtor country may have an export surplus owing to the discharge of its liabilities, and a creditor country may have an import surplus owing to the receipt of interest on its investments abroad. To avoid misunderstanding of the balance of international payments, we must bear in mind that exports are both visible (commodities) and invisible (services). The latter include the income from oversea investments, shipping freights, insurance premiums, bankers' commissions and charges, brokerages, tourist expenditure, emigrants' remittances home, authors' royalties and other items. Great Britain had an adverse balance of trade in respect of visible exports, but she had a favourable balance in respect of invisible exports which not only cancelled out the adverse balance on merchandise but gave her a net surplus. This surplus was considerable. In the three pre-war years 1907, 1910 and 1913, the credit balance amounted to £138, £153 and £181 millions respectively. After the war the amounts were as follows :—154 (1922), 153 (1923), 86 (1924), 54 (1925), 9 (1926—the year of the coal strike), 114 (1927), 137 (1928), 103 (1929). Incidentally these figures do not lend support to recent statements that, owing to the return to the gold standard at the pre-war ratio in 1925, " the British balance of payments was labouring in difficulties ". The favourable balance was due principally to the interest on investments abroad coupled with shipping freights, which enabled Great Britain to maintain a higher standard of life than would otherwise have been possible. Accordingly they must occupy a prominent place in all discussions on the future of our national economy.

The value of our oversea investments on the eve of the first world war is estimated at £4000 millions. During the war of 1914–18 over £600 millions were requisitioned and sold by the British government, and it is believed that £150 millions were lost in the belligerent countries. However, owing to the increased yields from old investments, combined with new investments, there was only a slight falling off in the total income—it was £210 millions in 1913 and £200 millions in 1920, while it averaged £240 millions between 1922 and 1929. The value of the investments on the eve of the second world war is estimated at £3750 millions. The receipts from shipping were also very large, because about three-fourths of our imports and exports were carried in British ships. They amounted to £94 millions in 1913 and averaged £130 millions between 1922 and 1929. The surplus on international revenue transactions was one of the sources of capital for new investments. Another source was the sinking funds on and maturity repayments of oversea loans ; and a third was the money derived from foreign purchases of British home securities. Altogether a considerable sum was rendered available year by year for making fresh investments abroad.

Let us now see what happened in consequence of the great depression. The credit balance of our international payments sank to £28 millions in 1930, and in 1931 it was converted into a debit balance of £104 millions. Hence Great Britain had an adverse balance not only on merchandise but on her total current account, and in five out of the next seven years she continued to have deficits although they were much smaller. These debit balances were usually offset by the proceeds which became accessible from the sinking funds on and maturity repayments of oversea loans. As a result the value of our capital assets abroad was impaired, yet this did not mean (as a chancellor of the exchequer deplored) that we were ' living upon our capital '. We might be making at the same time substantial additions to our capital assets at home, for instance, the erection of new factories and plant. On the eve of the second world war (1938), when the debit balance of our external payments was £55 millions, internal investment in capital equipment was increased by £376 millions, so that the net investment at home and abroad in this year was £321 millions. Thus an adverse balance often gives ground for needless alarm. In any case the disappearance or reduction of our former credit balance was mainly due to the decline in the yields from oversea investments and from shipping and financial services, caused by the slump in world prices and the contraction in international trade. The significant conclusion may be drawn that the income enjoyed by Great Britain from her international revenue transactions was affected less by the first world war than by the great depression, of which the protracted consequences were largely the fruits of her own errors of policy.

§ 5. *The Abandonment of Free Trade*

The suspension of the gold standard was immediately followed in Great Britain by the abandonment of free trade. As early as 1921 a Safeguarding of Industries Act afforded protection to certain 'key' industries, officially described as " articles of a pivotal character which were regarded as vital to the national safety or of outstanding importance to industry ". Thereby a breach was made in the ramparts of the fortress, however justifiable may have been the occasion, and it facilitated the subsequent capitulation to the besieging forces. The nation became accustomed to a marked modification of its traditional fiscal practices, and grew disposed to accept without demur the more drastic changes for which the ground was being prepared. Nevertheless the Conservative government which appealed to the electorate in 1923 in favour of protection suffered a reverse, showing that at heart the country still remained wedded to free trade. When protection was eventually adopted, it came in by the side door : it was a hasty improvisation born of panic. Just as free trade itself owed its final victory over the last defences of mercantilism to " the rain that rained away the corn laws ", so the nation was stampeded into protection by the collapse of the great bulwark of British credit, the pound sterling. In the face of a dire calamity, their minds filled with dark forebodings that English money might follow the way of the German mark (although the circumstances were completely different), the British people accorded to the 'national government' the blank cheque, the free hand which it demanded. After the general election in 1931 the 'national government' proceeded to fill in the blank cheque with the word 'protection'. It was explained that protective duties were necessary to reduce the volume of imports, and " redress the highly adverse trade balance which was one of the main factors in the flight from the pound in 1931 ". A doubtful proposition : but in any event the argument was invalidated by the depreciation of the currency which at the time afforded substantial protection. The Import Duties Act (1932) provided that each industry should present an application for its own requirements to a body known as the Import Duties Advisory Committee. By entrusting the responsibility into the hands of a technical commission, it was hoped to eliminate the discreditable practices prevalent in other countries of exerting political pressure upon the administration with the object of manipulating the tariff schedules.

The extent and character of the protective system may be indicated in general terms as follows. Whereas only one-seventh of our imports had formerly been taxed (for purposes of revenue) the proportion was now increased to nearly three-fifths, and those remaining on the free list were mainly Empire products. The average duty on manufactured goods approximated to one-fifth of their value. In the case of agriculture conflicting needs made themselves felt. The aim of protecting the British farmer was at variance with the desire to encourage imports from the Dominions ; and the interests of countries like Denmark, whose economy had become dependent upon the British market, could not be entirely ignored. A variety of devices was adopted. The best method of assisting an 'infant' industry, or any other industry whose maintenance is considered necessary for national reasons, is the payment of a subsidy—raised from general taxation since the burden ought to fall on the community as a whole and not on the section which consumes a particular product : this method was adopted in the sugar beet industry. More open to criticism was the Wheat Act : it imposed a levy on flour to establish a fund out of which British wheat-growers received a subsidy to make up the difference between the guaranteed price and the market price. The levy was a tax on bread of which the poor are the largest consumers; however it was preferable to an import duty, for the subsidy was only paid on the quantity produced at home which was one-fifth of the total supply. Subsequent measures extended the system of guaranteed prices to barley, oats and milk. Other foodstuffs—meat, dairy products, vegetables and fruit—were made subject to tariffs. Lastly, the quantitative restriction of imports was introduced. Some foreign commodities were assigned 'quotas' which limited the amount admitted into Great Britain: they included bacon, meat, potatoes and sea-fish. Subsidies, tariffs and 'quotas'—supplemented by the concession of immunity from local rates and by favoured treatment in the payment of income tax—failed to arrest the decline in the number of agricultural workers: cultivated land continued to shrink although the acreage under wheat and sugar beet was expanded.

The ultimate consequences of the revolutionary change in British fiscal policy may not work themselves out in one generation. Perhaps for several decades to come they will continue, as hitherto, to be masked by counteracting influences. None the less, as economic conditions throughout the world return in the fulfilment of the years to the normal, the renunciation of free trade must exert on Great Britain its cumulative and far-reaching effects. One immediate result was to alter the proportions of Empire and foreign trade. The proportion of our imports from the Empire increased by one-third (they rose from 30 per cent. to 40 per cent.); that of our exports to the Empire increased by one-seventh (they rose from 43·5 per cent. to 50 per cent.). This diversion was the outcome of the Ottawa Agreements concluded between Great Britain and the Dominions in 1932. The former undertook not to levy duties on Empire products already on the free list; to strengthen the duties on certain foreign imports; and to adopt the 'quota' system for meat. Six years later the Anglo-American Trade Agreement secured concessions for farmers in the United States, which modified the preferential position accorded to the Dominions. The real criterion which should be applied to the new commercial policy is whether it will leave unimpaired the total volume of commerce, the extent of the carrying trade, the vitality of the banking and insurance services, and the maintenance of the present standard of living. The shape of things to come lies hidden in the future. The historian can only place on record that during the first decade of protectionism our visible and invisible exports remained on a lower level, and unemployment on a higher level, than they were before the institution of tariffs. It would be wrong to isolate a single factor, however important, and to overlook other contributory factors in a complex situation ; yet at any rate protective duties and bilateral trade agreements have not succeeded in solving our economic problems.

Already it is possible to measure the reaction produced upon other states by Great Britain's renunciation of free trade. To begin with, it had a restrictive influence on their commerce and so contributed to the resurgence of economic nationalism. Moreover it had a marked psychological effect, inasmuch as it profoundly discouraged the forces throughout the world which were inspired by the British example to work for the breaking down of the barriers to international intercourse. So long as Great Britain adhered to her century-old policy, she was the outstanding argument in favour of a universal reduction or abolition of tariffs : her failure to maintain this policy in a grave emergency seemed to her former admirers almost in the light of a betrayal. Again, the reversal of British trade practices focussed attention upon the vexed problem of raw materials. While Great Britain offered an open door to imports, all countries were enabled to purchase their requirements in any part of the British Empire by the sale of their products to the motherland ; hence there was less disposition to challenge the British monopoly of a vast sector of the globe with its wealth of raw materials and foodstuffs, when the trade of other nations suffered from no handicaps. And lastly, British oversea investments amounted to several thousand million pounds, and both interest and repayment were made in goods. In a long view of the situation Great Britain's fiscal policy needs to be shaped by the broadest conception of her fundamental interests—and these concern her position in international trade, her shipping and financial services, and the obligations of her world status.

Nothing evinces more clearly the decay of the traditional maxims of commercial relationships than the trend towards bilateral trade. Here, also, Great Britain returned to an older viewpoint, the doctrine of 'the particular balance' of trade, which was held by some of the early mercantilists but was eventually discarded in favour of the doctrine of 'the general balance'. On the face of it, it is specious to say—the fallacious argument is repeated in every parliamentary debate on the subject—that we should buy only from those who buy from us. (On this principle a grocer should purchase his clothes or shoes from those who purchase his provisions !) A simple illustration will serve to show the difference between the multilateral (or triangular) and the bilateral system. Under the former country A buys from country B, which buys from country C, which buys from country A. Under the latter country A seeks to equalize its purchases and sales with country B ; as a result country C (debarred from selling to country B) cannot afford to buy from country A.

Observe now the effects of bilateralism in which commodity imports and exports are balanced for each pair of countries. In the first place, it is manifestly destructive of the multilateral system in which a state strikes the balance on the whole of its international transactions. In an expressive seventeenth-century phrase, bilateralism breaks "the links and chains by which all traffics hang together". In a multilateral trade India, who made large debt payments to Great Britain, was enabled to derive the funds required for these payments not from Great Britain (where she bought more than she sold) but from other countries (where she sold more than she bought). In a bilateral trade these other countries would have limited their demand for Indian products to the amount of India's demand for their products. This would have forced India to turn her import surplus with Great Britain into an export surplus in order to meet her obligations. Similarly, if we exclude the goods of nations which do not buy a sufficient quantity of our goods, they are no longer able to make purchases from our customers; and the latter in turn must restrict their consumption of British wares. Thus bilateralism deprives our customers of potential markets for their own exports, and so compels them to cut down their imports from us. In the second place, when a country cannot supply its former customers (owing to their being compelled to buy from Great Britain), it competes with us in neutral markets. Hence the volume of our exports will not be expanded by these expedients. Indeed it is more likely to suffer contraction, for the stream of international commerce is diverted into artificial channels. One example will serve to point the moral and adorn the tale. An agreement with the Scandinavian and Baltic states stipulated for an increase in their imports of British coal, which consequently rose from 5 to 8½ million tons (1932-36). In the same period the total exports of British coal declined from 39 to 34½ million tons because German and Polish coal, partially excluded from its usual markets, competed with us in other markets.

A third effect of bilateralism is that international financing (which is essential for the development of backward territories) is discouraged, since the balancing of exports and imports must ultimately make it impossible for debtors to have surpluses with which to discharge their debts. A fourth effect is that the international exchange of merchandise becomes based not upon economic considerations of price and quality but upon agreements made under political compulsion. Multilateral trade is the pre-requisite of international specialization, because there are fewer obstructions to the passage of specialized wares. On this account the Report of the Bank for International Settlements (1937) was justified in claiming that " the advantages of the international division of labour are not compatible with a system which forces trade into defined channels ". A fifth effect is that the national economy is rendered less stable, for the precarious framework of bilateral treaties is liable to be shattered by changes of government or changes of circumstances. Multilateral trade is more steady, inasmuch as unfavourable developments in one part of the globe may be balanced by favourable developments elsewhere. The wider the area of commerce the greater is the likelihood of repairing losses. Finally, the encroachments of bilateralism can only be viewed as a retrograde step. It sets up false criteria which measure the benefits of a world economy not by the advance in the standard of living but by 'the particular balance' of trade with each country. Thus it poisons the atmosphere of international economic co-operation.

No nation was more deeply concerned in the maintenance of multilateral trade than our own. By offering a market to the products of every land we provided them with the means to buy foodstuffs, raw materials and manufactures from our customers, our debtors and our colonies. All this was to our direct advantage, but in addition we received back a considerable share of our payments for imports in the form of shipping freights, while we drew a large income through financing the movement of commodities by short-term credits. The trend towards a bilateral trade policy was part of the short-sighted opportunism which jeopardized the enduring factors of national prosperity in order to snatch at a temporary benefit. The claim that the use of a bargaining weapon—namely, the threat to restrict imports from a state which resisted pressure to buy British goods—would enable us to increase our exports, by forcing them upon reluctant markets, is refuted by the fact that our exports failed signally to recover.

In another direction this country, which had once led the world in economic thought and (more important still) in enlightened economic practices, displayed during the inter-war period (1919–39) a remarkable avidity for absorbing the most fashionable economic nostrums. We not only showed a preference for bilateral in place of multilateral trade but we also adopted the practice of ' quotas '. We limited the importation of foreign agricultural produce into Great Britain, and of foreign cotton and rayon into most of the crown colonies. Furthermore the British government announced (in 1933) that it reserved the right to omit the ' most-favoured-nation clause ' in future commercial agreements. In virtue of the clause we had enjoyed, under free trade, the benefits of tariff reductions effected elsewhere since concessions granted by one state to another were automatically extended to British exports ; so that we were treated at least as favourably as any other nation. But the clause was reinstated in the Anglo-American Trade Agreement (1938), of which the terms were not confined to the two signatory powers. The United States opposed bilateral treaties which were discriminatory in character ; and in this respect the New World redressed the economic heresies of the Old.

§ 6. *Recovery*

Great Britain emerged eventually from the trough of depression, yet official policy can claim little of the credit. Primarily our recovery was due to the natural forces of recuperation. After all, neither booms nor slumps are permanent, and there is bound to be a swing of the pendulum. As stocks became exhausted, the demand for foodstuffs and raw materials and manufactured products revived, and the wheels of economic activity were once again set in motion. The movement was world-wide, and of all countries Great Britain was the least likely to be unaffected by world forces.

Other factors, though not negligible, were subsidiary. Expenditure for rearmament, while it came early in Germany, was delayed here until some years after the great depression ; in any event it tended to divert the national resources from civilian to military production. A more important element, which has always been a consequence of trade depressions, was the reorganization of industry—technical improvements and the elimination of incompetent producers—since the ability to survive depended upon efficiency of management and labour. Monetary expansion also played a part. In order to make money plentiful and cheap, the Bank of England bought securities and enlarged its gold reserves (which facilitated bank credit), and it lowered the rate of interest in 1932 to 2 per cent. (which diminished the cost of borrowing). Too much stress is apt to be laid upon the significance of monetary policy. It may increase the means of payment, but the advantage taken of them is a matter of business confidence, and entrepreneurs are influenced by the state of trade rather than by the price of borrowing. However the fall in money rates did combine with the cheapness of materials to occasion a substantial boom in house-building. Credit expansion should have led to an upward movement in internal prices, but the government at the same time pursued a deflationary policy by its conservative finance as shown in its handling of the currency and the budget. Yet it also reinforced the banking system of cheap credit by carrying through a conversion operation which lowered the rate of interest on the national debt from 5 to 3½ per cent., and it imposed tariffs on imported commodities partly with a view to bolster up prices at home. Thus it alternated between deflation and inflation in a makeshift policy which lived from hand to mouth. The same contradictory tendencies were evinced in the advice given to the public to economize, thereby still further contracting the volume of trade and employment and depressing prices, although consumers should be encouraged to spend more in a slump and less in a boom. The government itself set an example of official economy by cuts in wages and salaries and by the reduction of capital expenditure on public works [1], in

[1] It is estimated that capital expenditure by the central and local authorities on public works fell by one-third, whereas in Sweden it was nearly quadrupled.

the hope that private enterprise (presumably stimulated by a consumers' buying strike !) would create the conditions favourable for the revival of trade.

It is evident that there was considerable confusion in authoritative circles as to the proper mode of dealing with an exceptional situation. First and foremost it was essential to check the fall in world prices and restore international trade, upon which our export industries, our mercantile marine, our oversea investments and our receipts from banking services abroad, all depended. Instead we adopted (as we have seen) a currency and fiscal policy which had the diametrically opposite effects. Nowhere in the economic sphere was the absence of clear thinking responsible for a more fatal series of maladroit expedients than in our efforts to cope with the great depression. We succeeded in making the worst of both possible worlds—those of a planned economy and of free enterprise. The only fitting parallel lies in the political sphere in which vacillation and irresolute policy brought us remorselessly nearer and nearer to the supreme catastrophe of a second world war.

Whatever the causes of Great Britain's recovery from the great depression, it was only partial. The staple export industries manifested a melancholy decline ; our income from invisible exports (investments, shipping, banking) contracted ; and the balance of our international payments ceased to be in our favour. The percentage of unemployment did not return to its pre-depression level—whereas formerly one in nine was unemployed, in 1938 one in eight was out of work. There is, however, another side to the picture. Between 1929 and 1937 the home market expanded. The volume of industrial production was 24 per cent. greater. The number of insured workers was growing all the time : excluding agriculture it was 2 millions higher in 1938 than in 1921 (when it was about twelve millions). Thus British industry continued to develop sufficiently to absorb most of the increase in the working population, but it failed to absorb the 'hard core' of unemployment, partly perhaps because the unemployed in the declining trades tended to become unemployable. Moreover the great depression, while it augmented the amount of unemployment, had in compensation a beneficial influence on the standard of living of those who remained in work. In spite of the depreciation of sterling, the fall in world prices was so sharp that imports of foodstuffs and raw materials were substantially cheaper. The cost of living was reduced by 15 per cent. (the cost-of-living index fell 24 points between 1929 and 1933 : taking 1914 as 100, it was 164 in 1929 and 140 in 1933). Money wages were only reduced 4 per cent. (the wage rate index fell 6 points : taking 1913 as 100, it was 170 in 1929 and 164 in 1933). Hence 'real' wages rose, and the workers therefore had a wider margin for extra expenditure. The average diet in the worst year of the depression was actually better than in the relatively prosperous years preceding it. Between 1929 and 1938 the quantity of butter imported into this island was increased as much as 50 per cent. and there was a similar growth in the consumption of tobacco. Altogether if we compare the condition of the working community on the eve of the two world wars, it is officially estimated that the average rise in real income per head was about 25 per cent. while there was also a marked extension in the size of the working community since the total number of persons in employment was much larger.

§ 7. *The Revival of Economic Nationalism in Europe*

The outstanding feature of the troubled decades which bridge the two world wars was a momentous departure from the orthodox principles that held sway in the nineteenth century. This was the revival of an unbridled economic nationalism which in the space of a few years placed in jeopardy all the cherished hopes that 'the great caravan of humanity' was 'once more on the march'. In its origin economic nationalism was the offspring of a distorted political nationalism inflamed and over-stimulated by the war of 1914-18 ; though it did not definitely assume the form of ' autarky ' (that is, economic self-sufficiency) until world prices crashed during the great depression of 1929-33 and every country sought to protect itself from the consequences. Its general effect was not only to stifle genuine economic collaboration after the first world war, but also to fan the flames of the age-old political animosities which eventually culminated in a second world war. Let us begin by reviewing the impediments which strewed the path of international economic co-operation on the very eve of the second world war.

Among the numerous obstacles to international trade the most important was the high protective duties, to whose malign influence was attributed the primary cause of the disturbed economic aspect of Europe after peace was restored in 1918. As a result of the fresh frontiers created by the Treaties of Versailles, St. Germain and Trianon to satisfy national aspirations, no fewer than twelve thousand miles of additional customs barriers came into existence on a continent exhausted by a war of unparalleled magnitude ; and the new states vied with one another in the emulous pursuit of a commercial policy which had successfully wrecked the relations of the old states. The failure to counteract the economic mischief entailed by the territorial adjustments was the really serious flaw in the peace treaties : it perpetuated a malaise which was the root cause of the political instability of Europe during the next two decades (1919-39). In these fateful years the world's foremost need was the enlargement of its markets, in order to enable the different nations to absorb a greater share of each other's products, improve their industrial processes, and provide guarantees against over-production and unemployment. The implied condition was whole-hearted co-operation based on a rational division of labour corresponding with the situation prevailing in the various countries. Nevertheless, in spite of the argument that " an endeavour to restrict the armaments of customs policy is as important as an attempt to reduce armies and navies ", circumstances were not propitious for stemming the rising tide of tariffs. Following the lead given by the United States who erected a 'Chinese wall' around her manufactures, the European powers continued to raise their customs barriers still higher.

The second impediment to international commerce was the institution of 'quotas', by which limitations were placed on the quantity of imports which a state was willing to accept. The practice was widely adopted during and after the great depression, with a view to prevent the domestic market being flooded with cheap foreign wares coming from realms which had depreciated their currencies or drastically reduced their prices. Quantitative control of trade re-introduced, in a modified form, the mercantilist device of prohibition since it involved a stoppage of imports once the 'quota' was exhausted. The third impediment was the system of reciprocity, under which the exporting country undertook to make purchases of a stipulated value from the importing country. The bilateral method of balancing exports and imports with each territory—a rediscovery in the twentieth century, as I have already mentioned, of what was known in the seventeenth century as 'the particular balance'—deprived commercial intercourse of its triangular character by which a nation buys from one and sells to another, thus enabling all parties to choose the markets best suited for their requirements. In diverting the natural currents of trade, it militated against the expansion of international commerce which is regulated by its elasticity—by its degree of immunity from any kind of restraints tending to make it rigid and exclusive. The fourth impediment was the logical corollary of the third—the direct exchange of goods for goods. The return to the primitive system of barter revealed the shifts and devices to which in our own day some of the advanced peoples of the world had recourse.

Another group of influences of a financial nature also served to impede the circulation of commodities. One was the manipulation of the monetary exchanges. In many states the central bank took possession of the foreign money received in return for exports and released it for approved imports. This enabled the government to control external trade, since all transactions involving payments abroad had to be submitted to official scrutiny ; thus it interrupted the normal course of buying and selling as moulded by the interplay of the forces of supply and demand. The second was the violent fluctations in the exchange value of currencies belonging to states which imposed no restrictions on the export of money. When, owing to the repudiation of the gold standard, paper currencies ceased to be redeemable in gold, their mutual relations came to depend (in the absence of official control) primarily upon the confidence which they inspired abroad. Erratic quotations of exchange rates were caused by the abnormal movements of fugitive or 'nervous' money born of panic or distrust. Monetary disturbances injured a country's credit and exerted an unsettling influence on its foreign trade, for they affected both the volume and profits of business transactions. The third was the decline of international financing, that is, the flow of long-term capital from richer to poorer lands. Great Britain had been accustomed to make investments abroad, which had the consequence of stimulating her exports through the creation of new markets. The locking-up of large funds in Germany, a debit balance of international payments and the suspension of the gold standard led the Treasury to impose an embargo on foreign loans. In the absence of a credit balance which could be re-invested, lending abroad meant drawing on savings at home, thereby curtailing home investments and raising interest rates. Similarly the United States had made heavy advances—of which nearly one-third went to Europe—until the collapse on the stock exchange and subsequently the disturbed international situation reduced her financing to a minimum. Inasmuch as foreign loans are credit facilities, which are utilized by the borrowers for the purchase of goods, the shrinkage of the international capital market must be counted among the obstacles to international trade. The fourth was the diversion of national resources from the normal channels of production to meet the devouring needs of rearmament which in the thirties took place on a vast scale. While the nations continued to arm against each other, they had less to spend on merchandise imported for domestic consumption. Preparations for war served incidentally to intensify the prevailing sense of insecurity, which in destroying confidence hampered the revival of trade and finance.

The counterpart of the restraints which hinder the circulation of commodities is the restraints on immigration which hinder the circulation of labour. A country requires outlets for its surplus people as well as for its surplus products. When the economic structure of a state temporarily loses its elasticity and cannot be expanded to absorb the whole of the working community, serious complications are liable to ensue. Productive capacity is taxed to support the burden of those who are non-productive : labour unrest is fostered by the existence of an army of unemployed with its potential menace to the standard of life of the workers : political instability is generated by the psychological effects of economic disequilibrium. Germany affords a striking example of the dangers of mass unemployment, for it was the mounting waves of social distress that carried the National Socialists to power. Now prior to the war of 1914–18 emigration from Europe took place on a considerable scale. I have already contrasted the extent of British emigration before and after the war. The number of Italians who emigrated before 1914 averaged approximately half a million a year. Their remittances home constituted an important item in Italy's balance of international payments, though against this must be set the loss occasioned by the drain of enterprising and energetic elements. Subsequently Italian emigration fell off for reasons which also affected other nations—namely, the restraints laid on admission into the United States, the British Empire and South America.

Of these the first had been Europe's most important outlet. "America", wrote Israel Zangwill, "is God's crucible, the great melting pot, where all the races of Europe are melting and reforming ". In the decade 1901–1910 nearly nine million immigrants entered the United States. To check influx on such a scale, quota laws were enacted after the first world war which limited the annual number of emigrants from outside the western hemisphere to 150,000. It was not perhaps a coincidence that the decade which witnessed this restrictive measure also experienced the greatest depression in the history of the United States, whose industrial structure being based on the mass production of standardized wares demands an expanding population to prevent saturation of the market. Meanwhile a serious problem was created by the fact that the New World had ceased to encourage free emigration from the Old World. The pressure of population in Europe produced two notable effects. Firstly, in conjunction with the obstructions in external trade it intensified the trend towards self-sufficiency, for a country which is unable to exchange domestic for foreign goods or relieve itself of surplus labour must reorganize its economic system. Hence the stoppage of migration leads to the development of industrialism and the imposition of tariffs. Secondly, it strengthened the demand for colonies both as outlets for emigrants, and as sources of foodstuffs and raw materials which could be directly bartered for the manufactures and services of the motherland.

Already within a few years of a war which was designed to inaugurate a new era of universal peace and plenty, a mushroom growth of fungi was enveloping the very life of commercial intercourse. A formidable series of impediments obstructed the circulation of goods, the circulation of persons and the circulation of capital ; it interfered with the liquidation of trading debts ; it prevented the stabilization of the monetary exchanges ; and it checked the restoration of financial and business confidence. It bore all the traits of hasty improvisation and it intensified the chaos of which it was the fruit. The cumulative result was to circumscribe the sphere of international economic co-operation and to throw the countries back upon their own resources. The crowning disaster of a major depression which lasted for four years, instead of leading the nations back to economic sanity, had the reverse effect of stimulating economic nationalism since it eliminated the only great power adhering to free trade and threw the currencies of the world into utter disorder. A political factor—the rise of the totalitarian states—introduced fresh complications and powerfully reinforced the movement towards self-sufficiency. To a totalitarian state which sought to gather up all the political, economic and cultural forces in the life of the community and place them under the rigid control of the dominant faction, it appeared anomalous that the existence of the nation should be dependent upon alien sources of supply, and it sought to escape from its reliance on a world economy. The European dictatorships had experienced the dangers to which their economic position exposed them upon the outbreak of war. The collapse of Germany in the war of 1914–18 was accelerated by the naval blockade which ultimately brought the people to semi-starvation. The imposition of 'sanctions' on Italy during the Abyssinian war lacked the time element to be effective, but it served as a useful reminder of her economic weaknesses. Foreign support of the enemies of the Bolshevik Revolution convinced the rulers of Russia that the survival of the Soviet Union in a capitalist world necessitated a policy of rapid industrialization.

The significant conclusion follows that the resurgence of economic nationalism in our own day was not due purely to economic causes. The driving force behind it lay in its twofold objectives—insulating the national economy from the consequences of the great depression, namely, a dwindling foreign trade coupled with the collapse of world prices; and buttressing national security with the pillars of a strategic economy. The economic and political factors created by straitened resources and nationalist sentiment combined to bring it about that, over a great part of

Europe, economic nationalism marched hand in hand with political nationalism. Indeed the interaction of these two forces became so involved that one cannot distinguish between cause and effect. The economic rehabilitation of Europe was unquestionably an essential condition of its political pacification, yet no substantial measure of economic recovery could be achieved so long as it remained distracted by political acrimony. This was Europe's 'Gordian knot'; and in the general instability produced by the repercussions of these disturbing influences the peace of the world was once again shattered.

The widespread reaction against a world economy based on international specialization dominated the economic situation after the first world war. If we inquire whether the reaction is likely to persist after the second world war, then we must take account of a variety of factors which serve to impress a more permanent character on what might otherwise prove a temporary phenomenon. First: the progress of science in the twentieth century has made the ideal of economic self-sufficiency less visionary than it formerly appeared in the nineteenth century. Nations with meagre resources are still upon the threshold of unexplored possibilities of reorganizing their national economy by the discovery of substitutes, which may redress the balance between them and the owners of natural monopolies. The prospect foreshadows a fresh stage in man's conquest of nature, although the dependence of the newer industries (especially automobiles and aircraft) upon materials drawn from world-wide sources promises to increase in the future rather than diminish. Secondly: the industrialization of backward regions is facilitated by the spread of technical knowledge; and Soviet Russia affords a striking example of swift advance attained with the aid of foreign experts and foreign equipment. Thirdly: it is believed that a self-sufficing economy may provide a partial solution for the problem of unemployment, if additional labourers are wanted in their own country or its colonies to carry out the reconstruction schemes projected under a planned economy. Such a development would be in harmony with the mercantilist doctrine which treated productive labour as a national asset to be kept at home. The effort to promote domestic manufactures, in which the surplus population can be absorbed, has assumed a more compelling aspect in view of the liability to mass unemployment in a world depression, the curtailment of emigration, the reduced demand for men in mechanized agriculture, and the plight of the European peasantry struggling to maintain a precarious existence on the land. Certainly in so far as primary products—foodstuffs and raw materials—require less labour than formerly, the agricultural countries are bound to turn to a less homogeneous economy, and some disturbance of the international equilibrium based on the division of labour is inevitable. Fourthly: the scope of modern warfare impels states to develop the heavy industries needed to supply them with armaments.

I have drawn attention to the complex forces which are responsible for the growth of neo-mercantilism, because it is essential to dispel the idea that the destruction of Fascism and National Socialism will suffice to re-establish an era of international collaboration with its tradition of a world economy prescribing the conditions which regulate the national economies. Economic nationalism was not due exclusively to any one set of causes, and some of the factors which I have mentioned may be expected to operate in the days to come—the requirements of a strategic economy; the maintenance of agriculture in industrial countries and the stimulation of industry in agricultural countries in the interests of a more diversified economy; the attempt to insulate the domestic price level against rapid movements in world prices and to insulate domestic employment against the erratic course of international trade; and finally the deepening of national consciousness generated by the struggle for survival.

§ 8. *The German Example*

Germany affords the leading example of economic nationalism. I shall give some account of her system partly because it will enable the reader to see how economic nationalism worked in practice when carried to a logical conclusion, partly because it was held up to admiration in other countries, and partly because it drew into its orbit of activities the whole of south-eastern Europe in which German economic penetration raised an acute political problem. I am not concerned with the Treaty of Versailles, though it may be observed *en passant* that the cardinal principle of the territorial settlement was ethnic, and on purely nationalist grounds the majority of the frontier changes could be defended. Taken as a whole, it could scarcely be denied that the map of the new Europe was based on a sense of justice in a greater degree than that of the old Europe. As regards reparations, the sympathy lavished upon the vanquished as the victim of unconscionable taskmasters may be tempered by the reflection that—apart from deliveries in kind to make good the wilful and systematic ruin of the industrial regions in northern France—reparations were discharged by the victorious powers themselves. The McKenna committee of experts reported in 1924 that the amount of foreign money lost through investment in German paper currency was equal to the total payments which the German government had furnished in cash. Between 1924 and 1927 the influx of loan capital into Germany, attracted by a high rate of interest, exceeded the payments transferred abroad under the 'Dawes plan'. The nominal amount of her indebtedness was scaled down within a few years to less than one-third, when the Allies demanded only the equivalent of their own debts to the United States. Eventually she undertook to pay the relatively insignificant sum of £150 millions in final settlement of her reparation liabilities: this pledge also was repudiated.

The economic policy of Germany took formal shape and substance in 1936 when the 'four-year plan' was put into operation. Its purpose was expressed in the slogan 'Guns in place of butter', which embodied in a phrase the economic programme of National Socialism. It was intended to establish the new rulers in a position to pursue their aims at home and abroad with complete indifference to their reaction upon public sentiment in other countries. In peace-time they would be enabled to ignore the threat of 'sanctions', while in the event of war they could withstand a naval blockade even if it endured (so it was vaunted) 'for thirty years'. The crux of the problem of economic self-sufficiency is the production of domestic supplies of raw materials. The 'four-year plan' was intended to make the Third German Reich "entirely independent of all such materials as can in any way be home-produced by means of German ability, or by means of her chemical and mechanical industries as well as mining". Artificial substitutes for foreign commodities were invented, such as synthetic wool and rubber: low-grade iron ores were utilized: liquid fuel was distilled from coal: more intensive cultivation of arable land was encouraged in order to restrict grain imports: the growing of potatoes and sugar beets was stimulated. The general result was to lower the standard of living, since the consumer found that commodities were not only more expensive but also inferior in quality; nor did flour and other foods escape adulteration.

The conduct of this policy served for the moment, in conjunction with other factors, to diminish unemployment. These other factors were the lavish expenditure on armaments and public works (including land reclamation), the revival of military conscription which took hundreds of thousands of men off the labour market, the institution of labour camps, the compulsion put on employers to enlarge their staffs beyond their actual requirements, the discouragement of female labour, and the shortening of hours coupled with reduced earnings. The number of unemployed workers, which was 1,900,000 in 1929 and rose to $5\frac{1}{2}$ millions in 1932, fell to 900,000 in 1937; but despite the shrinkage the number of employed workers was only 4 per cent.

higher than in 1929. Let us contrast Great Britain. Here the number of unemployed workers was greater in 1937 than in 1929, yet the number of employed workers was 12 per cent. higher: industrial production had expanded by a quarter (in Germany it expanded by a sixth): 'real' wages had increased by 10 per cent. (in Germany they fell by 2 per cent.). Thus contrary to the general belief National Socialism did not eradicate unemployment, though the 1929 figures were halved partly by transferring workers from productive to non-productive (military) occupations; while the purchasing power of those in employment declined.

The strict regimentation of German economic life appeared to be the outcome, not of a constructive effort to remould the economic system on the principle of the corporate state (as in Italy), but of a provisional arrangement designed to place industry and agriculture on a war-footing as part of the country's military preparedness. An agricultural corporation, whose membership included all engaged in the production, manufacture and sale of foodstuffs, was charged with the function of regulating agriculture on the lines laid down by official policy—for example, controlling prices and fixing the quantities of produce to be furnished to the market. Through the medium of an economic corporation the government was endowed with complete authority over industry, commerce and banking. It had, for instance, the right to forbid the expansion of industrial plants or the opening of retail shops, and to limit dividends by investing the surplus in public loans. Recalcitrant employers could be eliminated from the direction of their businesses, and labour unions were deprived of their independence.

Notwithstanding her efforts to achieve self-sufficiency Germany was unable to escape dependency upon international trade. She still needed to import foodstuffs and raw materials, and her leaders therefore declared that she 'must export or die'. In order to establish a complete control over all international transactions in which she was implicated, foreign trade and the monetary exchanges were virtually nationalized. The principles which guided her economic relations with other states were announced in the flamboyant claim that " the new economic order of the world would be different from the past; especially the system of international division of labour would have lost much of its importance ". The basic feature of the ' new economic order ' was the bilateral system. Germany entered into clearing agreements with many countries under which exports and imports were balanced—each exporting country being required to buy German goods to the value of what it sold to Germany. England once had a similar system; it was known as the ' statute of employment ' because alien importers had to ' employ ' the money which they received here on buying native wares; but it had fallen into discredit four centuries before it was rediscovered in our own day as a ' new plan ' of international trade. In 1937 there were about 170 clearing agreements in operation between different countries. Germany also developed the device of ' blocked accounts ', by which payment for foreign merchandise was made in domestic currency which could not be transferred abroad. The system worked as follows. She bought foodstuffs and raw materials particularly from south-eastern Europe, and paid for them in blocked currency which could only be used in the purchase of German products. Thus she was not only provided with a market for her industries but the latter were financed by her creditors without her incurring the obligation of interest (since the blocked marks paid no interest). The president of the Standard Oil Company of New Jersey stated at the annual meeting (1936) that the company had bought with its blocked marks forty million mouth-organs! In addition the monetary exchanges were manipulated to give marks a high value in terms of foreign currencies: this enabled Germany to sell her exports more dearly and partially compensated for the high prices which she paid for her imports. Much admiration has been lavished upon the ingenuity displayed in the ' new plan ' of clearing agreements and exchange control, but it is only possible to be dishonest successfully when one preys on honest men. Obviously the old-established mechanism of international trade must eventually have broken down when states prevented the transfer of funds in payment for the goods which they bought.

The question is often asked how Germany financed her rearmament and public works. One method was credit expansion. Short-term bills were issued, of which part was subsequently funded (that is, turned into long-term government loans). A special feature of the arrangement was the strict check on inflation, because the level of wages and prices was kept steady and individual purchasing power was not allowed to expand. Another method was the raising of large loans in the United States and elsewhere and then making default on the debt service. A third method was the adoption of a trade policy under which Germany deliberately concentrated her main resources not on producing suitable exports to pay for imports but on her industrial development. Her creditors furnished the means for this expansionist programme by supplying foodstuffs and raw materials on credit which was interest-free, and which was subsequently liquidated in purchases of mouth-organs or other superfluous commodities. Further sources of income were taxation, which grew *pari passu* with the increase of output, a levy on domestic industry used to subsidize the foreign trade, and the offer of German marks to alien tourists at favourable rates of exchange.

CHAPTER SIX

A RECONSTRUCTION PROGRAMME

In the first world war men of vision were moved by the high resolve to make an end of war, to exorcize the spirit of militarism, and to fashion a world safe for democracy. In the second world war the Atlantic Charter voiced the universal aspiration for a better social order. It is natural that the titanic nature of the conflict, the magnitude of its casualties, the sufferings of the civilian population and the immense financial burdens, should all combine to nurture a passionate desire that these grievous sacrifices might yield fruits for which it was not only worth dying but for which it is also worth living. It would be easy to construct on paper ideal schemes which satisfy an abstract sense of justice yet bear little relation to our matter-of-fact world. My purpose in this chapter is more modest but at the same time more difficult. I shall endeavour to elucidate in broad outline the framework of a reconstruction programme which seeks to apply the lessons of history to the solution of the practical problems that confront us in the immediate future. We must ask ourselves the questions : what are the objectives to which our policy should be directed, in the pursuit of these objectives which is preferable—a planned economy or free enterprise, and if the former what should be its scope and character ? It is only with extreme diffidence that I venture to leave the safe and charted channels of history, in order to embark upon the hazardous undertaking of suggesting some possible answers to these fundamental questions.

§ 1. *The Effects of War*

At the outset a doubt may arise in the mind of the reader. It seems a paradox that war, which takes from us the fine flower of our youth and the gifted leaders of the coming generation, which leaves behind it shattered lives and embittered memories, which wipes out the accumulated fruits of human labour and ingenuity, which burdens posterity with the mortgage of astronomical debts—that this evil affliction should be viewed in the light of an instrument of regeneration. There are many who speak with inspiring optimism of the creation of a new order which will provide a remedy for the faults of modern society. They are possessed by the conviction that the losses entailed by war can only be justified if they result in commensurate changes. Others, again, deprecate the notion that war, which interrupts the normal processes of evolution, has any claims to be considered a prime agency in social amelioration. What is the truth of the matter ? To begin with, our victory would not be fruitless even if it were unaccompanied by any substantial modification of the economic structure. To have preserved our liberties, and retained our right to live our own way of life, would be compensation enough for the unparalleled exertions demanded of us. Moreover war in itself does not alter the basic elements of economic existence : these are still dependent upon natural resources and man's skill in utilizing them. Nevertheless we should not under-estimate the formative influence of a human eruption. It unleashes a driving force which may accelerate the tendencies already at work in the social and economic spheres, just as did the Black Death in the fourteenth century. One thinks of the lava which flows from Vesuvius spreading devastation as it pours down the slopes of the volcano, yet enriching the soil with properties that induce the peasants to return again and again to their ruined homesteads and vineyards. To make this admission is not to detract in the least degree from the folly of war, but to heighten the regret that civilized man still appears to require an orgy of indiscriminate destruction and an incalculable toll in human suffering to awaken him from the sloth and inertia of routine.

Wars may have lasting effects in several ways. Firstly :

strategic considerations—that is, preparations against future wars—may shape national policy and determine the direction of a country's resources (for instance, the stimulation of agriculture and other 'key' industries). Secondly: industrial developments abroad, in countries cut off from their normal channels of supply, may alter the character of our oversea markets and consequently the nature of our export trade. Thirdly: the redistribution of national income (one of the inevitable legacies of war) may affect the accumulation of private capital and so circumscribe the scope of private enterprise. Fourthly: the training of great masses of men and women in technical occupations may provide a reservoir of labour for mechanized industries. (The first world war made us automobile-minded; the second will probably make us aircraft-minded.) Fifthly: the increased adaptability of the nation to new conditions, new modes of thought and new policies, may prove a powerful dissolvent of traditional ideas, customary usages, inherited prejudices and obsolete conventions. A community which has experienced a complete transformation of its economic practices and social habits is mentally prepared to accept a fresh standpoint and a novel approach to the solution of its problems. Its resistance to change has been weakened by war-time innovations, and it develops versatility and a more flexible habit of mind. Sixthly: to whatever extent war establishes a buttress of security against future aggression as well as a psychological setting favourable to the adoption of a progressive attitude, it may offset the material ravages which are usually repaired in a few years.

The possibilities of extracting good out of the present world convulsion depend largely upon the crucial point whether the enthusiasm and spirit of sacrifice generated by the national emergency can be evoked in the task of rehabilitation after the war, and whether the energies released by the appeal to patriotic sentiment can be turned to the increased production of wealth and its more equitable distribution. One obstacle which may prove a serious handicap in the work of reconstruction is the emotional reaction that follows war, when the eagerness to forget its horrors and discomforts leads to supineness and indifference. Another is the exaggerated expectations of a new heaven and a new earth, soon succeeded by disillusionment and apathy. We must also take into consideration the cost of the war. An extreme view holds that we shall be utterly impoverished by a tremendous load of indebtedness and by the loss of our oversea investments. Actually war depends on men and material, and it cannot consume future wealth but only current production (together with accumulated stocks). War expenditure does not cause impoverishment when it merely replaces expenditure on consumers' goods (food, clothing, tobacco, etc.), but only when it replaces expenditure on producers' goods (repairs and renewals of capital equipment—factories and machinery). National debts contracted at home involve the transference of wealth (by means of taxation) from one section of the community to another which in turn is taxed, but the nation as a whole is neither richer nor poorer in consequence except when property has been destroyed or damaged by enemy action. In so far as oversea investments are sold, holdings of gold wiped out and debts piled up abroad without compensating assets, the future national income is affected. If the weight of taxation influences public opinion against fresh commitments, the expansion of the social services may be checked—though the lavish outlay of governments during a war tends to create an attitude of mind which is not conducive to cheese-paring economy after the war. Finally, when the rate of savings is reduced by a high income tax or capital reserves are absorbed in taxes, it limits the funds available for risk-taking in new enterprises. Thus the post-war generation does not escape paying part of the price of war, but the obligations incurred by the state to its own citizens do not directly diminish the national income though they lead to its redistribution. The national resources—our mineral wealth of coal and iron, together with the qualities of energetic leadership, inventive talent, technical skill, financial experience and other intangible assets—remain unimpaired, and these are the basic elements in national development.

§ 2. *The Case for a Planned Economy*

Now that free enterprise is passing under a cloud, it is proper to recall the services which it has rendered to the cause of economic progress. It helped to make this country a great seat of industry, commerce and finance. On the eve of the first world war Great Britain maintained a population which had increased threefold within a century, and enjoyed a standard of living higher at the end of the century than at the commencement. Even in the disturbed years 1919–39 the number of workers in employment was considerably expanded, 'real' wages rose, social services were improved, and hours of labour were reduced. The great depression (1929–33) itself bore testimony to the ability of the economic system to survive a world crisis of exceptional magnitude and to mitigate the worst effects of the 'blizzard'. Critics of our social system are apt to do something less than justice to these remarkable achievements, yet in the eighteenth century a growth of population was commonly associated with a growth of destitution, as readers of Malthus's famous *Essay on Population* will remember. It is by reason of its willingness to take risks, and to try out new methods of increasing wealth, that free enterprise has been enabled to make so monumental a contribution to the advancement of human society.

It is natural, and in a large measure salutary, that public attention should be focussed less upon the achievements of free enterprise in the past than upon its competence to handle the complex problems of reconstruction in the future. It is confidently asserted that free enterprise has 'collapsed', and in support of this thesis is adduced the chaos into which the economic system drifted between the two world wars. Nevertheless the failure of the economic mechanism in these troubled years proves only that it could not cope with an abnormal situation for which it was never designed. In normal conditions the economic mechanism with all its short-comings functions in a way which cannot reasonably be described as chaotic. Totalitarian war must be conducted on a basis of war-socialism ; and reconstruction after a war similarly requires central direction. But whether we should contemplate a gradual return to a free economy, or lay long-term plans for state control, depends on the view which we take as to the character of the decades that lie ahead. If our programme of national security involves economic preparations and if we cannot afford to run the risk of another great depression, then we may fairly conclude, not that free enterprise has ' broken down ', but that in the special circumstances it needs to be supplemented by the collective agencies of the community.

Whether or not we believe that free enterprise has outlived its day, admittedly it is attended by defects of which a critical public opinion is becoming increasingly aware. A democratic society is reluctant to submit to social and economic maladjustments as though they were ' Acts of God ', and it is impatient of the acknowledged evils of our industrial system. It is not difficult to frame a formidable indictment in which pride of place would be accorded to the prevalence of poverty. The term is ambiguous since standards of measurement vary in progressive communities ; yet it is undeniable that a substantial portion of the human race is under-nourished and lives in a degrading environment. In Great Britain the pressure of trade unionism has been largely responsible for raising the standard of living, but this involves a conflict between capital and labour which serves to diminish the total amount of wealth available for distribution. It is here that the authority of the nation might be fittingly invoked to make a fair wage one of the fundamental rights of a charter of labour. Another influence detrimental to the increased production of wealth is the deliberate restriction of output. Workers sometimes follow a policy of ' ca-canny ' in which they refrain from exerting their full powers for fear of rate-cutting. Capitalists sometimes curtail supplies to prevent a fall in prices, like fishermen who throw part of their catch back into the sea to avoid a ' glut '. It is the feature of our economic system, which is based on organized scarcity, that it is demoralized by plenty—producers of foodstuffs, raw materials and manufactures alike are liable to be ruined by abundance. Temporary restriction of output in a particular industry may be justified if the capacity is redundant, provided the surplus capacity is eventually eliminated. But general restriction, which destroys nature's bounty or militates against maximum productivity, means an impoverishment of the community. In the category of ' anti-social ' acts must be included the practice of taking out or buying up patents without any intention of using them but to stop others from doing so. Here, again, the authority of the nation must impose a solution.

Next to poverty ranks insecurity of employment. Between the two world wars the public consciousness was deeply stirred by the spectacle of the depressed areas, and the unwillingness to return to an uncontrolled economy is primarily due to the spectre of mass unemployment. The alternation of booms and slumps, throwing immense numbers of men out of work and bringing ruin upon business undertakings, has created the impression that free enterprise is deficient in foresight, and that it is content to make progress by the wasteful method of ' muddling through ' without any clear vision of the direction in which it is moving. Furthermore, regularity of employment is closely bound up with the whole financial system—the stability of the price level, the volume of bank credit, the monetary exchanges. In these intimately related aspects of finance the case in favour of some form of control has been strengthened by the experiences of recent decades.

It is generally recognized that free enterprise has shown itself in the past to be extravagant in the use of human resources by its frequent indifference to social conditions, and in the use of natural resources—for instance, mineral wealth and forests. Economic wastage also results from periodical depressions in industry when the productive processes are only in partial operation ; from the deliberate policy (noticed above) of not working to full capacity in order to maintain high prices ; from fraudulent undertakings ; and from the disproportionate concentration of capital and labour for the purpose of providing for the more prosperous consumers. Inefficiency in methods of production and marketing is another important cause of the misuse of resources. Much is heard of the peaks in a free economy as represented by outstanding ' captains of industry ', yet there is also a distressing level of mediocrity. Arthur Young, an eminent authority on agriculture who lived in the reign of George III., relates that " when I passed from the conversation of the farmers I was recommended to call on, to that of men whom chance threw in my way, I seemed to have lost a century in time or to have moved a thousand miles in a day ". This observation can be applied to not a few business men in our own day. They provide a modern parallel to the eighteenth-century ' statesmen ' (yeomen farmers) of Cumberland, who handed on their patrimony to their children together with their notions of cultivating it.

The critics of our present economy have other strings to their bow. It is represented that business conduct is content with low standards. In reality the best business standards are not inferior to the best professional standards. Individual business men take the same pride in building up enterprises on honourable lines as doctors and lawyers in building up their practices. At the same time competition to sell goods is keener than the competition to sell services, partly because goods are often perishable, large capital funds are locked up, overhead charges and other costs are greater. Moreover discipline is more lax since (outside the factory acts and legal restraints on adulteration, etc.) it is self-imposed, whereas in the liberal professions the rules of ' etiquette ' are coercive. The prestige of industry and commerce would be heightened if they became once again, as in the middle ages, an ' art ' (profession) in which indulgence in certain practices was frowned upon and incurred the penalties levied by the craft gilds. Industrial leaders are beginning to realize that a business career is a *métier* and not simply a means of accumulating wealth. The change of outlook is assisted by the fact that capital is becoming increasingly impersonal. Those in whose hands rest the direction and management of large companies are often animated by a sense of the public interest and pride in the reputation of their wares. In this development we may perhaps see a reversion to mediaeval gild principles.

One of the favourite charges levelled against free enterprise is that it is dominated by the profit-making motive. In point of fact industry is not carried on just for profit. Its primary aim is to satisfy the needs of consumers in the most efficient manner ; in addition it is a way of life to those engaged in it, and a means of livelihood to all who share in its earnings. The true measure of an industry is the degree to which it fulfils these essential purposes, yet the measure normally applied is the presence or absence of the profit-making motive. Profit-making, which is usually considered the mainspring of free enterprise though it may be merely incidental, is singled out for special condemnation. It carries with it a certain moral stigma. Nevertheless even professional men do not pursue their vocation for the benefit of their health. Business and professional men alike seek a gainful occupation, and in respect of motive there is no difference between fees, salaries, wages and profits. Obviously there must be remuneration for all the factors of production—for land (rent), labour (salaries and wages), and capital (profit). The share which goes to capital provides for interest, depreciation, losses and expansion. No doubt profits are sometimes excessive, especially when competition is eliminated by monopolies or trade agreements ; and recourse may be made to nefarious ways of profit-making such as misrepresentation and cornering supplies ; but 'profiteering' must not be confused with fair profits based on a 'just price' (to employ a mediaeval term). In Soviet Russia all industries are expected to show a margin between the cost of production and selling price except that certain industries may be intentionally run at a loss—but even in Great Britain agriculture is now subsidized by the state.

The dislike of profit-making as an economic incentive is prompted mainly by the belief that free enterprise produces for 'profit' and not for 'use'. This presumably means that the entrepreneur is concerned to ask, not what things are most needed in the community, but what things are most in demand by those who can afford to pay for them. If it is more profitable to employ labour and materials in making cosmetics than articles of primary necessity, he prefers the former. As a result the national resources are utilized for the satisfaction of wants which are in the nature of luxuries, while basic needs may go unsatisfied. The moralist adds his condemnation in the conviction that frugality and a 'Spartan' mode of existence fortify the national virtues. In a general way it is doubtless true to say that when capital and labour are set free from the luxury trades, they become available for the non-luxury trades, and consequently the necessaries of life are rendered more abundant and cheaper. And of course there are some kinds of luxuries in which wide indulgence is neither possible nor desirable. These forms of expenditure should undoubtedly be discouraged in a country where a section of the people is sunk in poverty, and heavy taxation which is bringing about a greater equalization of income is proving a potent influence in this direction. None the less it must be remembered that many of our present-day necessities and certainly all our amenities originated as luxuries enjoyed by the few until they came into common use. Through the ingenuity and enterprise of entrepreneurs most luxuries are speedily made available for the masses at prices within their reach. Human wants are infinite in their variety: progress consists, indeed, in creating new wants just as enlightened progress consists in elevating the nature of our wants. Luxuries diminish the danger of a uniform world with 'utility' food, clothes, houses, culture and amusements, because they set a higher standard of living which is an incentive to work harder. They also offer scope for individuals whose talents claim something different from the ordinary routine. Our exports comprise luxuries in part, and a domestic trade is usually necessary as the basis for an export trade. The most effective mode of securing the right employment of the national resources is not by an indiscriminate ban upon luxuries which would check economic advancement, but by raising the standard of living throughout the community in order to ensure a steady and regular demand for necessities and amenities.

Much of the criticism directed against free enterprise is concerned with the vexed issue of competition. One school of opinion holds that competition is excessive and tends to reduce the economic system to chaos. Unquestionably attempts are sometimes made to force rival producers off the market by fixing prices below their remunerative level. The practice is an abuse, and in the public interest it is preferable that competition should be focussed on the quality of wares and services rather than on price-cutting. However statistical evidence appears to support the view that the competitive risks of industry are diminishing and are not unduly detrimental to the survival of business undertakings. Another school contends that powerful trade bodies are eliminating competition altogether and with it the advantages claimed for a free economy. The truth is that 'pure' competition has seldom if ever existed, and even 'imperfect' competition has often been conspicuously absent. As I have already mentioned, agreements to restrict output and control prices have a continuous history from the beginning of the seventeenth century, when they first began to excite adverse comment. The report of the Committee on Trusts (1919) drew attention to the fact that there were more than five hundred associations of producers in the United Kingdom "all exerting a substantial influence on the course of industry". One object which they shared in common was to regulate output and maintain or raise prices. In recent decades public opinion has grown less unfavourable to industrial combinations. It is recognized that concerns in which a large amount of fixed capital is invested, and in which price-cutting militates against the maintenance and replacement of equipment, may be constrained to enter into agreements that will provide an assurance of stable prices and regular output, as well as facilitate co-operative research and export selling agencies. Furthermore it may be found necessary to reduce the redundant capacity of an industry by extinguishing small and inefficient firms ; and under the name of rationalization this procedure is widely advocated as a means of avoiding economic wastage. Accordingly the government itself has taken steps to bring about a reconstitution of industries on a basis which involves the concentration of resources and co-operation. Thus in the coal industry it established a commission to lower costs of production by encouraging amalgamations, and it created machinery for regulating prices and output expressly in order to limit competition. In the shipping industry it made the union of the Cunard and White Star Lines a condition of financial aid. In the iron and steel industry it exerted pressure upon the producers to reorganize themselves in more efficient units.

It is obvious that the existence of industrial combinations gives rise to a situation which the state cannot afford to ignore. It is desirable to prevent over-investment of capital, that is, surplus capacity in an industry ; prices are higher when the overhead charges are spread over a smaller volume of business ; nevertheless the erection of a fence against new entrants would create virtual monopolies. Strong combines are also in a position to squeeze out competitors already in the market, by selling goods at uneconomic prices or by boycotting customers who buy from others. There is nothing novel about these competitive devices—they were known in the seventeenth century—but modern technique has doubtless extended their field of application. Moreover it is contrary to the principle of a democratic society that economic power should be usurped by a group of ' economic royalists ' as they have been called, for it gives them a stranglehold upon the community which enables them to exploit consumers and to exercise undue political influence. An important consideration is that large enterprises are usually established by entrepreneurs gifted with exceptional powers, but their successors into whose hands control eventually passes are often men of more mediocre talent wedded to routine. As a result these overgrown structures lose their original dynamic qualities and become static and unprogressive. At the same time they may retain the strength to stamp out small enterprises which endeavour to struggle into existence ; yet the opportunity which the latter present to men of initiative and driving force makes them an indispensable factor in industrial progress. Another development furnishes ground for misgivings, namely, the growth of international concerns and international agreements. The practice of setting up branch factories abroad, and of concluding agreements with foreign cartels either to create a monopoly in the home market or to control the output and prices of raw materials, raises an issue of vital consequence to national security. The disregard of territorial frontiers in the organization of business undertakings may harmonize with the trend towards a world economy, but its manifestations need to be closely supervised.

These various considerations lead to the conclusion that the argument in favour of a free economy assumes hypothetical conditions of pure competition, which in fact are largely non-existent. We have heard much in the past about ' economic laws ', ' economic harmonies ' and ' the invisible hand ', and we are lulled into the comforting belief that a free economy is beneficient because it is presumed to be guided by impersonal forces which are automatically set in motion. Actually under free enterprise there is a vast amount of planning ranging from amalgamations to ' gentlemen's agreements ' which restrict the scope for individual initiative. This planning, however, is devised to satisfy sectional interests. Hence our practical choice does not really lie between a free and a controlled economy, but between an economy which is regulated by vested interests and one regulated by the collective interests of the community. None the less state intervention need not necessarily take the form of replacing a private monopoly by a public monopoly. It is possible that the appointment of official members on certain boards of directors may provide a guarantee against the pursuit of an anti-social policy by large establishments. There is a historical precedent for linking the state with private enterprise—after the Restoration a corporation of clothiers was set up in the West Riding of Yorkshire and assigned the power of framing by-laws for ' the better making ' of woollen cloth. Its membership embraced not only the clothiers but also the local authorities, and thus foreshadowed a type of industrial structure in which control is shared between industry and the state. The Port of London Authority instituted early in the present century is a more recent example of the inclusion of public representatives on the governing body of an undertaking [1]. In addition trade associations could be required to submit their agreements to an official tribunal for approval or rejection, just as the craft gilds lay under a legal obligation to seek confirmation of their ordinances.

Apart from the specific criticisms levelled against free enterprise, positive arguments may be advanced in support of a planned economy. It seems to lie in the logic of history, for we have obviously reached a stage in economic evolution in which the pendulum is again swinging in a fresh direction. Free enterprise has not exhausted its potentialities for increasing the production of wealth, but it has developed the defects of its qualities, and the demand for applying suitable correctives has become insistent and widespread. The evils of a free economy can only be remedied or avoided by returning to an older tradition which did not shrink from

[1] There was an independent chairman of the British Iron and Steel Federation, but the Import Duties Advisory Committee has recommended the erection of an independent body. This proposal for a state agency provides another method of safeguarding the public interest without superseding private enterprise.

the attempt to control economic forces. Moreover problems relating to world prices, domestic employment, foreign trade, etc. are grown so immense, their repercussions are so extensive and complicated, that individualism tends to lose its bearings. The state already covers a wide field of activities embracing the relations of employers and employed, utility services, price-regulation, immigration, commodity imports, currency, monetary exchanges and the export of capital. Indeed the alternative no longer rests between *laissez-faire* or an increasing measure of state interference. It rests rather between conscious and co-ordinated direction of the national resources, or an opportunist policy producing a mass of contradictory expedients to cope with emergencies without due regard to their ultimate reactions.

The fact must also be recognized that the phenomenon of a planned economy promises to be in the nature of a universal tendency. It was particularly in evidence in the inter-war epoch (1919–39) when a variety of circumstances—the aftermath of the first world war, the great depression and war preparations—led many European countries and even the United States to extend the province of state control in the economic sphere. National planning was most marked in Russia, Germany and Italy, but manifestations of a controlled economy were found in regions extending as far east as Turkey, as far west as Portugal, as far north as the Baltic. The tendency may be expected to persist after totalitarian states have ceased to strut on the stage of history. As I shall explain presently, social pressure and the requirements of a strategic economy are likely to remain potent influences in compelling governments to assume a larger and more immediate responsibility for the functioning of the economic mechanism. In the international sphere a planned economy offers the opportunity (one must not put it more strongly) of removing the sources of economic friction. The peace settlement of 1919 demonstrated that a new political framework is not enough to preserve the tranquillity of the world ;

and together with machinery for the enforcement of treaty obligations must go a systematic effort to abolish the economic causes of war. A new international order cannot be constructed on a political basis alone : it will be rudely shattered (as in 1929–33) when exposed to the blasts of an economic blizzard.

Most of all, the growing volume of opinion in favour of a planned economy is due to the determination of democracy to set its house in order, and to show the world that ' dictatorships ' are not alone in their power to organize the community for economic objectives—though in place of the totalitarian state it exalts ' the common man ', whose interests a planned economy endeavours to serve. Our generation is unwilling to acquiesce in the maladjustments of a peace economy. It is impressed by the paradox that war while it lasts should solve the most baffling economic problems—the elimination of unemployment and the harnessing of the man-power and resources of the nation for purposes which are clear and defined. In war-time the will of the community is concentrated on specific ends : its productive forces are directed by state action into the appointed channels : nothing is allowed to stand in the way —the vested interests of ideas and of people must yield to the paramount needs of national safety. The questions inevitably arise why we cannot eliminate unemployment in peace-time and harness man-power and resources for the abolition of poverty. Is human sagacity incapable of controlling economic processes except under the stress of extreme national peril ? If the issues involved were purely economic, there might be some justification for leaving these processes to work themselves out unimpeded, but economics are part of a larger whole and we cannot afford to ignore their social reactions. Those who hold that the state ought to stand aside deprecate government intervention in the belief that it is best to let things pursue their own course. It is true that many of the remedies applied during the great depression retarded instead of aiding recovery. Our sudden abandonment of free trade and the devaluation of our currency are signal examples of an ill-planned economy in which far-reaching changes are effected, not as part of a wider programme of reconstruction, but in capitulation to a temporary wave of adversity. Yet this only proves that measures hastily improvised in the midst of an economic crisis may cause the situation to deteriorate rather than ameliorate. It does not prove that a long-term policy for preventing an economic crisis is necessarily ill-judged. It is quite certain that if economic affairs are left to themselves the alternation of booms and slumps will recur in the future as in the past. Furthermore the interdependence of nations will intensify their severity. The economic mechanism may function reasonably well in normal times. It is the fear of periodic phases of economic anarchy, of world chaos as in 1929–33, that makes it worth while to see if a controlled economy can offer on balance a greater contribution to human welfare than the method of 'muddling through'. It would fufil in the economic sphere the purpose which social medicine is designed to achieve in the sphere of public health. It would seek to create conditions in which economic maladies were less likely to happen, and to be less severe if they did happen.

The coming of peace presents a unique possibility of making a fresh start. There is general agreement that it is impossible after a world war to return at once to a free economy. The steps taken abroad to rehabilitate the occupied territories and put Europe on its feet, coupled with the steps taken at home to rebuild the devastated areas and liquidate the problems arising out of the transition from war to peace—all these complex adjustments will make it necessary for the state to retain in its hands some measure of control over the economic system. None the less public opinion in this country is unlikely to tolerate the continuance of war-time restrictions unless they can be justified as part of a comprehensive programme of reconstruction; the demand for their rapid disappearance will become irresistible; and there will be no guarantee that the economic malaise which preceded the second world war will not recur again after a temporary period of fictitious prosperity. Above all the collaboration between governments, which will be needed to cope with the immediate post-war situation, affords an exceptional occasion for laying the foundations of an improved economic order. It would be a misfortune if the opportunity were irrevocably lost. For one thing, if the nations learn to work together in handling their economic problems, it may create an atmosphere that will dispel the suspicions and mistrust which have hitherto proved a fatal handicap to international co-operation. For another thing, the principles which are applied and the machinery which is improvised to deal with emergency conditions can be utilized on an ever-broadening basis so long as there exists a genuine desire for concerted action. We must choose one of two policies. We can make it our aim both in domestic and external affairs to restore as quickly as possible the economic *status quo* of 1939. Or we can endeavour to perpetuate the good will which our common sacrifices have fostered by carrying into the peace years the cordial collaboration of the war years, and strive to crystallize it into a system of permanent co-operation. The decision must be made at the outset, since it will deeply colour all our plans for the post-war world.

§ 3. *Drawbacks of a Planned Economy*

We shall commit a profound mistake if we wilfully close our eyes to the drawbacks of a planned economy. Its adoption will bring in its train certain dangers, which if left unchecked can be gravely detrimental to the long-term interests of the community. It is essential to devise safeguards for the purpose of ensuring that the good which may be achieved by a planned economy is not neutralized by the harm which it may do. Economic conduct involves a nice balancing of gain and loss, and we should therefore be prepared to sacrifice something in the effort to attain the larger ends visualized by a reconstruction programme;

but we ought not to plunge blindly into a maze of restrictions on private enterprise. There are indispensable conditions to be satisfied before we embark upon a new and hazardous adventure. We must know precisely our goal, that is, what it is we wish to plan: of this I shall speak elsewhere in this chapter. We must also establish provision (as far as human fallibility will permit) against the defects which are latent in any economic system controlled by the state. These defects will be discussed in the paragraphs that follow.

One criterion of a planned economy is the nature of the machinery by which a paper programme is translated into economic realities. In a twofold respect the modern state is in an infinitely stronger position to carry out a comprehensive economic policy than it was under England's first planned economy. In the first place, it can draw upon the accumulated experience of many generations of entrepreneurs in the realm of industry, commerce and finance; and it has at its command the advice of experts trained in the school of economic analysis though less deeply versed in a knowledge of past economic development. In the second place, it possesses an able body of civil servants accustomed to frame and administer a vast and complicated body of legislation. In former centuries the state was unable to enforce the industrial code, or to stop the drain of gold, or to prevent smuggling. To-day the apprehension is not that state control will be ineffective but that it will be too effective. There is undeniably a widespread feeling against putting the economic system into the hands of a bureaucracy. The civil service is better suited for administering the law than for path-breaking. The personal equation, the fear of making mistakes, often combines with Treasury control of the public purse to deter government departments from striking out in new directions. The danger is not confined to departments of state. Private concerns may also develop a routine, and their administration may become stereotyped and bureaucratic. Yet the economic world does not stand still—it must either move forward or backward; hence it is vital for a dynamic society to preserve the spirit of initiative and enterprise. I have designedly quoted the pregnant sayings of Thucydides in order to show that the greatest of our political historians was able to derive lessons from history, which more than two thousand years later can be studied with profit. He wrote : " Constant necessities of action must be accompanied by the constant improvement of methods ". The officials who discharge economic functions will need to combine the admirable qualities of the civil service with breadth of vision in the conception of bold designs and a willingness to take risks and break new ground. The business community, apprehensive of red tape and excessive delay in making decisions, should not allow itself to be unduly influenced by war-time experiences, when new ministries were quickly improvised and their staffs—recruited from many different sources—were called upon to undertake novel responsibilities. There is no valid reason to doubt the feasibility of building up in peace-time a bureaucracy skilled in the expeditious handling of business affairs.

An economic system is judged, largely though not exclusively, by its ability to organize the factors of production in such a way as to attain the maximum output of which they are capable. The supposition that the standard of life can rise in a community where the standard of production is static or even falling is the most hopeless of illusions. When this crucial test is applied to a planned economy, it at once raises a doubt as to whether the decline of a sense of personal responsibility will not put a premium on incompetence. It is evident that the maintenance of a high degree of efficiency is essential if our second planned economy is not to share the fate of the first. It should be frankly recognized that in the long run no economic system is likely to survive in a country where public opinion is critical and powerful, unless there is a general feeling that it is able to ' deliver the goods '. Accordingly we ought to make sure that central planning does not weaken the personal incentives to economic effort nor impair productive capacity. Some method must be found of creating the stimulus which is provided in war by the presence of imminent national danger. Unless the spiritual appeal of service for the community proves an adequate substitute for self-interest, a planned economy may achieve order and regularity but only at a considerable cost.

While a planned economy will doubtless begin on a modest scale, it may be expected to grow in stature. The confidence bred of success or the mere momentum of events will enlarge the scale, and for good or evil the nation will find itself committed to an ever-increasing sphere of official regulation. The grasp of the state, at first experimental and tentative, is all the time tightening. This is perhaps inevitable. Piecemeal control invariably provokes in other parts of the economic structure a series of reactions which necessitate an extension of control.

> " The Moving Finger writes ; and, having writ,
> Moves on : nor all thy Piety nor Wit
> Shall lure it back to cancel half a Line,
> Nor all thy Tears wash out a Word of it ".

The prospect may seem depressing to those who are prepared to accept only a strictly limited amount of government interference. We cannot hope to bind the future but we can at least take steps in view of eventualities ; and I believe that the best safeguard is some kind of apparatus through which public criticism of bureaucratic administration may be made effective. As to the apparatus appropriate for the purpose something will be said later.

I have pointed out that an economic society is in the nature of a living organism, and that it functions by the process of unceasing adaptation to an environment which is always dissolving and reforming. This constant readjustment to the complex requirements of a progressive community is the hall-mark of a really free economy, in whose self-regulating mechanism a complicated sequence of impersonal forces is automatically set in motion. It is less readily achieved in a planned economy, which (like a written constitution) tends to become rigid since it is subject to central direction and pursues a well-defined course. Economic progress is more rapid in a free economy, though it is often accompanied by grave social friction. It is likely to be slowed down in a planned economy, though there will be compensation in increased stability. In a word the potential defect of a planned economy is that it will be prone to inflexibility. If it developed into a static economy, if it discouraged change because it shrank from disturbing vested interests, its efficiency would be fatally impaired. Economic stagnation is a very high price to pay for a larger measure of social security. Thus the question at issue is whether the state can introduce greater order and regularity into the economic system without stultifying progress. The most practical and least hazardous solution appears to be that, whatever the character of our future economic arrangements, they should not too hastily discard the dynamic qualities of individual enterprise in experiment and risk-taking.

The English people have a profound aversion to anything which savours of economic regimentation. In war-time they submit to state control with greater willingness than is commonly displayed in countries accustomed to authoritarian rule. In peace-time when the danger has subsided they are impatient of departmental regulation. While the national economy continues, as at present, to be based in the main upon private enterprise it is indispensable that there should be co-operation between the government and the business community. Lack of confidence in the economic policy sponsored by the state can neutralize all the efforts made to bring about an improvement in the general economic situation. Of this the recent history of the United States affords an example—and a warning. On their part industrial leaders, however much they may dislike the notion of a planned economy as the thin end of the wedge, should recognize that the choice which confronts them is co-operation or compulsion—either to assist in the shaping of the new order or to have it thrust upon them in a more drastic form. A 'die-hard' attitude will not save free enterprise but can destroy it completely. If the spirit of compromise which has enabled the English constitution to adapt itself to a changing society is carried into the sphere of economic affairs, it may be found that a controlled economy is not incompatible with reasonable scope for the best qualities of individualism. It is a happy augury that many 'captains of industry' in Great Britain have expressed in no uncertain terms their approval in principle of a planned economy. Their attitude signifies two things—a return to an older standpoint which recognized the right of the community to control the economic manifestations of individualism, and the rejection of the doctrine of *laissez-faire* that the state has nothing to do with industry except to leave it alone. At the same time it must not be overlooked that the door might be opened to the exercise of undue political influence, and that governments might submit to pressure and allow their course of action to be virtually dictated by sectional interests acting behind the screen of an official façade.

The most serious drawback to a planned economy lies in the possibility that, if it involved eventually the extinction of economic liberty, it might involve also the decline or extinction of political liberty. This does not mean that there is an historic or organic relation between economic freedom and political freedom in the sense that the one is the measure of the other. Actually political freedom is not only compatible with, but is generally conditional upon, reasonable restraints on economic freedom. Nevertheless should the state, like an octopus, completely envelop the life of the community, it will be in a position to menace the rights of the individual. It ought not to be hastily assumed that the danger is negligible. I have shown in a previous chapter how England's first planned economy became mixed up with an authoritarian system of government, and in consequence the struggle for economic freedom was merged in the struggle for constitutional freedom and religious freedom. In our own day the most conspicuous examples of a planned economy were to be found in countries with a dictatorial form of government.

In a community where the economic system was brought within the dominating grasp of the state labour might gain in dignity and prestige, in stability of employment, in a high minimum standard of living, in increased opportunities of economic advancement ; but it would undoubtedly suffer in personal freedom, for the state cannot permit indiscipline or strikes. In a community where private enterprise is maintained in an extensive field of economic activity, employees may compete with employers for a larger share of the business's earnings, and producers may compete with each other for a larger share of the consumers' purchasing power ; but the state tolerates no competitors nor is there any appeal from its authority. Hence the change from a free economy to a planned economy is fraught with loss as well as with gain. Excessive economic regimentation threatens to involve political regimentation —that is, the virtual supersession of democracy—when vast economic power is concentrated in the hands of an omnipotent state which may ride roughshod over the rights of the individual. The economic state can be a greater menace to human freedom than either the feudal or the theocratic state. The latter were destroyed by the rise of a middle class, but the former can prevent a middle class from functioning independently outside its own orbit. If the middle class, from which in the past has come the most effective opposition to an autocratic state, develops into a managerial class pledged to its support, individualism will be left too weak to stand up to the state. The fundamental problem is to reconcile political liberty with the necessary restraints on economic liberty. Unless we devise adequate safeguards, we shall find that a greater measure of social security will not compensate for the destruction of our cherished privileges.

In weighing up in the light of past experience the merits and defects of a free economy and of a controlled economy, our conclusion must be that salvation lies neither in unrestricted enterprise nor in a planned economy which leaves no room for the legitimate play of individualism in seeking out 'fresh woods and pastures new'. A compromise between the two extremes, which combines the best in each, can establish the necessary checks and balances which will correct the defects of both. In such a manner it may be possible to harmonize social security with economic progress and preserve political freedom. The two traits in the English character, the communal and the individualist, must be fused together. Each has been tried in isolation : each has developed abuses. The village communities, the urban gilds, the oversea trading companies and the first planned economy involved the danger of economic stagnation. Individualism has often displayed indifference to human welfare, and if left unchecked it involves the menace of social revolution. The Greek maxim of the golden mean (*μηδὲν ἄγαν*) offers us a rule of conduct dictated by the lessons of history.

It is with this sense of moderation and objectivity that we should approach the much-canvassed issue of nationalization. We must refrain from treating it as a matter of principle or appealing to doctrinaire theories which can only provoke acrimonious and sterile controversy. There is no 'natural right' at stake in the choice between public management and private management. It is entirely a question of determining on its merits whether any branch of the national economy should be left in the hands of individuals or entrusted to the state. It is generally agreed, for instance, that utility services which are in their nature monopolies ought to be vested in the community. Adam Smith himself conceded that the state should maintain 'certain public works'. The phrase may be held to cover especially commodities and services which are uniform in pattern—water, gas, electricity, post, telegraph, telephones, among the rest. The only criterion to be applied is whether public or private ownership is the more effective instrument in promoting the general welfare, and viewed from this angle it involves a careful balancing of pros and cons in each particular case.

The practical genius of the English people is already working out a compromise between individualism and collectivism. Great Britain has long abandoned in principle, and to an increasing extent in practice, the doctrine of *laissez-faire*. Her repudiation of an uncontrolled capitalist system is in harmony with a universal tendency which is being manifested even in the United States. Eventually, indeed, the whole national economy may be placed under state direction to the extent that central planning will regulate the nature and scope of production in such a way as to ensure that the country's resources are utilized in the collective interest and not for the exclusive benefit of private owners. As regards the actual management of business undertakings no hard and fast rule is likely to be laid down. In many spheres it may be expected that private enterprise will be retained. In other spheres, where private enterprise is completely superseded, it is probable that nationalization will take the form of public corporations. This promises to be Great Britain's specific contribution to the constitution of a new economic order. A public corporation is an organ of the state which is not bureaucratic: it is moulded in the shape of an autonomous self-governing institution. It differs from a government department because it is managed not by civil servants but by nominees of the state who enjoy independence within the terms of their charter. As a non-profit-making institution with no shareholders and serving the interests of the community, it fulfils the purpose of nationalization: as an autonomous body it is shielded from political influence, ministerial vacillation, Treasury control, and conventional procedure. The public corporation was foreshadowed in the creation of the Port of London Authority, whose members represented both public and private interests. After the first world war there followed the Forestry Commission, the Central Electricity Board, the British Broadcasting Corporation, the London Passenger

Transport Board, and various other bodies. It may be safely assumed that the system of public corporations will continue to grow in the years to come. Moreover its underlying principle of a national economy controlled and guided in many of its branches by professional corporate bodies will doubtless exert a profound influence upon the remaining branches in which private enterprise is allowed to survive. If this forecast is borne out by the course of events, individualism will undergo a gradual transformation and develop more and more into an instrument of public policy. The net result will be the concentration of national effort in a rationally organized economy framed to give effect to whatever may be the accepted programme of national needs.

§ 4. *Principles of a Planned Economy*

There is no magic in the phrase 'a planned economy': it is not a key which will spontaneously unlock the door to Utopia. It means embarking upon uncharted seas, for everything depends on the nature of the planning. If we are to think clearly about the problems which lie ahead, we must not allow our minds to be hypnotized by slogans like capitalism, socialism or communism, as though economic salvation is to be found in any particular 'ism'. We should set ourselves well-defined objectives, and decide how they can be best attained within the shortest compass of time while avoiding the disturbances which may bring in their train a host of unsuspected reactions. Two guiding principles should determine the range and character of a planned economy. The first principle is that it ought to create conditions favourable to the proper utilization of the national resources subject to other considerations. In the long run the acid test of an economic system is whether it fulfils its primary function of ensuring the efficient use of the factors of production; and this criterion claims its due weight when the feasibility of any contemplated change is under scrutiny. Idealism—as the ill-fated settlements founded by Robert Owen over a century ago amply demonstrated—will not compensate for a drastic fall in productivity. The second principle elucidates the proviso attached to the first. A planned economy cannot be exclusively shaped by the calculus of profit. The maximum output of wealth does not comprise the whole field of a new economic order. Other considerations are equally vital, notably, national security and 'social justice' (an elastic conception which needs to be translated into concrete realities—stability of employment and a rising standard of living).

In the public mind these twin aspirations, national security and social well-being, constitute the principal reason for the widespread interest in a planned economy. I propose to examine them in some detail, but first of all I must point out that the pursuit of either involves some sacrifice of the other. National security is bound up with a measure of self-sufficiency; while the abundant enjoyment of the fruits of the earth demands international specialization. Thus the antithesis between 'power' and 'plenty' once more confronts the statesmen of the twentieth century as it formerly did those of the mercantilist era. For instance, foodstuffs grown at home—in the interests of national security—may be dearer than imported foodstuffs and so increase the cost of living. Again, the promotion of domestic at the expense of foreign trade—in the interests of employment—may mean a smaller mercantile marine, on which naval strength (as well as a substantial part of our oversea income) largely depend. It is not enough, therefore, to satisfy ourselves that a particular solution will solve a particular problem. Always we should ask the question: how will it affect other branches of the national economy? And if an excessive concentration of our resources on purposes which were non-economic caused a serious decline in the production of wealth, we might ultimately find ourselves unable to support the burden of an Empire or the maintenance of a population of nearly fifty millions in its present standard of living. All these aspects deserve to be kept in view if we seek to prevent the clash of conflicting objectives. Hence the initial stage in formulating a planned economy is to frame the broad lines of policy, making sure what exactly it is we want to plan, in order to establish a gauge by which every proposal may be judged. I stress the point because it is precisely the one most conspicuously ignored between the two world wars; and the unfortunate results which ensued teach a lesson that we shall be very ill-advised to disregard.

§ 5. *National Security*

For a century after the fall of Napoleon this country felt itself free from the menace of invasion: it could cultivate the arts of peace and allow the untrammelled development of the economic system without apprehension of sudden hostile attack. British strategy was based upon the assumption that in our impregnable island home we could build up our strength in the midst of war behind the shield of our navy and our continental alliances. The rapid progress of the science of war has presumably dispelled once and for all a dangerous illusion. The generation which has witnessed two titanic convulsions can no longer share the complacency displayed in the confident lines of W. S. Gilbert:

> " Sleep on, ye pale civilians.
> All thunder-clouds defy.
> On Europe's countless millions
> The sentry keeps his eye ".

We shall do well to anticipate that in the event of another conflict the enemy will have learnt his 'lesson of history', and that he will strike at Great Britain first with all the overwhelming force of new methods and devices. Thucydides, painfully anxious that posterity should profit by the experience of the past, observed that " it is a common mistake in war to begin at the wrong end, to act first and wait for disaster to discuss the matter ". The remark was uttered more than two thousand years ago, and the state of unpreparedness in which we braced ourselves to meet the expected *blitzkrieg* of 1939 suggests that these words might be fittingly inscribed upon the portals of our legislative chambers. According to Thucydides preparations against war should embrace " the acquisition of allies and the development of our home resources ", that is, both political and economic means must be employed. Once again the ebb and flow of events have brought us back to an older standpoint. Economics can no longer be divorced from politics, and as in the age of mercantilism it assumes a prominent place in the array of strategical factors which govern the direction of national policy. Bacon's famous antithesis mentioned in an earlier chapter—between a strategic economy ('power') and a welfare economy ('plenty')—after being forgotten during the past hundred years, takes on a new lease of life when the economic structure is treated as one of the pillars of national security. If we incline to the opinion that the chances of another war are remote, we should be willing to accept in the immediate future disarmament on land, on sea and in the air ; if we are not prepared to run so stupendous a risk, then we ought to recognize that war is not merely a matter of men and ships but of heavy artillery, tanks, aircraft, as well as food for the population at home. The mechanical character of modern warfare is such that, now more than ever, victory will go to the side which possesses the most 'money'—interpreted to mean the greatest economic strength.

Accordingly in the future organization of our national resources, industrial and agricultural, adequate provision is needed to enable the nation to be ready at any moment to withstand the shock of arms. This includes all kinds of economic preparations—factories for the production of aircraft, tanks and munitions together with ship-building yards and 'key' industries (dyestuffs, optical glass, etc.) ; it also involves the maintenance of agriculture to meet the dangers of excessive sinkings at sea, and the dispersion of home industries to meet the dangers of air raids. The distinction between a 'war economy' and a 'peace economy' will tend to be blurred when the latter is based on strategic considerations ; and from the new development one major consequence may be expected to flow. The discussion whether state direction of industry is desirable or not will become purely academic when the supreme law of national safety over-rides all the theoretical arguments in favour of *laissez-faire*—for Adam Smith himself acknowledged that " defence is of much more importance than opulence ". Thus the province of state action will be greatly enlarged ; in course of time the public mentality will grow accustomed to the close association of state and industry ; and the frontier between private enterprise and collectivist enterprise will lose its present sharpness of outline. The momentous prospect opens up a vista of pregnant and far-reaching possibilities. *Laissez-faire* was practicable in an age when Great Britain was relieved from the fear of invasion and sea-power gave her an unchallenged pre-eminence. These conditions have ceased to prevail, and a situation parallel to that which existed before the nineteenth century has restored the state to its former position of authority and control in the economic order.

The place of agriculture in our national economy raises one of the most controversial issues of a reconstruction programme. There is endless debate over the questions whether our aim should be to grow more food or to promote the settlement of more people on the land ; whether ' industrialized ' farms or small holdings constitute the ideal unit of production ; whether we should yield to the importunity of English farmers for protection against all imports whatever their source, or recognize the right of the Dominions to imperial preference ; whether we can afford to sacrifice the interests of our commerce and mercantile marine in an artificial stimulation of a moribund industry. These vital issues are discussed with an acerbity which, as we have seen, is traditional ; and the differences of opinion are acute in the extreme.

I may begin by reviewing the essential facts which are not in dispute. In 1871 (before the United States poured cheap grain into Europe) there were in England and Wales approximately a quarter of a million farmers and a million employees. Two generations later (1931) the number of farmers was unchanged but the number of employees had been halved. The decline in the wage-earning population was due mainly to the replacement of manual labour by machinery and to the conversion of arable land into grass on account of the drastic fall in prices (the arable area diminished from 15 million acres in 1871 to 9 millions in 1938). Subsidiary causes of the rural exodus were the economic opportunities and social amenities of the towns, the lack of cottages, etc. yet the migration from the country was in general compulsory rather than voluntary. An extensive literature has grown up on the present state of British agriculture. Its themes are that the industry is starved of capital owing to the inability of the landlords to keep the land and buildings in good condition ; that small farms prevent the adoption of scientific methods and labour-saving machines ; that there is insufficient specialization of functions, scanty organization on modern business lines, little infusion of new blood (especially men with brains but no capital), and no ladder of opportunity for the labourer on the land. The net result may be expressed by saying that two-thirds of the foodstuffs (in the case of bread four loaves out of five) consumed in this country were not produced here. The diversion of the national resources from agriculture into other channels was dictated by the fact that it was cheaper to import food from abroad in exchange for exports than to grow it at home. In peace-time the nation accepted the situation with equanimity, though in war-time the submarine menace introduced a new and ominous factor. During the second world war it was found necessary to expand arable cultivation by several million acres, and eventually the pre-war output of food supplies was doubled.

We have to make up our minds whether we intend to regard agriculture—as we formerly regarded the woollen industry—in the light of a favourite child of the legislature and shelter it from the fierce blasts of world competition ;

or alternatively to leave it at the mercy of uncontrolled economic forces. If the latter solution is adopted, agriculture may still remain a prosperous industry but it will become a shrinking industry, for the farmers will adjust themselves to economic realities and again lay down millions of acres to grass. The former solution is advocated on grounds of national security by those who believe that good land must not be allowed to go out of cultivation since several years are needed to restore neglected land to fertility. The contention that agriculture should be treated as one of the pillars of national defence has met with criticism. When the question was examined after the first world war it was decided by the responsible authorities that it was the navy's function to safeguard our food supplies, and if the navy lost command of the seas, then all was lost. This view appeared to overlook the necessity of preventing starvation in the event of a temporary stoppage of imports due to the fortunes of war ; moreover the available shipping space might be required for the transport of troops and munitions. In short, all the representations which are advanced during a war to induce farmers to increase home production seem also valid in making preparations against war. Another view holds that the solution of the problem lies in the storage of imported wheat and sugar, etc., rather than in reliance on ' uneconomical production at home '. Over three hundred years ago James I. sought to establish corn magazines on a national scale for ' the well-storing the realm with corn '. The London authorities pointed out the practical difficulties—the expense of erecting granaries and the loss of stored-up grain ' by vermin, shrinking and screening '. To-day we should add the exposure of elevators to air attack. The ' defence ' argument put forward in favour of agriculture is sometimes reinforced by another plea of more doubtful validity. It is alleged that a rural stock is healthier than a town-bred, but the claim is apparently unsupported by statistics ; we cannot therefore assert that an infusion of country blood is necessary to prevent the deterioration of the urban population.

The case against the maintenance of agriculture can be stated briefly. It is detrimental to the principle of international specialization, for it substitutes self-sufficiency in the place of world division of labour ; it is detrimental to our export industries, for if we buy less food we shall sell fewer manufactures ; it is detrimental to our mercantile marine, for there will be fewer imports and exports to be carried across the seas ; it is detrimental to our investments abroad, for the returns from the debtor countries come largely in the form of food ; it is detrimental to the standard of life of the masses, in so far as they may have to pay higher prices for the essentials of life. It must be frankly recognized that an economic loss is incurred when the national resources are employed on less profitable forms of enterprise—raising food at home which can be bought more cheaply abroad. Yet this admission is not decisive provided it is considered advisable on broad national grounds to extend the margin of home-grown foodstuffs. An economic loss, as measured by the criterion of maximum productivity, may be offset by other fundamentals such as national security or the desire to preserve a more balanced and diversified economy. And after all, it cannot be pretended that under the present system all our resources are being used to the best national advantage. Some of the capital and labour now devoted to producing manufactures in exchange for luxuries could be diverted to the land with a certain measure of justification ; moreover there would be a market for our manufactures at our door, since the home producers of food would have greater purchasing power. Quite apart from these general considerations, the case against the maintenance of agriculture is based upon assumptions which are not necessarily tenable. A rise in the price of food can be avoided if state assistance takes the form of subsidies raised from taxation. Even an economic loss in one branch of the national economy can be made good in other branches by improvements in industrial technique, better organization of production, and economies in transport and distribution. Lastly, both financial aid and economic loss may be eliminated altogether if agriculture, while fulfilling the requirements of a strategic economy, could be put on a self-supporting basis.

Agricultural experts are convinced that the land can be made to pay its own way without recourse to either subsidies or tariffs. Subsidies are preferable to tariffs because they do not add to the cost of living when they come out of taxes. It is right that the burden of national defence in all its forms should be borne by the tax-payer ; if a subsidy falls on consumers it will lead to a demand for higher wages, which will be injurious especially to the export industries, and it will necessitate an increase in pensions so that ultimately part of the burden would be shifted to the state. Nevertheless subsidies should be regarded at best as a temporary measure intended to tide over the period of adjustment, for they are attended by serious drawbacks. It is represented that their benefit may not go to the farmer since it is liable to be intercepted by the landlord who increases the rent as soon as an opportunity presents itself ; and also that they perpetuate inefficient methods of farming.

Those who reject subsidies and tariffs as an unsatisfactory solution of the agricultural problem also condemn the policy of ' a closed market ' for wheat with limited supplies and high prices, which curtails the consumption of meat, dairy produce, vegetables and fruit. Instead they advocate abundant supplies and lower prices, which would lead to an improvement in the national health (consequent upon a more varied diet) as well as to an increased use of arable products for animal feeding. To accomplish this, it is proposed in effect to return to the mediaeval system of communal control over the lay-out and exploitation of the land. A reconstruction programme for agriculture, as contemplated in some quarters, provides that the state should acquire the land by purchase—issuing stock on which the interest would be paid out of rents—and furnish the capital for putting it into good condition. The management of the farms would be left to private enterprise under the supervision of a public corporation, which would be responsible for laying out the land and for choosing tenants. The general aim would be the promotion of mechanized farming on the basis of large 'industrialized' farms in preference to small holdings. These proposals raise many controversial issues which cannot be discussed here, but they have at least one merit. They conceive the possibility of making British agriculture self-supporting instead of eleemosynary.

§ 6. *Social Security*

National security constitutes one of the essential planks of a controlled economy: another is social security. The latter implies two things—a minimum standard of living and what is now commonly termed 'full' employment. The drawbacks of free enterprise are the uneven distribution of wealth and the liability to unemployment; and the test of a planned economy will be its ability to remedy these twin defects of the existing order. The ultimate criterion of an economic society is no longer exclusively its maximum productive capacity; it depends also upon the nature of the minimum standards which it prescribes for its members. I have said that the conception of a national minimum of well-being as the inalienable right of every individual was steadily gaining recognition in the closing decades of the nineteenth century. The experience bred of two world wars lies at the root of the demand for a concerted effort to abolish poverty in all its forms, and the time is clearly ripe for the state to assume larger responsibilities in the direction of safeguarding the interests and welfare of the industrial masses. This is not simply a matter of the better distribution of wealth: the removal of the existing inequalities will only partially solve the social problem. The present output of wealth is insufficient to supply the needs of the country as a whole, and one of the purposes of a planned economy is to devise ways and means of increasing production on an adequate scale.

The standard of life of the community was raised between the two world wars, and the improvement was accompanied by a marked decline in the numbers of those whose level of subsistence fell below the ' poverty line ' as defined by social investigators. Unfortunately progress in one direction has been offset by retrogression in another, for in the same period the numbers of those who suffered from unemployment were doubled. The knowledge that for two decades more than a million men and women at a time were unable to find work—and that during the great depression an increase of one hundred per cent. was registered—has deeply coloured public opinion which regards unemployment as the outstanding social evil of our day. And rightly, because continuity of employment is the indispensable basis of a well-ordered society. The authoritarian state of the early seventeenth century insisted on the provision of work for the unemployed : free enterprise preferred relief in the form of ' doles ' as a cheap price to pay for the maintenance of a labour reserve : a democratic society is returning to an older standpoint in its unwillingness to accept ' doles ' as a substitute for work.

Many weighty treatises have been written on the subject of unemployment and the trade cycle. It is not my purpose in this book to examine in detail the various theories favoured by economists nor to review the merits of the panaceas confidently propounded by different schools of thought. An official investigation, which brought together all the relevant economic data set against the historical background, and which elucidated all the possible explanations of the genesis of unemployment and the remedies, would serve at any rate to put the picture in focus and clarify the public mind. Here I may touch upon some general considerations.

Unemployment has been a feature of our national economy since at least the sixteenth century. Its long history serves as a warning against the facile optimism which suggests that there is any ' cure ' known to economists or to anyone else. The problem bristles with complications due to the highly complex nature of the economic system. Nor is the prevalence of unemployment to be attributed solely to the workings of an individualist economy. A certain amount of unemployment would occur in a collectivist economy : the turn-over of labour is stated to be considerable even in Soviet Russia. Spells of unemployment are inseparable from technical progress, from variations in the bounty of nature, from the alternation of the seasons, from the satiability of human wants, from the caprice of human desires, from the interdependence of the various parts of the economic mechanism. This does not mean that unemployment must be tolerated as an inescapable fact, any more than we are now prepared to tolerate war or disease or famine ; but it does mean that it calls for the highest qualities of human organization and perseverance in the effort to circumscribe the scope and mitigate the rigours of a grave social malady.

A distinction needs to be drawn between the immediate post-war situation and the long-term factors. The cessation of war liberates from the services and from a group of industries many millions of men and women who have to regain their former place in the economic order. It may be taken for granted that demobilization will be gradual in order to prevent the labour market from being swamped and to facilitate a smooth process of absorption. Some of the economic consequences of the first world war may be expected to be repeated after the second world war. Certain industries have been expanded to meet war exigencies, and the task of beating swords into ploughshares, in other words, adapting these industries to peace-time requirements, involves painful adjustments. The shortage of raw materials and finished products will inevitably lead to inflated prices and a trade boom (unless the state exercises effective control), followed as inevitably by a slump. The war of 1914–18 provided us with many lessons : these are doubtless being carefully studied. One new feature merits attention. The state is likely in the future to exert a powerful influence both upon the supply of labour and the demand for labour. By maintaining larger armed forces and instituting a term of training, it will diminish the supply of labour ; by its equipment of the three services it will increase the demand for labour ; thus it will help to bridge the gap between the one and the other, a process which would be assisted by raising the school-leaving age and by lowering the pensions age. The rebuilding of the mercantile marine, the restoration of devastated areas, urban and rural housing, roads, etc. should also serve to open up many avenues to employment and to tide over the period of transition from a war to a peace economy. The distribution of ' post-war credits ' earmarked for income-tax payers will doubtless be timed to take place when trade begins to slacken : this will avoid the danger of inflation which might occur if the purchasing power of the community were expanded while there remained a serious deficiency of commodities.

After the legacies bequeathed by the war have been liquidated, we shall still be confronted with the normal problem of unemployment, whose incidence may be the more severe because of the cataclysmic disturbances in the economic world. To see the problem in its true proportions, we must notice the different kinds of unemployment. Some are inherent in the industrial system. Whatever the organization of society it could not escape fluctuations in foreign trade due to circumstances over which the home government could have no control. Similarly domestic trade is exposed to fluctuations consequent upon changes in fashion, intermittent supplies of raw materials, the extended use of machinery, alterations in processes, and so on. Moreover many trades are seasonal in character : there are always times in the year when some trades are busy and others are slack. Yet one important cause of unemployment proceeds directly from a capitalist regime. Instead of a single employer Great Britain has an indefinite number, and the demand of each employer for labour is never fixed —it keeps expanding or contracting. This irregularity makes unemployment inevitable, for the lack of co-ordination spells lack of stability. The practice of short-term engagements introduces another element of insecurity. It will be recalled that in the middle ages it was usual to engage workmen for long periods—sometimes for three or four years: in the Yorkshire textile industry it was not uncommon, down to the nineteenth century, to hire journeymen for twelve months: in agriculture the custom of annual hirings still persists in parts of the country. Nowadays in general a wage-earner is taken on for the shortest possible period: he is usually employed by the week or by the day or for a single job. It is impossible to measure precisely the loss of stability which the existing system involves, but it means that the workers are always face to face with the menace of unemployment, and the effects are demoralizing.

The ordinary phenomena of unemployment do not attract much attention. The ebb and flow of labour due to variations in fashion, seasonal fluctuations and want of co-ordination among employers, appear an inseparable feature of the industrial order. In vivid contrast the phenomenon of a ‘special area’ or of a general depression seizes upon the popular imagination. The former is the result of structural changes in industry. The latter is the outcome of the trade cycle, the alternation of booms and slumps, whose influence is not restricted to a single industry or group of industries but is widespread.

Structural changes in industry are in constant operation: they are caused by new methods of production or by loss of markets. Thus in the course of the last century the handicrafts were virtually extinguished by the competition of machinery; and between the two world wars the export industries (textiles, coal, etc.) underwent a considerable contraction. Again in agriculture, where the short-term liability to unemployment is less than in manufactures, there is a long-term liability due to mechanization or alteration of processes such as laying down land to grass. An economic system dominated by free enterprise is necessarily in a perpetual state of flux. The individual branches of industry are always growing or shrinking, often to the accompaniment of much social distress—though the manner in which collectivist farming was instituted in Soviet Russia shows that a planned economy can be more ruthless than competitive forces. Long-term trends in industry cannot be arrested except by stultifying economic progress, yet the harmful effects of short-term oscillations can be partially neutralized provided measures are taken in time to check excessive dislocation. The economist's ideal of highly mobile labour, which moves freely about the country from declining to expanding industries, represents a hypothetical condition which in fact is only slowly realized ; nevertheless industrial training should be developed on lines which will facilitate the more rapid transference of labour from one occupation to another. It must be remembered, however, that (in the words of Adam Smith) " man is of all baggage the most difficult to be transported ". The shortage of housing accommodation combines with attachment to local ties and with inertia to keep the unemployed from migrating to other localities. A partial remedy may be found in bringing light industries into the regions where the staple industries are in a state of decline : at present new industries tend to gravitate to the more prosperous areas. An Industrial Development Board could control the location of industries with a view to assure a more even distribution of the nation's resources. A historical precedent points the way. Towards the end of the sixteenth century some of the older centres of the woollen manufacture (for instance, York), which had begun to decay, endeavoured to set up fresh industries by inviting entrepreneurs to settle in their midst on favourable terms. It is on these lines—increased mobility of labour and the introduction of alternative occupations—that the problem of the declining industries can perhaps best be handled. The more usual method of working short-time in order to spread a limited amount of work over a larger number keeps the redundant labour where it is no longer needed and lowers the level of earnings.

Cyclical fluctuations, more commonly termed the trade

cycle, are as old as the industrial system itself. Current discussions are mainly centred on this source of unemployment largely because the great depression of 1929–33, like a memorable earthquake, will be long remembered until it is eclipsed by a successor of similar or even greater magnitude. Not all commercial crises occur on so impressive a scale, yet the regularity with which booms and slumps alternate is viewed both as an indictment of free enterprise and as a challenge to man's powers of organization. Instead of a continuous flow of goods and services economic activity assumes an intermittent aspect and proceeds by spurts followed by periods of slackness. The regularity of the phenomenon is one of its features : another is its wide range. A crisis spreads swiftly like an all-devouring fire from industry to industry and from country to country : starting like a cloud no bigger than a man's hand it eventually covers the sky and blots out the landscape. Its catastrophic character is generally attributed to the waning of business confidence. Apprehension that their turn may come next induces entrepreneurs to reduce their commitments and throw their stocks on the market. The consequent fall in prices leads buyers of materials and finished products to delay their purchases until prices appear to have reached bedrock. Many undertakings are able to finance themselves ; in their case profit deflation need not curtail enterprise if the loss is distributed over a large number of shareholders or if they can draw upon reserves ; and though the general rate of profit declines, the rate in particular industries may still prove attractive. Other business concerns, however, rely upon advances made by the banks and their position rapidly deteriorates when the banks under the spur of falling prices begin to call in their loans.

A favourite explanation of the trade cycle ascribes it to psychological causes. The governing factor is considered to be the fallibility of the judgment of business men, who alternate between errors of optimism and errors of pessimism involving over-production and under-production. When trade is brisk, producers are eager to make hay so long as the sun shines but they have no means of gauging the extent or duration of the market, nor do they know what preparations are being made by their competitors. When the boom is halted, buoyancy swiftly succumbs to panic until eventually demand once more revives. This theory is criticized on the ground that even if the judgment of entrepreneurs were never at fault, it would not prevent cyclical disturbances. Nevertheless, while it may not explain the origin of the trade cycle, the 'state of mind' of the business community manifestly cannot be ignored in view of the fact that industry and commerce are conducted by private enterprise. The conclusion may be fairly drawn that the 'herd' instinct of business men provides a very unstable basis for an ordered economic society. The necessary correctives may be found in the formulation of a long-term programme, together with the accumulation of statistical data on actual stocks, current production and potential needs. With their aid speculative guessing in business activities may yield place to more scientific methods of appraising the nature and extent of the market.

Another hypothesis lays stress upon the monetary element in the trade cycle: variations in prices are held responsible for variations in the volume of production. During a boom capital investment (that is, the creation of producers' goods which are used to create or transfer consumers' goods) may be stimulated in excess of savings (which represent the surplus of income over expenditure and are embodied in bank balances of individuals, company reserves, etc.) by means of credit expansion (bank loans). This is one form of 'over-investment', which occurs when people—instead of diverting a sufficient part of their income into the channels of savings—continue to expend freely at the same time as the constructional industries embark on a large spending programme financed by bank credit. The consequent growth in the community's purchasing power produces inflation, which occurs when money increases faster than the supply of commodities. (In the second world war state expenditure developed enormously, but excessive inflation was avoided since the community abstained from consumption on a pre-war standard and transferred a substantial portion of its purchasing power to the government in the shape of taxes or loans [1].) Inflation causes a rise in prices, which at first swells profits and so encourages production [2], until the upward turn of wages leads to a further advance in prices; demand then begins to fall off, production shrinks, and the credit system is contracted. The chain of interlocking movements constitutes the trade cycle. Hence the proposal is made for a monetary system which is immune from short-term disturbances in the value of money, though not from long-term trends as reflected in a gradual rise or fall in the general level of prices. Admittedly an increase in the volume of purchasing power affects the price level, but the monetary explanation serves to show what may happen during a trade cycle rather than what actually generates it. Nor in any event is it certain that, if savings were adequate to provide for capital investment without any danger of inflation, industrial fluctuations would thereby be avoided.

A much-debated theory of the trade cycle finds the root of the evil in under-consumption. People do not spend enough on consumers' goods either because they lack purchasing power or because they save more than is really needed for the accumulation of capital. The deficiency in the community's demand for consumers' goods (which means less employment) is not repaired by an additional outlay on producers' goods, for the latter are ultimately dependent on the former. Accordingly the motive for capital investment is weakened, and the volume of labour in the constructional industries—building, engineering, iron

[1] In the later years of the second world war about one-half of the government expenditure was covered by taxation, as compared with one-quarter in the first world war.

[2] During the period of industrial adjustment prices may rise even though the output of commodities is increased. Ultimately prices fall provided the costs of production per unit are reduced and competition is effective. The reason why prices did not rise during the boom of 1925–29 is that there was a world recession from the high level of 1920 and but for the boom this recession would have been more pronounced.

and steel, etc.—is reduced below the proper level to maintain 'full' employment. In short the effect of under-consumption, whether it is due to inadequacy of income or excess of savings, is to discourage the steady flow of capital equipment. (It may, of course, happen on occasion that owing to lack of foresight some entrepreneurs misjudge the situation and produce new capital goods which are relatively excessive. This helps to create the phenomena of 'over-production', which may also arise if the normal demand for consumers' goods falls off for any reason.) Historical support may be adduced for the view that, as a general practice, expenditure on capital equipment presupposes 'effective demand', that is, willingness and ability on the part of the consumers to purchase what is produced. One main reason why the 'Industrial Revolution' came first to England was that the general diffusion of purchasing power supplied the inducement to invest capital in factories and machinery.

Two different schools of thought have propounded remedies. One school proposes to bridge the gap between the consumers' purchasing power and the community's productive capacity by expanding the former. In this connexion ingenious schemes have been framed which are not easily distinguishable from an inflation of the currency. It is certainly important that, particularly in a depression when the gap is widened since many more people are out of work, measures should be adopted to support the purchasing power of the unemployed. It is the volume of consumption that determines the volume of capital investment, and a decline in the demand for consumers' goods involves a decline in the demand for producers' goods. The other school approaches the problem from the opposite angle. Instead of increasing directly the expenditure on consumers' goods, which would presumably necessitate a state subvention, it advocates an increase of capital equipment. The latter (runs the argument) can be taken in hand just as occasion requires; indirectly, by what is termed the 'multiplier', it enlarges the volume of consumption;

and it may not necessitate a state subvention. The call is therefore made for an investment policy which will promote a regular instead of an intermittent demand for producers' goods, and so ensure steady employment and earnings and in consequence a stable demand for consumers' goods. To check cyclical fluctuations, the expenditure of the community needs to be distributed in given proportions between capital investment and consumption. There must be sufficient saving—that is, abstention from consumption—to create an adequate supply of capital goods ; and there must be sufficient consumption to create an adequate demand for capital goods. One of the functions of a planned economy would be to establish the true balance between capital investment and consumption, and determine (the crux of the problem) what must be considered disproportionate. Then in accordance with its findings it would regulate the volume and character of capital investment, which at present are largely shaped by casual influences.

All the various theories of the trade cycle contain elements of the truth : each draws attention to some factor which affects the course of its development. If we seek to ascertain the primary influence which gives rise to the trade cycle, it is perhaps to be found simply in the fact already stated that in a progressive community the volume of economic activity is not constant but expands and contracts in a sort of rhythm. After a spurt of energy to meet a new demand there is naturally a pause until a fresh demand arises. We tend to think of progress as a continuous process : if we take a long-term view this is doubtless true, but over a short period the reverse is true. It works up to a climax, loses its original momentum, precipitately declines, then starts all over again. Thus there was a boom in the cotton industry when machinery was invented, in the railways when the steam engine was introduced, in the automobile industry when the internal combustion engine was adopted, and in the case of other large industrial projects. In an individualist society the periodical recurrence of phases of stimulated activity followed by quiescence is inevitable, unless some corrective is applied through the instrumentality of a planned economy in order to make the road more level with fewer sharp gradients.

The state cannot afford to hold itself aloof from the problem of unemployment. Apart from humanitarian considerations, its intervention can be justified on economic grounds. It is as wasteful to allow the capital invested in human beings—their technical skill and physical qualities—to deteriorate, as it is to neglect the up-keep of factories and machinery. Moreover unemployment in restricting the purchasing power of those out of work affects the industries which cater for immediate consumption and eventually the constructional industries. The state can appropriately apply remedies, because in a slump private enterprise contracts its operations and therefore needs to be supplemented by collective agencies which may serve to keep the wheels of trade in motion.

Several ways are open to a government which seeks to avert a trade depression or to mitigate its severity. It can come to the rescue of private enterprise, yet here the utmost caution must be exercised lest harmful consequences ensue from ill-advised methods of assistance. In particular we should reject a short-sighted policy which militates against the interests of other nations. The principle is fundamental that whatever is detrimental to the world economy must in the long run react adversely upon our own situation. The imposition of tariffs, the institution of 'quotas', the provision of subsidies on exports, the manipulation of the monetary exchanges, are all measures which are injurious to other countries, breed resentment and invite retaliation. However some forms of subsidies do not come within this category, though they are liable to put a premium on inefficiency. Similarly loans on favourable terms and export guarantees may be useful in appropriate cases. The government could help trade and industry by a more flexible mechanism of taxation which lightened the burden on the tax-payer in times of depression and increased it in times of prosperity.

If the surpluses of ' the fat years ' were utilized to meet the deficits of ' the lean years ', the fiscal system could be made into a valuable instrument for correcting the maladjustments produced by the alternation of booms and slumps. Relief in taxation in a depression would not only encourage enterprise but also sustain the consumers' purchasing power; in addition the latter should be supported by adequate grants of unemployment benefits and perhaps by ' instalment buying ' [1]. Propaganda for thrift and economy in a slump is a mistake—the public should be encouraged to spend more freely when trade is declining and to curb expenditure when trade is booming.

In the search for a solution of the problem of unemployment, other possibilities of state action have been widely canvassed—especially an extension of the market through the medium of credit expansion and low rates of interest. It is believed that the trade cycle can be controlled by manipulating the terms and facilities of borrowing. Merchants are enabled to hold larger stocks when the rate of interest falls: manufacturers are enabled to broaden the scale of their operations when the volume of credit expands. The policy of ' cheap money ' was tried during the great depression. The bank rate (discount rate) which in previous years had been 4 to 5 per cent. fell in 1932 to 2 per cent. and remained at this level, but the assumption that the reduction was a primary cause of revival is debatable: recovery in general was tardy and governed by world factors. The influence of the bank rate as an instrument for smoothing out industrial fluctuations is liable to be over-stressed. For one thing, the rate of interest at which industry is financed by the joint-stock banks does not fall (except by special arrangement) below 5 per cent. In a boom high money rates do not deter producers unless they swallow up all expectations of profit—though manufacturers will suffer if an increase in bank charges leads traders to

[1] There are proposals for ' consumers' credit '. The term is variously interpreted but is understood to cover a direct money subsidy to the consumer.

hold smaller stocks and limit their orders to their immediate requirements. In a slump low money rates do not attract producers unless there is general business confidence that prices have touched bedrock and are on the upward grade. Entrepreneurs are concerned with prospective costs. Their problem is to determine whether, if they enter now into fresh commitments, their costs will be higher or lower than those of their competitors. Accordingly they react quickly in a boom and slowly in a slump. Cheap credit doubtless makes it easier for merchants and manufacturers to take fuller advantage of a revival of trade, but banking policy does not appear to be the mainspring of recovery. Indeed it is normal for rates of interest to decline in the course of a slump, since the demand for capital is less than the supply. Confident assertions that unemployment can be cured by the creation of credit overlook the fact that the willingness to lend must be reciprocated by the willingness to borrow. Moreover one may question the soundness of a policy which relies upon successive doses of fresh credit to keep the industrial mechanism in motion [1].

Discussions on credit turn largely on the rate of interest; but there is another aspect which has been ignored. It is imperative not to discourage necessary enterprises by 'dear money' during a boom (incidentally it may provoke the slump). The proper method of preventing misdirected investment—that is, a redundancy of investments in a particular sphere—is not to impose a heavy burden on all investments alike but to apply discriminatory measures. At present the banks in lending money are guided largely by the financial standing of their customers rather than by the suitability of further investments in certain directions. The chief executives doubtless receive periodical statements of the amounts loaned to each industry, and doubtless also information is disseminated informally among the banks, yet apparently there is no machinery which operates from

[1] A delegate to the World Conference of 1933 asked: if low prices are due to excess of capital equipment, how will an increase of equipment by credit expansion help?

day to day. Furthermore banks are commercial institutions, and it is natural that they should wish to lend freely during a boom, especially if they have to recoup themselves for losses sustained during a depression. Thus, without superseding the private banks, there appears to be a need for a national authority which not alone regulated the volume of credit—as is now done by the Treasury and the Bank of England—but also determined its general distribution among competing claimants in accordance with the genuine requirements of industry and trade. One may envisage the possibility that capital investment will be brought under control not by raising either the price of money or the price of commodities but by the rationing of constructional materials. This is an instrument by which the state can ensure an economical use of the national resources as well as a more even flow of goods and services.

The state can make a contribution to the prevention or alleviation of unemployment not only indirectly by stimulating private enterprise but directly by its own expenditure. Here a distinction must be drawn between relief works and public works. Relief works are intended specifically to find jobs for the unemployed. The Unemployment Grants Committee frames schemes of which their usefulness is not the primary consideration—just as in the eighteenth century destitute weavers might be put to stone-breaking merely to keep them occupied. Public works are undertaken by the central government, local authorities and 'public utility' bodies in connexion with the services for which they are responsible. The category of public works covers a wide field, for it embraces water, gas, electricity, railways, roads, harbours, housing, schools, libraries, the post office, the maintenance of the public health, the requirements of the armed forces, and the rest. Public works, unlike relief works, are not an alternative to relief in money ; nor is there any employment of the unemployed as such, because they are carried out in the ordinary way. They embody vital needs which have to be met in any event ; but if (so far as is practicable) they were taken in hand when trade was slack they would help to steady both the volume of activity in the constructional industries and the labour market itself. The Minority Report of the Poor Law Commission of 1909 proposed that the government should regularize the aggregate demand for labour over a long period by a more deliberate arrangement of its orders for work of a capital nature. A public investment policy may not achieve all that is claimed for it yet it fills a gap, while its influence on morale is likely to prove considerable. It may serve to counteract the paralyzing tendency of a Micawber-like philosophy. Instead of 'waiting for something to turn up' the community is in a position to attempt some measure of self-help. Moreover the effectiveness of a public investment policy would be immensely strengthened if it were reinforced by a private investment policy (mentioned above) designed to regularize the demand of individual entrepreneurs for capital goods. Nevertheless the constructional industries cannot be expanded beyond the normal requirements of the community if an excess of productive capacity and economic wastage is to be avoided: a balance must be preserved between producers' goods and consumers' goods. In order to maintain employment among the workers engaged in industries which cater for general consumption, it may even be found expedient for the public authorities to buy consumers' goods during a crisis, and either distribute them to the necessitous or gradually release them as demand revives.

Experience will doubtless demonstrate that a combination of remedies is required to cope adequately with an emergency. Yet whatever the methods adopted by the state, it is imperative that intervention should not be delayed. To postpone action until the depression is well under way is to reduce almost to vanishing point the chances of its being effective. A depression is like a fever: once it has gained a real hold it must take its course. Promptitude in applying appropriate remedies before business confidence is destroyed, and the situation has passed beyond control, is the essential condition of success. On this account the careful preparation of plans in advance, and the accumulation of data to furnish a sound basis for exact timing, merit a leading place in the programme of a planned economy. It must be recognized, however, that the working out of a complete policy to control the trade cycle will involve virtual control of the economic mechanism.

§ 7. *Other Aims of Reconstruction*

Although the defence of the homeland and social security are the most insistent of our problems, they must not be allowed to obscure other important issues—for a planned economy should take into its purview all facets of the national life. The housing of the people constitutes one of the leading planks in any reconstruction programme, since it is incumbent upon the state to mould the environment which will make possible a healthy and vigorous community. It is not enough to remedy the shortage of houses : it is not enough to clear away the slums that have been left too long to adorn the perorations of platform speakers. Our towns have grown monstrous in size, but overcrowding is the legacy of conditions which happily no longer exist. The dispersion of industry is now made feasible by electrification : a wider distribution of the population is facilitated by light railways and motor transport. The chairman of one of the most progressive enterprises in this country, alluding to the view that the creation of derelict districts is the greatest crime of capitalism, has recommended that no factory of any kind be started anywhere without government permission—on the ground that the responsibility of forecasting future development for generations ahead is too serious to be left to entrepreneurs. I have drawn attention to the outstanding merit of the older industrial system that it was not concentrated in urban areas ; and we have it once again in our power to ensure, by controlling the location of industries, that the coming generations shall grow up in healthy surroundings instead of in depressing streets and wretched ' homes '. The ravages of illness and disease may then be greatly circumscribed. In the early days our fields and meadows were laid out by communal agreement : here is a precedent for town-planning schemes under which our manufacturing and mining towns may be redeemed from the ugliness which makes them disfiguring scars upon a fair landscape.

Another vital issue is education. If ever we yield place to other nations in the capacity for leadership, it will be to those better educated than our own. We still stand upon the threshold of the Promised Land in which the English genius may find its fullest expression, because our educational system lags behind the national needs. In view of the demands of modern industry, we have to face the question whether technical education should be made compulsory as formerly under the apprenticeship system ; and whether some official direction is requisite to promote the flow of labour into industries wanting skilled workers, a flow which is at present haphazard and casual. In view of the fact that we are a democracy, we have to face the question how far education should be concerned with cultural values and not merely with utilitarian values as measured by the power to earn a livelihood. Fundamentally these two aims are not incompatible since modern industrial technique as well as the administrative side of business enterprise call for a flexible habit of mind and ability to turn readily to other processes, and these qualities are stimulated by an education on broad lines. We can perhaps best define the purpose of education by saying that it is intended to form character, develop the intellectual faculties, lay the basis for vocational instruction, and create an intelligent interest in public affairs. A lesson may be drawn from the past, for the institution of mediaeval apprenticeship had a twofold aspect as a system of social training and a system of technical training. Yet the expenditure lavished upon education of the mind will be largely wasted if it is not accompanied by attention to the body. I have little doubt that the day will come when children will be the nation's care, and the state will assume responsibility for the child from birth (and by making provision for expectant mothers, even before birth) to adolescence in respect of medical requirements, nutrition, clothing and recreation in addition to education. Parental responsibility, relieved of financial anxieties, need not cease to be any the less a formative influence in the child's life.

There are many desiderata of a planned economy to which I can only make the briefest reference. A long-term view of national development must take account of population trends, which raise a question of far-reaching significance. The rapid expansion of population in the nineteenth century was one of the outstanding factors in the growth of industry. A stationary or declining population will affect both the supply of labour and the character of the market. Automatic machinery may overcome the shortage of labour; and a higher and more diversified standard of living may compensate for a contraction in the demand for necessaries. In this connexion it is worth while to remark that there is room for considerable improvement in the statistics of infantile mortality. Again there is urgent need to frame a comprehensive labour policy in which wages, participation in control, social security, hours of work and holidays will no longer be treated in a piecemeal fashion but will constitute integral elements in a charter of labour rights. The importance of effecting substantial economies in the distributive trades and in transport must not be overlooked, for they would materially lower the cost of living. The relation of finance to industry, the safeguarding of standards of quality (a return in principle to an older standpoint), and the adoption of measures to prevent the stifling of inventions, are among the other numerous issues which would find their place in a comprehensive treatment of our national problems.

In co-ordinating these various postulates of a planned economy in a general scheme, a realistic approach to our task may offset a certain loss in symmetry and idealism. Yet the crucial gauge of a planned economy will not be its basic principles—on which agreement is not improbable—

but their practical application. And here one thing can be said with confidence. No reconstruction programme can be constructed on a *tabula rasa* or blank surface : if it is to survive as something more than a paper programme, it must harmonize the traditional forces which have moulded economic life with the changing needs of a virile community and the demands of an awakened social conscience. A planned economy will also need to satisfy other requirements. While it must lay down guiding principles and the broad method of giving effect to them, it must be fluid in the working out of its details or it will inevitably break down. Flexibility is essential since a nation is a living organism, and rigid schemes springing from the brains of experts will eventually stifle progress. Yet at the same time it must not be opportunist in its fundamentals, for a plethora of 'ad hoc' measures to suit particular occasions will produce a fatal jumble of conflicting devices.

§ 8. *Commercial Policy*

I have shown in the previous chapter how Great Britain developed a tendency as a result of the great depression to model her commercial policy upon that of her neighbours. Tariffs, 'quotas', bilateral treaties and currency manipulation figured among the continental practices which were imported wholesale into her economic system. In the shaping of our future policy we should be guided by the long-term factors of our national development and reject a slavish adherence to the fashionable economic nostrums of the day. We adopted free trade in the nineteenth century not in imitation of other countries but because it suited our interests. We should retain it—or as much of it as is practicable in present circumstances since vested interests have grown up under the protection of tariffs—irrespective of the policy pursued elsewhere if on balance it still suits our interests. These interests are complex, and their scope extends far beyond the benefits which protection may confer on particular industries. First and foremost Great Britain is vitally dependent upon the maintenance of a world economy functioning in conditions of the utmost freedom. Economic isolation is as impracticable for her as political isolation. Four loaves out of five came from abroad to feed her industrial population, together with many other foodstuffs and indispensable raw materials. They were largely paid for by her carrying trade, her entrepôt trade, her investments, and her banking and insurance services overseas—all of which are jeopardized by the modern trend towards economic nationalism. The words of Charles Davenant, written two hundred and fifty years ago, have not lost one single grain of their profound truth : " England never throve by trade but while she was an universal merchant ". The common view of world trade as a feverish scramble for markets can perhaps be applied to the years of the great depression, but it hardly represents normal conditions. What can scarcely be questioned is the fact that a wide range of markets abroad makes for stability inasmuch as it offers compensatory factors if any one market declines. And there is a non-economic consideration which ought to influence our economic relations with other states. As a world power Great Britain cannot afford to adopt racial discrimination, religious discrimination, or economic discrimination. Her international and imperial status imposes upon her the obligation to set a standard to those countries which have learnt to look to this island for leadership and inspiration; the obligation to avoid measures which militate against the ' good neighbour ' policy ; and the obligation to facilitate access to the world's raw materials of which she controls a considerable portion.

In discussions of our commercial policy the traditional fear of imports is certain to become articulate. Actually from the point of view of the producer it is immaterial whether the demand for his wares suffers from a change of fashion, a new process, under-selling by a native rival, or imports. There is no difference, so far as he is concerned, between foreign and domestic competition ; yet it would scarcely be proposed that both forms of competition should be prevented in order to safeguard his business. If an enterprise, in which a substantial amount of fixed capital is invested, may claim the exclusion of cheap imports, it can on like grounds buy up and stifle inventions that might depreciate the value of an existing undertaking. In the long run a nation which pursues these tactics will stagnate, for they are applicable to all new developments. Moreover in so far as a reduction of imports results in a reduction of exports, it follows that protection is afforded to one set of producers (the domestic industries) against another set (the export industries). Eventually the latter will be forced to compete against the former by invading the home market ; and in any case they are bound to curtail their own purchases from the accessory industries at home. Furthermore a tariff on imports increases their cost to the industries which consume them. It must not be forgotten, also, that if we resent the competition of foreign goods other states will resent our competition, and on balance we shall be the poorer. Finally a word may be said about the familiar argument that manufacturers should be protected by 'scientific' tariffs against the 'unfair competition' of nations whose wages and other costs of production are on a lower level. International specialization exists precisely owing to varying costs of production in different territories. If they were identical everywhere there would be no motive for international trade except in certain natural products. Apart from the latter, we buy imported goods because they are cheaper in price or better in quality than those made at home. If the United States is protected against the 'pauper labour' of Europe, and Great Britain is protected against the lower wage-levels of her best markets, there will be few countries left in the world with which to trade. Ardent supporters of commercial restrictions lose sight of the fact which goes to the root of the whole controversy over imports—that imports are paid for by exports (merchandise and services), unless they constitute the proceeds of capital assets abroad.

I have indicated some of the general considerations which

should govern our future trade policy, but in addition there is a financial problem—we must find the means of payment for the commodities which we receive from abroad. In Great Britain's international balance-sheet her income is represented by visible exports (commodities) and invisible exports (services). How far will these sources, on a long view, enable us to support our normal standard of living?

Our export industries are affected by structural changes due to industrialization and population trends abroad. Countries which raise primary products (foodstuffs and raw materials) have learnt to engage in manufactures; and Lancashire, in particular, has suffered from the growth of the cotton industry in India and Japan. Several factors combined to bring about this important transformation, which is having a profound effect upon the basic export industries of Great Britain and is fast destroying the unique position which they once enjoyed in world trade. During the first world war our inability to supply our oversea markets led other nations to start their own manufactures. Although war furnished the stimulus, it was a natural evolution since all communities begin with primary products and then advance to the next stage. In recent years the process of industrialization has been accelerated owing to—the desire to absorb the surplus of population released from the soil by the mechanization of agriculture and retained in the homeland by the obstacles to emigration; the effort to attain the higher standard of living associated with an urban economy; the promotion of heavy industries in order to provide the armaments needed in war; the fall in the prices of foodstuffs and raw materials as a result of the agricultural revolution, which diminishes the ability of the states affected by it to buy foreign manufactures; the protection given to European agriculture, which restricts the market for oversea produce; and finally the dissemination of technical knowledge, which facilitates the erection of industries in the backward territories (of this Russia is the outstanding example).

These developments have proved detrimental to our export industries, where large capital structures and specialized labour forces cannot overnight adjust themselves to a new situation. However, if the long-term consequences are analysed, the prospects are not discouraging. The industrialization of agricultural countries will lessen their importation of the simpler products (for instance, cotton goods), but their increased wealth will eventually react favourably on the older communities in providing the latter with markets for the highly-technical products. Even in the nineteenth century industrialized nations carried on more trade with each other than with agricultural nations. As the standard of life rises throughout the world, the demand will inevitably grow for expensive consumers' goods (automobiles, etc.), which the advanced countries are best equipped to supply owing to their technical competence and efficient organization. In addition the backward countries will need producers' goods (machinery, etc.) for their local industries. This involves a change in the industrial structure of the advanced countries—that is, a change in the nature of their products—yet not necessarily a decline in the volume of their production as a whole. I think that we can look forward with reasonable confidence to an increase in world trade on the assumptions that narrow restrictive policies do not hamstring the international exchanges of goods and services, and that not only war but even the fear of war is effectively exorcized. On these assumptions, which must not be taken for granted, the question naturally arises as to how Great Britain may hope to ensure a fair share of world trade.

I shall begin by specifying five unsound methods of stimulating commodity exports, which run counter to all the lessons of history. The first is the reduction of wage rates. If we turn the export industries into 'sweated industries', we shall repeat the mistake which formerly tolerated 'sweating' in tailoring and other occupations. We shall put a premium on the adherence to inefficient and obsolete practices in the spheres of production and marketing ; while other states will either follow suit or subsidize their exports. The notion inspired by Japanese competition, that it is possible to capture the markets of the world on the basis of cheap labour, terrifies the West but is purely chimerical. A community which exports largely must import largely because its purchasing power increases and its standard of life improves [1]. Labour unrest then begins to drive up wages—Japan was not free from communist agitation in the thirties, which was the reflex of unsatisfactory economic conditions that could not have persisted indefinitely on a rising tide of prosperity. The second method is currency depreciation, and the third is the grant of a bounty or subsidy on exports—both arouse resentment, invite retaliation, and at best can only confer temporary advantages. The fourth method is bilateral bargaining, which endeavours to force the sale of our goods abroad by balancing exports and imports with every state with which we trade. I have described the injurious effects of this system, and here it is only necessary to say that in the long run whatever diminishes the elasticity of trade must inevitably diminish its volume. The fifth method is an indiscriminating assimilation of American technique. The United States has a home market three times as great as our own ; her population drawn from every part of the globe is responsive to scientific management and other devices of increased production ; her entrepreneurs are encouraged by the extent of the market and the flexibility of the workers to scrap machinery long before it is worn out and to introduce the latest mechanical appliances ; for these various reasons she is adapted for the mass production of cheap commodities. Great Britain leads the world in certain specialized products which require craftsmanship of a high order. She should not sacrifice the benefits which she enjoys from the traditional skill of her artisans by competing in a field where she does not possess the same unique advantages. And the more

[1] If a low-wage country refused payment in goods, it must take gold, and this will raise prices and eventually wages.

prosperous the world grows the more it will desire articles of superior workmanship. Accordingly Great Britain should concentrate her energies and resources on quality goods in preference to cheapness [1].

It is not by reliance upon low wages, currency manipulation, subsidies, bilateralism or mass production that we can re-establish our oversea trade on a firm basis, but rather by the promotion of new industries to meet the changing demands of the international market. The crisis through which the basic export industries passed between the two world wars has its parallel in the situation which existed in the early nineteenth century when the growth of machinery displaced the handicrafts. A mistaken policy of submitting to repeated reductions of wages in the vain hope of averting their doom postponed, though it could not prevent, the ultimate extinction of the handicrafts, and it was responsible for one of the most tragic episodes in our social history. The long-drawn-out sufferings of the handloom weavers afford a classic example of the folly which persists in a refusal to make the adjustments necessitated by economic progress. Incidentally the need for adjustments is strengthened by population trends to which I have alluded. In the nineteenth century, when population was growing rapidly, entrepreneurs could look forward to an ever-increasing demand for machine-made products of the simplest type: now, with the prospect of a stationary or declining population, a higher standard of life with more complex wants ought to be developed in order to provide another outlet for surplus activities. Far-sighted planning should recognize betimes the shift which is taking place in world trade, and encourage the transference of redundant capital and labour from the older industries into fresh and more productive channels. The growth of new industries as well as the maintenance of the established industries call for ingenuity and enterprise—qualities in which Great Britain is not

[1] The United States (where 'ring' spindles are mainly used) imports the higher grades of yarn and cloth (the product of 'mule' spindles) from Great Britain.

deficient—coupled with the harnessing of science in the service of industry ; but they also require the creation of economic units of production (in which efficiency of organization may compensate for high money wages), greater adaptability in supplying the requirements of oversea markets, and less obtuse methods of selling goods abroad. In this connexion I may refer to the report of the Sheffield Industrial Mission which undertook a market investigation under the auspices of the Overseas Trade Development Council. The mission, which visited South America in 1930, stated that Sheffield had lost the trade there owing to general neglect of the market; for instance, failure to appoint representatives or to offer convenient terms of payment or to issue catalogues in the language of the country. The government can assist the export trade not only by a negative policy—the avoidance of measures which have a restrictive influence on trade—but by a positive policy which manifests itself in practical ways. These include the provision of commercial credits, insurance against risks, detailed information on the state and prospects of trade, and (most important of all) the encouragement of scientific and technical research. Moreover the volume of world trade is ultimately determined by the prosperity of the domestic trades ; it therefore follows that government action to prevent depression at home ought to have beneficial repercussions upon the international situation.

Visible exports are supplemented by invisible exports, which make a substantial contribution to our national income. Let us look at our international accounts on the eve of the second world war. In 1938 the value of our retained imports amounted to £860 millions of which half represented food, drink and tobacco, one-quarter raw materials and articles mainly unmanufactured, and one-quarter articles wholly or mainly manufactured. The value of our produce and manufactures exported abroad amounted to £470 millions of which one-half went to British and the other half to foreign countries. The gap of £390 millions was bridged by oversea investments (£200 millions), shipping (£100 millions), banking and insurance services (£35 millions), and the realization of capital assets abroad (£55 millions). We may expect considerable changes in the coming years. It is impossible to estimate at the moment the value of our oversea investments, but it is known that the second world war has necessitated a very large 'disinvestment' (that is, sales of investments) which—apart from accumulated external liabilities—accounts for over one-quarter of the pre-war total. To measure the effect on our income we must allow for the possibility that our surviving assets may furnish larger dividends if post-war reconstruction brings prosperity to particular industries or public utilities. The losses of our mercantile marine can eventually be made good, and shipping freights will doubtless rise in consequence of the increased volume of the carrying trade, though as the demand slackens they will presumably fall again. The London money market is likely to retain its position owing to its unique experience of world conditions, and insurance and banking services should be well maintained. The prospects of diminishing our retained imports are not very rosy, for as already noticed food, drink, tobacco and raw materials comprise three-quarters of the whole (and some of the raw materials are used by the export industries)—indeed a boom in industrial activity would stimulate the demand for imports. As a partial solution we could doubtless raise more foodstuffs at home ; but this will affect our exports, since if we buy less from other countries their power to buy from us is impaired, and our carrying trade will also suffer. To liquidate debit balances, we are confronted with the alternatives of selling our remaining oversea investments or expanding our commodity exports. If the excesses of a boom can be avoided, and if the leaders of the export industries display energy, imagination and flexibility, there is no reason why we should not play an active part in meeting the needs of a world impoverished by war.

§ 9. *Machinery of a Planned Economy*

A planned economy, in these days of a highly complex economic system, presupposes the existence of a body of experts or planning commission, charged with the duty of laying down the general lines of policy and framing four or five-year ' reconstruction ' plans. Its scope would include the following—(1) to ensure that the resources of the country were directed into the channels best calculated to promote the national welfare—in this sense production would be for ' use ' and not for ' profit ' ; (2) to fulfil the requirements of national security especially as regards agriculture and ' key ' industries ; (3) to regularize the flow of production in order to avoid as far as possible the recurrence of booms and slumps, and to apply appropriate remedies for maintaining employment in a trade depression ; (4) to facilitate the diversion of capital and labour from declining industries ; (5) to afford guidance to the export industries ; (6) to encourage the dispersal of industrial establishments ; (7) to frame a comprehensive labour code relating to wages, hours, holidays, technical training, housing and general conditions of work ; (8) to exercise supervision over trade associations and monopolies ; (9) to set up public corporations in those industries which are not left to private enterprise ; (10) to formulate monetary policy affecting the price level, the rate of interest, the volume and distribution of credit, and the monetary exchanges ; (11) to control long-term investments abroad and the movements of short-term funds ; (12) to develop international economic co-operation. Some of these items already come within the province of various departments of state, but they need to be integrated in the general framework. A planning commission could also serve another purpose. The Macmillan report (1931) stressed the need for " a complete inventory of the economic life of the community ". Our knowledge at present is empirical not scientific, and it is imperative to accumulate a full and ordered body of statistical and other data.

Apart from the specific functions assigned to the planning commission it would have the merit of taking national planning out of the arena of party strife. There is a serious danger that a planned economy may become the shuttlecock of political parties, each of which has its own programme. In the heat of controversy comprehensive schemes of reconstruction will soon wilter away and a series of compromises will produce a coat of many colours designed to placate all the vested interests. It is supremely necessary that the energies of the community should not be frittered away in barren disputes, and that the public mind should be freed from the shibboleths which with extreme partizans usurp the place of clear thinking. If those who are now ranged in opposing camps will rise to the height of a great occasion, they will discover in the economic and social spheres an unexpected number of essentials on which an agreed programme is possible. The alternative is endless debate over slogans and ideal schemes in which enthusiasm will soon evaporate in an atmosphere of disillusionment and indifference. A planning commission, like the tariff commission, would be detached from politics and so exert an influence which parties and governments would be bound to respect. There is the added advantage that as a permanent body it could shape a continuous policy and frame long-term plans, upon which governments (particularly in their last years of office) are less likely to embark. Hitherto four or five-year plans have been associated only with totalitarian states, and it remains to be seen whether they are practicable in a democracy based on the party system. I think the difficulty of securing agreement on economic planning in democratic countries can be exaggerated. Actually ' his majesty's opposition ' when in office does not proceed to destroy the work of its predecessors : in the social services, etc., continuity is preserved. An authoritative body may therefore expect to enjoy the general support of successive administrations.

The indispensable condition of a planned economy is a planning commission—by whatever name it may be known. Sitting in permanent session, it would differ from a royal commission whose existence terminates when it has completed the 'ad hoc' investigation for which it is appointed. Yet inasmuch as economic planning implies something more than cut and dried plans worked out by experts, since it involves a continuous adaptation of the existing order, we may conclude that some additional mechanism is needed to focus the economic activities of the nation and bring them under central direction. Parliament is not a suitable body for deliberations on economic matters. Its members in general have not the qualifications or technical competence, and economic issues tend to be considered less on their merits than on the influence which they may exert on the party fortunes or on the prosperity of vested interests. The government of the day may fear to handle certain thorny matters on the principle followed by Walpole, *quieta non movere*—from apprehension of losing votes or of imperilling projects which it considered more important or more urgent. The opposition is anxious to discredit the schemes emanating from the government benches. Moreover Parliament is overburdened with a multiplicity of topics, and congestion of business makes it impossible to find the time to give them adequate attention. For these various reasons a planned economy is most likely to materialize in a national economic assembly, before which the ministries would lay their legislative proposals for debate and criticism. Parliament as the sovereign body would retain an over-riding authority, though in practice it would doubtless not ignore the recommendations submitted by the assembly. The national economic assembly should be representative of all manufactures, trades, services and professions, in order to prevent sectional interests from taking root behind a frontier of state control ; and if it were found feasible to organize electorates on an occupational basis for the choice of members, it would serve to supplement the present system of organizing parliamentary constituencies on the basis of locality. Furthermore the dislike of being governed by a bureaucracy would be mitigated if its actions came under the watchful scrutiny of a qualified body : this is the more essential in days when the executive is enabled to encroach upon the province of the legislature by framing ordinances. Public corporations which as autonomous bodies are largely shielded from parliamentary interference would also be exposed to healthy and informed criticism, without which a public monopoly can become unprogressive and inefficient. And if the community were organized separately for political and economic purposes, the danger of the complete absorption of the individual into the state might be wholly or in a great degree eliminated. Although a proposal for a national economic assembly may not come within the range of 'practical politics' at the present moment, it is put forward here as a basis for discussion in the belief that the trend of opinion is likely to move in this direction.

§ 10. *International Economic Co-operation*

Among the many problems which confront the framers of a planned economy, the most baffling is the reconciliation of the conflicting claims of national autonomy and international economic co-operation. This raises vital issues that go far beyond the province of purely economic affairs. The acid test of all schemes of reconstruction is whether they will work; and in a large measure the answer will be determined by the extent to which they can be fitted into the orbit of a world economy. Nations, like individuals, must pay heed to the distinction implied in Milton's noble lines:

> "Licence they mean when they cry Liberty,
> For who loves that, must first be wise and good".

Before the first world war an automatic price system, which functioned on the principle of buying in the cheapest and selling in the dearest market, regulated economic activities—that is, the flow of commodities and services; and the internal price level was accommodated to the external value of the national currency. When domestic prices were too high for world trade, the bank rate was raised and the credit fabric was contracted; when they were below the international standard, the bank rate was lowered and the credit fabric was expanded. The report of the Bank for International Settlements, in 1934, spoke regretfully of "the healthy and stimulating financial and economic internationalism which existed almost unnoticed in so widespread a degree before the war [of 1914–18]". High prices in one country attracted imports from other countries; the drain of gold to pay for these imports reduced the volume of credit; purchasing power was diminished; and prices fell. Thus international equilibrium was restored by a self-regulating mechanism. There was a reverse side to the medal in the injurious reactions on the domestic economy; but in any event after the first world war a more rigid price structure resisted change, and whatever might be said by economic purists complicated issues were at stake. Deflation lessens the capital value of undertakings and impairs the assets held by banks as 'cover' for advances; it augments the 'real' burden of fixed monetary charges; it discourages enterprise; and it causes unemployment. Accordingly no government can afford to look with indifference on a sharp fall in prices with its attendant consequences [1]—widespread insolvencies, wastage of capital, deterioration in labour skill, the increased weight of debtors' obligations, the pressure of taxation on a smaller national income. "A drowning man clings to a serpent". Confronted with the effects produced by deflation, a government may be driven to protect domestic prices from international competition by excluding imports, and to expand the credit system with the design of maintaining employment—even though this involved a fall in the exchange rates of the national currency.

The great depression brought into prominence the two alternatives of a stable price level at home coupled with unstable exchange rates [2], or an unstable price level coupled

[1] A different situation arises when the fall in prices is due to technical progress cheapening the cost of production.

[2] If the national price level is maintained above the world level, the exchanges become adverse. The preservation of fixed exchange rates may therefore necessitate deflation of the national price level.

with stable exchange rates. The antithesis is perhaps unduly simplified. The prices of imported commodities respond to sharp changes in the external value of the currency, so that in practice it might prove impracticable for a country vitally dependent, like our own, upon a large foreign trade to keep a stable price level in conjunction with rapid deterioration in the exchanges. In any case, the decision must be taken whether in our economic planning we should seek to preserve an international equilibrium in which domestic conditions are adjusted to the requirements of world trade—or whether we should endeavour to insulate the national economy against the disturbing influences that come from beyond the seas. Advocates of monetary autonomy are prepared to let the external value of sterling take care of itself, in the conviction that the remedy for a trade depression lies in an extension of the home market instead of a scramble for oversea markets by methods which breed international bitterness and provoke retaliation. They therefore favour a system in which credit expansion is deliberately encouraged with a view to facilitate full employment. It may be admitted that the practice adopted under the gold standard of varying the bank rate in order to safeguard the gold reserves was injurious to industry and trade, in so far as it involved a contraction of commercial loans or an increase in interest charges. Nevertheless the implications of a policy of financial nationalism need to be carefully scrutinized.

I have already referred to some of the consequences of unstable exchange rates. They promote competition in currency depreciation, impair business confidence, discourage long-term investments, and cause the hasty transferences of short-term funds. And when monetary autonomy merges into a general policy of national self-sufficiency based on high protective duties, 'quotas' and other impediments to trade, it virtually destroys international economic co-operation which alone makes possible a system of international specialization. Yet the importance of international specialization is beyond dispute—the division of labour ensures the most efficient use of the factors of production and in sum the higher standard of living to which civilized man has grown accustomed. On it, in fact, depends the structure of our present civilization. Natural resources—wheat, meat, tea, coffee, fruits and an immense variety of raw materials—are distributed unevenly over the face of the globe. Hence economic nationalism, which exhibits a preference for the domestic as against an international market, and strives to escape dependency upon a world economy, must renounce not only the flesh-pots of Egypt but many of the everyday necessities of an advanced community. It is true that foreign trade is but a fraction of the total trade of a country ; none the less its importance is disproportionate to its size because it provides the materials for a richer and ampler existence whether in the shape of necessaries or amenities. In short the value of foreign trade does not lie in an excess of exports over imports, but in the opportunities afforded for the acquisition of commodities superior in quality and more varied in character : accordingly, as the standard of life of the masses improves, the quantity of imports will tend to grow [1]. Indeed the notion that the volume of domestic employment can be maintained by a restriction of imports ignores the fact that employment itself is dependent upon imported foodstuffs and raw materials. Furthermore industry is always seeking to overflow national frontiers, for mass production demands mass markets. Thus social and industrial trends alike—the advance in the standard of living as well as in technique—are moving towards the economic integration of human society, and consequently they are opposed to a political congeries of state sovereign-ties and self-sufficing communities. Until these clashing tendencies are harmonized, a spirit of unrest will con-tinue to brood over the world and to retard its orderly evolution.

Economic planning must take account of world reper-

[1] Even the vast territory of the United States is not self-sufficing in respect of metals and many raw materials.

cussions not alone in the sphere of trade but in the sphere of politics. I have said that national self-sufficiency is destructive of international economic co-operation : it is equally incompatible with international political collaboration since it produces inter-state friction. It excludes men and merchandise coming from other countries ; it hinders the fair distribution of raw materials by making payment difficult ; it accentuates the division into the ' haves ' and the ' have-nots ' ; it makes the acquisition of territory an advantage by extending the markets and economic opportunities of the victors ; and in all these respects it creates an atmosphere which endangers the preservation of peace. No nation, however powerful, can afford to pursue an economic policy which stirs up discontent abroad ; and in this connexion it may be recalled that the high price of British coal exported to Italy in the early twenties caused the embitterment which disturbed the relations of the two powers. The argument that self-sufficiency would diminish the friction provoked by commercial jealousies is fallacious. Inasmuch as some foreign trade is indispensable the result would be a sharper struggle to obtain a share in a contracted volume, and it would intensify national antagonisms. Under a freer trade, with an expanding volume, every country may hope to have its place in the sun. Governments therefore, when they contemplate a particular line of policy, ought to weigh its anticipated benefits in the light of its international implications. They should recognize (as was pointed out by a world economic conference in 1927) that even tariffs, " though within the sovereign jurisdiction of the separate states, are not a matter of purely domestic interest ". The twenty years that lie between the two world wars have taught the lesson that economics and politics are indissolubly connected and cannot be divorced. The political pacification of Europe, which seemed on the point of complete attainment after the Treaty of Locarno (1925), suffered shipwreck partly because economic collaboration was precarious and short-lived. At the first signal of disaster there ensued a policy of *sauve qui peut* : each nation went its own way : tariff walls mounted higher and were reinforced by ' quotas ' : currencies were manipulated to serve domestic objects. No wonder the years that followed the great depression witnessed the wreckage of the political structure erected by the Treaty of Versailles. If the world aspires to eradicate the economic causes of war it must learn to approach its problems from a different angle, and pursue a policy of co-operation and fair distribution. The leadership in such a movement falls naturally upon the United States and Great Britain—upon the former on account of her wealth ; upon the latter on account of her political experience coupled with her position at the centre of world trade and world finance. The sacrifices which they may be called upon to make are likely on a long view to prove a fruitful investment in international good will.

The time still seems remote when national planned economies will be consciously co-ordinated within the framework of a world planned economy. Indeed the experience of the inter-war period (1919–39) suggests that state regulation increases the rigidity of the commercial system and so interposes obstacles to effective economic co-operation, just as state sovereignty has proved a barrier against effective political co-operation. However it is necessary in all our discussions to keep our ultimate goal steadily in view, if we wish to find a way out of the present impasse in which the modern trend of national economies appears to involve increasing disintegration of a world economy based on specialization. In any event we have clearly entered upon a phase where *laissez-faire* in international economic relationships is incompatible with domestic planning, and some positive approach to world planning is essential to keep the nations in step as far as is practicable. The economic functions of the League of Nations, the International Labour Office and the Bank for International Settlements, are indications that the need for establishing international agencies is gaining recognition. Yet neither these institutions, nor the convening of world conferences for special purposes, are adequate in themselves to furnish the means for concerted action in the economic sphere and for the working out of a systematic and continuous policy.

A world economic assembly meeting in regular session would provide a forum for the interchange of views and for the co-ordination of state projects : it would enable the national representatives who participated in it to become internationally-minded and see their own specific problems in relation to the world as a whole. Just as the Universities are linked together in a common brotherhood, in which knowledge acquired in one is placed impartially at the disposal of all, and in which the search for truth does not stop short at territorial frontiers, so we must endeavour to develop an international outlook on economic affairs in the realization that prosperity is indivisible and that a disaster for one may become a disaster for all. A world economic assembly could create an international public opinion, which would discourage the tendency to snatch at temporary advantages and substitute a sense of solidarity for the law of the jungle. It could call into existence the machinery which would give effect to the desire expressed in the Atlantic Charter " to bring about the fullest collaboration between all nations in the economic field, with the object of securing for all improved labour standards, economic advancement, and social security ". The assembly —whose composition ought to be other than that of a diplomatic body expressing the views of governments—should have specialized organs to deal with labour, agriculture (foodstuffs and raw materials), migration, tariffs, currency and monetary exchanges, oversea investments, commercial treaties and international cartels. The extent of its legal powers would naturally depend upon the willingness of nation-states to submit to limitations on their sovereignty for the sake of closer collaboration. An atmosphere of mutual confidence, security and solidarity would reinforce its authority in shaping a policy designed to re-establish order in international economic relations, to promote prosperity, and to improve the general standard of living ; but if national sentiment became too strong for genuine co-operation then isolationism would once again rear its malevolent head. Even amidst the chaos produced by the great depression there emerged hopeful signs of a more enlightened outlook on world problems. Thus the abandonment of the *de jure* stabilization of the exchanges (under the gold standard) was followed within a few years by its *de facto* stabilization. This evinced recognition of the fact that the paramount need for international co-operation remained unimpaired, although we may want to devise a more flexible mechanism for reconciling internal stability with external equilibrium.

One can scarcely question the utility of a world organization which focussed discussions on the international aspects of national policies—especially those detrimental to the movements of men and commodities (immigration laws, tariffs, ' quotas ', bilateralism, etc.)—and which fulfilled (if it did nothing more) the functions of a constitutional monarch in offering counsel and warning. I shall give three illustrations of the way in which it might eliminate potential sources of friction that were largely responsible for the economic malaise of the inter-war years (1919–39).

In the first place, whatever international monetary standard is adopted it must avoid the sacrifices exacted by a rigid gold standard, because if the choice lay between deflation of the domestic price level or the repudiation of fixed rates for the currency sold abroad, it is improbable that in the future public opinion will tolerate the former. At the same time the danger of fluctuating exchanges is widely recognized. An official declaration of the British government, announcing a Tripartite Agreement with France and the United States (1936), affirmed the intention " to avoid to the utmost extent the creation of any disturbance [of the system of exchanges] by British monetary action ", though it was careful to reserve the right to " take into full account the requirements of internal prosperity ". The necessary flexibility in working an international monetary standard could be attained by co-operation between the central banks. A world economic assembly could explore the possibilities of synchronizing the expansion of credit in different countries when the slackening of commercial activities heralded a general trade depression. By ensuring that national price levels were kept in their existing relation to each other, it could offset the dangers of unilateral action which—in 'managing' the level of domestic prices in one country—runs the risk of disturbing equilibrium in the monetary exchanges. National autonomy might be rendered compatible with stable exchanges if uniform monetary policies were simultaneously brought into operation. Concerted action between the central banks would also promote steadiness of the exchanges if they agreed to control the abrupt transfers of large fugitive balances, which played havoc with the international monetary system in the thirties.

In the second place, a world organization could (in the words of the Atlantic Charter) "further enjoyment by all states, great or small, victor or vanquished, of access on equal terms to the raw materials of the world". The uneven distribution of raw materials has raised an issue profoundly influencing the course of world politics. The common argument that no one is hindered from purchasing raw materials becomes irrelevant when a nation finds itself unable to buy them, since it cannot sell goods abroad to pay for them: in fact the problem of raw materials is primarily a problem of obtaining the means of payment. Furthermore restriction schemes which limit the output of primary products cause heart-burning. Between the two world wars the attempt to maintain high prices gave birth to more than thirty projects for curtailing the quantity of foodstuffs and raw materials—among others they embraced wheat, coffee, rubber and tin. It is difficult to write temperately of a procedure expressly intended to replace abundance by artificial scarcity in a world where the greater part of humanity is sunk in poverty. Yet it must be recognized that the cost of a primary product is only a fraction of the total cost of the finished product, and consequently a fall in prices will not materially affect an inelastic demand. In the seventeenth century the English economist, Charles Davenant, remarked that it was 'strange economy in our government' that abundance should make things a greater drug to the grower and very little cheaper to the consumer. As the economic system is at present organized, it appears that supply must be regulated in order to avoid a 'glut' of goods being thrown on the market at prices which are ruinous to the producers. It is not merely a question of the vested interests of a few capitalists, because a sharp fall in prices may spell disaster for the specialized workers engaged in the industry. Nevertheless it creates international friction when countries which have a monopoly of a particular commodity agree to raise its price by limiting its amount. It is evident, moreover, that the general adoption of a policy of restriction is bound to contract the volume of international trade and so to lower the standard of living. It would be preferable, in appropriate circumstances, to preserve the financial solvency of an industry by subsidies rather than by reduction of output, provided that the evil is not perpetuated by the retention of the surplus capacity and inefficient undertakings within the industry. Contrary to the common view, colonies are not an important source of raw materials. It was pointed out in a report of the League of Nations that "most raw materials are produced wholly, or to a great extent, in sovereign countries [1]. The total present production of all commercially important raw materials in all colonial territories is no more than 3 per cent. of world production". A reasonable solution of the problem of affording access to raw materials should not prove beyond the capacity of statesmanship, yet some international body is required to carry it into effect.

In the third place, the investment of capital abroad should be brought under supervision. In the nineteenth century Great Britain made loans to Australia and Argentina,

[1] This of course includes the Dominions.

which were used productively because she was repaid in wool and meat. After the first world war the leading powers poured immense sums into Europe and South America, but many of the loans were ill-judged and heavy losses were incurred. Moreover the danger arises that powerful financial interests may have a strong motive for advocating impolitic concessions to states where an economic collapse would imperil their loans. No doubt public regulation will restrict the scope of free investment, but here as in other directions it is a question of balancing gain and loss. Accordingly governments, instead of adopting an attitude of benevolent detachment, should exert control to prevent misdirection of foreign credits and to ensure that they are made only for productive purposes. Still more important, international co-operation could make international lending the basis of constructive measures for the development of the less advanced communities. One may conceive the possibility of a world corporation, in whose investments all industrialized nations are enabled to participate not by making money loans (which put a strain on the exchanges) but by credits in capital goods. If we think less in terms of currencies and more in terms of commodities and services, we can widen the field of investment ; and the investing countries, contributing their own products, would benefit by increased industrial activity and employment. The benefit would be permanent if a rise in the standard of living of the people in Asia and elsewhere were accompanied by an expansion of exports, which would augment the power of the East to purchase the manufactures of the West. This, however, assumes that some solution is found for the fundamental problem of reconciling international lending, designed to stimulate world productivity, with the high tariffs of the creditor countries designed to exclude the products of their debtors—one of the lessons of recent history is the futility of making loans abroad unless it is rendered less difficult for debtors to repay. The case for international co-operation in the sphere of investment is strengthened by the fact that governments are reacting against foreign control of national assets, while private investors are discouraged by the instability of currencies, by the liability to expropriation, and by general political uncertainties. It is of interest here to recall an early attempt at international co-operation. Over three hundred years ago, in the reign of James I., a group of European capitalists —Dutch, English and French—combined to finance an expedition to the East Indies though the government intervened to nip a promising venture in the bud. Proposals put forward by the League of Nations for international banks dealing in mortgage credit and agricultural credit furnish more recent historical precedents.

§ 11. *Conclusion*

Ultimately the mainspring of post-war reconstruction is neither political nor economic but spiritual. The acid test is whether the unparalleled energies which the nation has displayed in exerting all its strength to destroy a menace to human freedom, German National Socialism, shall be allowed to be dissipated, or whether forethought, sacrifice and conciliation can be fused together to create a new and better Britain. The struggle for survival has revealed unsuspected depths in human nature and brought to the surface qualities of a higher order. It is tragic that war alone should exhibit these finer traits of character on a national scale. Our task is to evoke in the peace years the spirit of altruism, the appeal of service for the community, so that it may be employed for constructive purposes in promoting aspirations for the common welfare. We are not likely to under-rate the difficulty of a task which seeks to import a touch of idealism into the grim realism of our everyday world. The moral exaltation born of imminent national peril is lacking, the clamour of vested interests is more vocal, individual self-seeking is more unashamed. And yet—the effort must be made. Its measure of success will depend on whether our leaders in politics, in industry, in commerce and in finance have the vision to grasp the uniqueness of the occasion, and will take the tide at the flood which leads on to national fortune. The faculties which these stirring times demand are those of a flexible habit of mind, facility in adjusting our ways of thought and methods to changing conditions, receptivity to new ideas, willingness to learn from experience, readiness to attempt experiments in processes of trial and error. In the alternative, will the lessons of history be once again ignored? As after the first world war, will an emotional reaction unsettle the outlook of the post-war generation; will the state pursue a fatal hand-to-mouth policy, waiting on events instead of anticipating them; and will industry erect its financial house on the quicksands of a fleeting boom? Eloquent perorations will not build the new Jerusalem; and it remains to be seen whether Britain will produce the statesmen who can convert the enthusiasm which has been the driving force of the war into a revitalizing and regenerating instrument, and who will escape the reproach that they have made up their minds—but they do not know exactly to what!

There is no single solution to our social and economic problems: a long and difficult road lies before us. We shall be the better prepared to confront and overcome the obstacles that present themselves if we avoid the facile optimism with which we blundered into economic chaos after the war of 1914–18. We must endeavour to extract from past experience the lessons, the warnings and the inspiration which may serve 'as a light to our feet' to illuminate our path. Once again a great opportunity awaits us to reconstruct the economic fabric and introduce into it a much needed degree of stability and regularity. If with the memories of the sacrifices which two world wars have exacted, we grasp this opportunity with both our hands, we may still cherish the expectation of preserving all that is best in our civilization and transmitting to posterity the priceless heritage of a community in which law, and not 'dictatorship', provides the framework of ordered progress.

In facing the uncertainties of the future we may derive courage from the fact that Britain surmounted her difficulties in the past despite the forebodings of those who then (as now) took short-term views. I have given in an Appendix a selection of these Cassandra-like utterances which may serve as an antidote to despondency and an exhortation to cast out fear. I conclude this book with the spirited and apposite words written in 1696 by J. Whiston in a work entitled *The Causes of our present Calamities in reference to the Trade of the Nation fully Discovered*: "Whilst England had few or no rivals in trade, and the riches of the world flow'd into her lap, she lived at ease (slumbering in the downy bed of peace), wallowed in pleasures, and had no other unhappiness but in being too happy. Her abundance begot idleness, and that a stupid security. . . . But now 'tis high time to awaken all the vital powers of state, and rouse the very soul of government from this slothful lethargy, to see the danger of our condition and provide for a remedy".

APPENDIX ONE

THE DEFINITION OF TERMS

In these pages I make frequent references to private enterprise (alternatively individualism), free enterprise (alternatively a free economy), and a planned economy (alternatively a controlled economy). It will be useful to indicate the meanings which I attach to these terms.

Private enterprise is the opposite of state or collectivist enterprise, which is usually called nationalization. It can exist under both free enterprise and a planned economy, provided the latter does not assume a form which completely eliminates individualism.

Free enterprise denotes a system in which there are many thousands of individuals engaged in the production and marketing of goods, whose operations—guided by the motive of profit-making in a market of competitive prices—are supposed to achieve the economic harmonies of a balanced system of production and consumption. The ultimate arbiter of a free economy is the consumer, whose control is exercised by his readiness to buy goods and services at the market price. A free economy is self-regulating in the sense that supply and demand are equated not by external authority but automatically by the workings of an impersonal force, namely, a competitive price system. A free economy is not of course incompatible with planning ; it does not function without foresight and organization ; but the planning is done by individuals or by groups, whose economic activities are dovetailed in a general framework. Furthermore a free economy is not entirely unregulated. It is conditioned by property rights, by legal restraints such as factory acts and laws against adulteration, by social conventions, by trade-union pressure, and by commercial agreements or combinations. Actually there is a great deal of ' management ' in a free economy, which in practice diverges widely from the postulates of the classical economists.

Lastly a planned economy implies central direction of the national resources. In essence it is distinguished from a free economy in its scope, that is to say, the difference between them is fundamentally a matter of degree rather than of principle. It need not supersede private enterprise, nor involve (as in totalitarian states) the absolute regimentation of the economic life of the community. Nevertheless it does not tolerate an uncontrolled private enterprise that functions under the dictates of 'natural forces', which virtually means self-interest. It supplements—and in a measure limits—the innumerable decisions of individuals by super-imposing upon them a co-ordinated and deliberately planned programme. For an economic jig-saw puzzle into which an infinite number of fragments are fitted (often haphazardly), it seeks to substitute a system in which conscious direction at the centre achieves unity of design and construction. And this system may prove the more flexible because it can do what is normally beyond the province of free enterprise—it can make allowances for social reactions.

APPENDIX TWO

AN ANTIDOTE TO DESPONDENCY[1]

THE economic malaise with which the nation is grappling at this moment is not without precedent in earlier times. When due allowance is made for differences of scale, one finds remarkable parallels to the situation which has arisen to-day; for the problems of unfavourable exchanges, an adverse balance of trade, widespread unemployment and heavy taxation have troubled and perplexed past generations not less than our own. Nor has the general attitude towards these problems undergone any conspicuous change. Every 'economic blizzard' which afflicts the country seems to create a spirit of what a French statesman the other day called 'economic defeatism'.

Throughout the course of our economic development runs a never-ceasing stream of complaints that industry is declining, that foreign trade is diminishing, that the country is being drained of its money by the excess of imports over exports, that the people can no longer support the burden of taxation, that poverty and unemployment are increasing, that the nation is on the brink of irreparable ruin.

In illustration, one might cull from the pages of the mediaeval statute-book repeated warnings that native textiles were losing their reputation in continental markets. Or one might turn to the fourteenth century, and listen to the officials of the Mint giving grave counsel that trade must be "well and rightly governed", that is, imports must not be allowed to exceed exports; or else, "where you think to have five shillings you will not have four". (Some are saying the same thing to-day.) And in the seventeenth

[1] My purpose in writing this Article (originally published in *The Times*, January 20, 1932) was to show that the pessimistic views of Britain's future, prevalent during the great depression, had been frequently re-iterated in former centuries.

century we should feel ourselves to be in a thoroughly familiar atmosphere. We should find England in 1620 in the throes of a trade depression which lasted four years, with a royal commission on unemployment propounding causes and remedies as diverse and contradictory as those with which we are assailed to-day. We should discover Malynes conducting an acrimonious controversy with Misselden over the foreign exchanges with all the heat, devoid of light, which that great mystery—" the greatest and weightiest mystery that is to be found in the whole Map of Trade ", so Scarlett called it in 1682—has a tendency to generate. We should certainly detect a familiar ring in the election address of a parliamentary candidate (1676) deploring the general poverty, " which if not quickly remedied will soon reduce us to the utmost misery ". We should hear even Petty, one of the fathers of political economy, describing the staple trade of the country (cloth) as " almost totally lost ", although later he recognized that the condition of England was not quite so bad as he and others had painted it, but that " men eat and drink and laugh as they use to do ".

A collection of economic predictions falsified by the progress of time would make instructive reading. It would help us to preserve a sense of proportion in appraising the flow of current events and fortify our minds against jeremiads of impending catastrophe. One collection of the kind was made near the end of the eighteenth century, when the country was in despondent mood and the prophets were busily employed—though their powers of prevision, oddly enough, did not enable them to foretell the great industrial expansion which was at hand. The collection was compiled by Sir John Sinclair, afterwards first president of the Board of Agriculture. It was appropriately styled : " An Antidote to Despondency ; or Progressive Assertions from respectable Authority, tending to prove that the Nation was Actually Undone prior to the Revolution in 1688 ; and that it has remained in a continued State of Ruin, or Decay, ever since that memorable Era ".

Our author starts by saying that " it has often been remarked that the English are more inclined than any other nation to view the dark side of the prospect " ; and that whoever seriously sits down to consider the situation of the country always ends by concluding, after mature reflection, that the country is undone. He rightly points out that such opinions are particularly injurious to a state that depends for its existence " upon credit ". To prove them groundless he appeals, first, to " the infinite resources of which the nation is actually possessed ", and which " have hitherto stood many a severe trial " ; and, secondly, to the fact that " similar desponding apprehensions " have been entertained for a century past, " during which period it is well known that the nation has enjoyed no inconsiderable degree of happiness and prosperity ".

The extracts quoted by Sir John Sinclair are taken from " works of authority " extending over a century. Their cumulative effect is certainly striking, for they all concur in stressing the miserable state of the country and in predicting its inevitable decline. Here we can take only a rapid glance at a few illustrations. A well-known economic tract, *Britannia Languens* (1680), sets the ball rolling with the pronouncement that " a kind of common consumption hath crawled upon us " : our poor are vastly increased, and the rest of the people generally more and more feel the want of money. The effects of our participation in continental wars are depicted by a writer in 1694 as " the utter beggaring of ourselves by the decay of traffic and unsupportable taxes ". Davenant, an eminent economist, solemnly warns the nation in 1699 that unless the budget were reduced we should languish and decay, our gold and silver would be carried off by degrees, shipping would diminish, industry would decay, " and we shall have upon us all the visible marks of a declining people ". Lord Lyttelton in 1739 contrasts the condition of England and France—the former with her revenues mortgaged, her credit sunk at home and abroad, her people exhausted and dispirited ; the latter rich and strong in alliances and reputation.

Postlethwayt, known for his *Dictionary of Trade and Commerce*, writes in 1757 : " The great bane of our trade is the high price of our commodities. And must not the augmentation of our debt and taxes still enhance their price ? " Hume remarks in 1776 : " I suppose there is no mathematical, still less an arithmetical, demonstration that the road to the Holy Land was not the road to Paradise as there is that the endless increase of national debts is the direct road to national ruin ", a goal which he considered to be " now completely reached ". And the Earl of Stair in 1783 comes to the " infallible, inevitable conclusion that the state is a bankrupt, and that those who have trusted their all to the public faith are in very imminent danger of becoming (I die pronouncing it) beggars ". It may be left to the author of *An Antidote to Despondency* to state the moral : " Even the ablest men may entertain ill-founded and groundless apprehensions respecting the political strength and financial resources of the nation. . . . Nothing but the grossest mismanagement . . . can possibly effect the ruin of so powerful an empire, inhabited by a race of people distinguished for strength, for courage, and for ability ".

After the lapse of a century and a half these words still convey a message for our generation.

Also by E. Lipson

EUROPE 1914–1939

Second edition. With 4 portraits and 2 maps

The twenty-five years between the two outbreaks of European war in this century were marked by momentous events which merit the attention of students and general readers who seek to understand the complex phenomena of our own age. These developments, which must profoundly affect the future evolution of Europe, are here set out in a book that clearly shows the interdependence of political and economic factors in shaping the recent history of Europe, and gives a detailed account of the influences which contributed in a vital degree to make inevitable the renewal of war in 1939.

EUROPE IN THE XIXTH CENTURY 1815–1914

Sixth edition. With 8 portraits and 4 maps

" Inspired with the conviction that historical fact should be made the subject of reflection." *Manchester Guardian.*

" An illuminating and attractive book. It exhibits in an eminent degree what is most valuable to the student, the gift of historical style."

Professor R. K. HANNAY in *The Scottish Historical Review.*

* These two books may also be obtained in one volume, *Europe in the Nineteenth and Twentieth Centuries*

ADAM & CHARLES BLACK : LONDON W.1